Hunted Through Fiji: Or Twixt Convict And Cannibal

Reginald Horsley

Printing Statement:

Due to the very old age and scarcity of this book,
many of the pages may be hard to read due to the
blurring of the original text, possible missing pages,
missing text, dark backgrounds and other issues
beyond our control.

Because this is such an important and rare work, we
believe it is best to reproduce this book regardless of
its original condition.

Thank you for your understanding.

Hunted Through Fiji

OR

'Twixt Convict and Cannibal

BY

REGINALD HORSLEY

Illustrated by J. Ayton Symington

LONDON: 38 Soho Square, W.1

W. & R. CHAMBERS, LIMITED

EDINBURGH: 339 High Street

Another and yet another until he had counted fifty-seven.

CONTENTS.

1925

Printed in Great Britain.
W. & R. CHAMBERS, LTD., LONDON and EDINBURGH.

PREFATORY NOTE.

It is, perhaps, unnecessary to remind my young readers that cannibalism, once so rampant in Fiji that as many as one hundred bodies were eaten at a single feast, now no longer exists there. Long before the formal occupation of the islands by the British, in 1874, at the invitation of the *Vu-ni-Valu*, Cacobau or Thakombau, the horrid practice had become almost obsolete, owing to the heroic efforts of the missionaries, who over and over again exposed their own lives in their determination to protest against the dreadful custom. Probably, however, it did not become wholly extinct in the interior until after the subjugation of the *Kai Tholos*, or Hillmen, by Sir Arthur Gordon, the first governor.

The scenes described are not overdrawn. Indeed, for obvious reasons, they are not fully drawn, nor must the escape of the fugitives by means of the under-river caves be regarded as extravagant invention. These caves exist, as the traveller—now freed from the fear of the cooking-pot and the cannibal fork—may see for himself among the cliffs of the Singatoka River; and some of them formed, during the war above referred to, the most inaccessible strongholds of the enemy.

PREFATORY NOTE.

The Tongans, always an adventurous race, were among the earliest visitors to Fiji; and the slight acquaintance with English possessed by Faatu is explained by the visit of certain missionaries to Tonga in 1797, and his probable contact with Mr Mariner during the latter's captivity there in the early part of this century.

For the convenience of the reader, the Fijian words used in the story are written as pronounced, thus:

B is pronounced Mb—*e.g.* Bauan = Mbauan.

C   „   Th   „   Cava = Thava.

D   „   Nd   „   Dran = Ndrau.

G   „   Ng   „   Turaga = Turanga.

Q   „   Ng or Nk—*e.g.* Yaqona = Yangona.

Bonavidogo = Mbonavindongo.

HUNTED THROUGH FIJI.

CHAPTER I.

CLEARS THE STAGE FOR ACTION.

N a glade in the forest, under the shadow, such as it was, of his own native gum-trees, a small Australian aboriginal was receiving a practical demonstration of the superiority of the white man over the black; and he did not enjoy it.

The black boy writhed in the grasp of two strong men, a third held him by the right wrist, twisting the arm until the dislocation point was almost reached. A fourth—a smooth-faced man with pale-blue, glittering eyes, and thin lips drawn into an ugly, mirthless smile—struck heavily with a knotty stick upon the swarthy stretched skin and tense, quivering muscles beneath. It was a form of punishment much in vogue amongst schoolboys of, let us hope, a past generation, and—it hurts.

At every stroke the black boy shrank and twisted his body in agony. He did not cry out, for the simple reason that a thick piece of bark, thrust

crosswise between his teeth, effectually prevented
any such expression of feeling; but his eyes, starting
from their sockets, streamed tears which ran down
his poor drawn cheeks, flowed over the gag, and
dropped upon the parched grass at his feet.

Half-a-dozen other men sat around upon logs or
the stumps of felled trees, or lay, lazily stretched
upon the ground, contemplating the scene with
manifest satisfaction.

They were convicts, one and all, with the exception of the black boy—he was one of the lords of
the soil—and their occupation was to clear the forest
from the selection of the settler to whom they had
been assigned. They had worked hard all morning
with axe and adze, and now, at noonday, when the
sun was at its hottest, their reward had come. A
black boy, an innocent, inoffensive, laughing black
boy, had chanced their way; they had caught him
and were amusing themselves with turning his
laughter into tears.

That was all. The black boy had done no wrong,
injured no one; but these men, these brutes rather,
whose coarse faces, with one exception, indicated
truly enough their yet coarser natures, were tired,
and desired a little recreation, and found it in cruelly
torturing a helpless shivering child.

The one exception was the man who struck those
measured, agonising blows. His face was not coarse
like those of his companions; indeed there were indi-
cations of refinement in the well-cut features and
the long slender hands, though the first were brown
and grimy and the second roughened by much toil.
But the blue eyes were too close together, the short

stubbly hair grew low over the brow, and the corners of the lower lip drooped in a perpetual sneer, fixed by long habit. It was a bad and vicious face, but not coarse. The face of a man who had fallen from his high estate and was at war with his fellow-men; a man who hated those whose equal he had once been, and despised the men amongst whom his lot was cast; a man who could scheme and plot and execute; a clever villain, who could set in the handle of his wit the rough knaves with whom he rubbed elbows, and use them for his tools how and when he would.

The heavy stick rose and fell monotonously, and the arm which had been slender and sinewy was swollen and shapeless now. But for the black boy the agony was past for the time being; his head hung down sideways upon his chest, his eyes were closed, and his knees bent limply under him.

'Leave him be, Bill; he's swounded,' growled one of the onlookers. 'Arsk me, I didn't think as he'd have held up so long.'

'You made more noise when you were tied up to the triangles, Thomas, I remember; though to be sure you had better opportunity, for your mouth was free,' answered the man addressed as Bill, as with a cold smile he allowed the stick to fall once more upon the poor bruised arm.

'Ay! And how did ye like it yerself when yer own turn came, Bill Larkin?' was the snarling reply. 'Same time there ain't no use flogging a dead horse. We've got all the fun out of him as is to be got.'

'I wonder if he thought it funny,' said Larkin

musingly. 'Well, as you say, there is no more to be got out of him. Carry him off and throw him into the bush, some of you.'

'Knock him on the head now and have done with it,' advised the man who had spoken first. We don't want him carrying tales to the cove,* and one nigger more or less don't matter.'

'Please yourself,' answered Larkin indifferently. 'That's your work, not mine. I have amused you long enough.'

The other fellow rose and reached for his axe, when suddenly a wrathful shout rang out; there was a sound of rushing feet, the bushes to the left were violently dashed aside, and a young man bounded into the circle.

At sight of him the convicts darted this way and that, and sped like scared rats into the undergrowth. Only Larkin remained, cool and sneering, though for one instant the blood fled from his face and came slowly crawling back again.

The new-comer was a fine, strapping young fellow over six feet in height, broad-shouldered, deep-chested, with fair, closely-curling hair, and strong sun-burnt, resolute face, which, ordinarily good-humoured enough, was now distorted with rage, while his blue eyes blazed furiously under their drawn brows.

For a moment the two stood face to face, the younger man with tightly clenched fists, his broad chest heaving, and his breath coming and going in short gasps, the convict outwardly cool, and with that shadowy sneer at the corners of his lips. Between them lay the senseless body of the black boy.

* The Master.

Larkin was the first to speak. 'A bad business this, Mr Hawkins,' he said smoothly. 'I fear the brutes have killed him. I wish I had come up sooner.'

Anthony Hawkins took a step forward, bestriding the huddled body.

'Liar!' he foamed. 'I saw you;' and he drove his fist full into the convict's face.

Down upon his back among the crackling ferns went Larkin, and lay motionless, while Anthony Hawkins, all the rage gone out of his face, stooped and gently lifted the little black body to one side.

'Guy!' he shouted. 'Guy! Coo-ee! Guy!'

Then he went forward and stood over Larkin.

'Get up, you monster of cruelty, you murderous sneak!' he said fiercely. 'Get up! No shamming now. Get up!' He stirred the fellow with his foot.

But Larkin was wise in his generation, and lay perfectly still with eyes closed. Besides, he really was half-stunned.

Anthony opened his clasp-knife and cut three stout saplings—willowy things that would curl and twist and bend, but would not easily break. 'Guy!' he shouted again, whittling off the leaves and twigs. 'Guy! Coo-ee!'

'Coo-ee!' came an answering cry far away.

Anthony strode over to Larkin once more. Two of the rods he threw on the ground, the third he took in his right hand, raising his muscular arm above his head.

'Get up!' he commanded again. 'What! You won't?'

Swish! The supple rod fell across the face of the
prostrate man, and the blood rose in a long red wale
upon cheek and brow.

With a shriek of pain the convict started into a
sitting posture, and raised his hands to his face, livid
with rage and fear. The position of things had
become swiftly reversed: the torturer had become
the tortured.

'I thought that would move you,' said Anthony
coolly. 'How do you like it yourself? Now howl
away as much as you please, for I'm going to give
you the biggest thrashing you ever had in your life.
If you try to get up any further, I'll knock you
down; if you lie down, I'll pull you up—Now!'

Swish! swish! swish! A rain of stinging blows
upon the shrinking quivering back, stripped to the
shirt as it was. Swish! swish! shrieks and curses.
And at the tenth stroke the rod broke. Swish!
Down came the second rod, and with a howl for
mercy the convict sprang up, only to be instantly
forced to his knees. Swish! The second rod
snapped; but as Anthony raised the third, a strong
hand caught back his arm, and a terrified voice cried,
'Anthony! Anthony! Good heavens! What are
you doing?'

'Doing!' echoed Anthony. 'Paying a brute in
his own coin. Look to the boy, Guy, and leave me
to finish this ruffian.'

Then for the first time Guy Trimball, who was a
slighter, darker edition of his cousin Anthony, saw
the little blackamoor, and with a cry of sympathy
fell on his knees beside him, and began to care for
the wounded arm.

'Oh, oh, oh!' he cried. 'Was ever such a brute? Give it to him, Anthony.'

Anthony needed no persuasion, and until the third switch gave out showered stinging stroke after stroke upon the shoulders of the cowering convict.

'There, I think you've had lesson enough for once,' he said as he threw aside the broken pieces. 'Make your way back to your hut, and tell the overseer what lie you please to account for your condition. This is the way you cut wood, is it? Humph. Well, considering that I've taken the law into my own hands, I'll not report you to Major Hawkins, which is more than you deserve, for I think a taste of the cat at the triangles would do you good, despite the licking you've had. Be off, you cowardly brute.'

Larkin picked up his jacket, which was lying close by, and for one moment stood facing the young man.

'Mr Hawkins,' he began in a trembling, far-away voice, 'you have beaten me black and blue. Mr Trimball, you came up and saw it done. You won't report me? You won't have me tied up at the triangles and flogged to death? Thanks! Thanks! I shall remember your kind forbearance. Oh yes, I shall remember.'

'See that you do,' answered Anthony haughtily. 'I am not the only one by whom you are suspected of fomenting mischief among the men. I have nothing to do with that; but if I catch you at your cruel tricks again, I'll serve you worse than I have served you to-day. Remember that as well.—Come, Guy.'

He raised the now moaning black boy in his arms

and strode away through the trees, followed by his cousin.

Larkin looked after them for a moment, and then through the grimaces of pain the ghost of his old sneering smile curled his lip.

'Suspect me of fomenting mischief among the men, do they?' he muttered. 'Thanks for the information, Mr Haughty Hawkins. We must be careful; it won't do to fail now when everything is ready, and we are only waiting for the right moment. As for to-day's business, I must put my feelings in my pocket for the present; but never fear, my fine fellows'—he shook his fist in the direction of the cousins—'never fear. I shall remember.'

Ere yet this century had left the last very far behind it, the infant colony on the shores of Port Jackson—Botany Bay as it was then commonly, but erroneously, called—received certain additions, respectable and otherwise.

First, news came to Major Hawkins (the right hand of his Excellency the Governor), already settled there with his young son Anthony, that his brothers-in-law, Captain Trimball of His Majesty's navy, disabled, and Dr Blake, a physician unable to cure himself, intended to follow the widowed major's example and seek health, if not fortune, in the new land to the south. And presently they came, these worthy gentlemen, bringing each a wife and a sturdy boy along with him.

Impressed with the beauty and believing in the future of the country, the brothers-in-law joined forces and obtained grants of land on the fertile and,

at that time, forest-covered rolling lands to the north
of the Parramatta River, the ground being cleared
for them by convict labour; for it was the custom
in those days to assign to each free settler as many
convict servants as he would engage to feed and
clothe.

Six months later a whaling brig, hailing from the
youthful republic of the United States, put in at
Port Jackson, where her captain asked and obtained
permission to land the carpenter's mate, one Eli
Banks, who had fallen into ill-health.

Dr Blake happened to be at the Settlement when
Eli was carried ashore, and pitying the poor fellow's
forlorn condition, took him under his own care and
speedily set him on his legs again; whereupon the
Virginian, shorn of this world's goods, but rich in
gratitude, offered his services to his benefactor, urging
in his own behalf that he could turn his hand to
anything from cooking a dinner to building a house.
So thoroughly did Eli make good his word and,
moreover, so heartily did he identify himself with
the interests of the brothers-in-law, that at last it
became a standing joke between them that it was
impossible to determine to which of them the American ought to apply for his pay.

But the boys were Eli's especial care, and it would
be difficult to say whether they were the more
devoted to him or he to them. At all events the
four speedily grew to be inseparables, and before three
years had passed away the lads had hardened under
the teaching of the gaunt Virginian into expert young
bushmen, and indeed bade fair to rival their teacher
in all the mysteries of wood and river craft.

Two of the cousins have already been introduced. Guy, who was a year younger than Anthony, was neither so tall nor endowed with such remarkable physical strength as the elder lad; while in disposition he was less impetuous and much more studious and thoughtful.

As for the youngest of the trio, Gerald Blake, better known as Jerry, he was, in the language of his devoted friend Eli, 'an outrajus imp.' At the same time an agreeable imp with a round, laughing, freckled face and plentiful crop of red hair. An imp who could assume such a comical expression of penitence, and who could on occasion twist his tongue so delightfully round the soft brogue of his native land, that whatever prank he played, no one could be angry with him for long.

For a month or two before turning into his 'teens' Jerry had drooped somewhat, but he speedily revived when it was suggested that he should join his elder cousins in a camping-out expedition to the then unsettled shores of Broken Bay. Mrs Blake demurred at first, holding up her hands and talking of wild black sand snakes and what not; but the Doctor overruled her objections, declaring that the trip would set the youngster up in health and make a man of him.

And so, on a certain day in November, before the fiercest heats of summer had begun, the lads set out, accompanied by the indispensable Eli; the imp in the wildest spirits and raising such a dust that even his anxious mother declared that she was glad to be rid of him. The Doctor ran them up the coast in his little lugger as far as Brisbane Water, as the salt-water lake or inlet on the northern side of Broken Bay was named in after years, and there landed them, promising to call at a rendezvous on the southern shore in three weeks' time. Whereupon, they gave him three cheers, shouldered their fowling-pieces, and plunged into the bush.

Meantime, while they were tramping here and there, enjoying themselves thoroughly, something was happening at Port Jackson with the issues of which, though they did not dream of it, they were soon to be seriously concerned.

Among the convicts assigned to Major Hawkins and his partners was one William Larkin—of whom mention has already been made—who had been transported for forgery, a crime which in those days was punishable by death. The social condition of the condemned man had been such that the most strenuous endeavours were made to obtain a commutation of the sentence, and these proving successful, Larkin, a gentleman and a man of education, had been transported for the term of his natural life to the penal settlement in New Holland.

The life which Larkin had led prior to the commission of the crime which brought him within the grasp of the law had been irregular and dissipated to a degree, and his nature, cold, cruel, and crafty, was not likely to improve in the company of the ruffians with whom he was now forced to herd. Nor did it. Though retaining to a certain extent the outward polish of his palmier days, his spirit coarsened; he chose, on the sly, the worst associates, and while playing up to the authorities, cherished in his heart a sullen hatred of those by whom he was held in bondage. Such double dealing was not safe, and at last he was caught in a flagrant offence.

Had the rough-and-ready justice which prevailed in the Settlement been allowed to take its course, the culprit would have been hanged out of hand, but Major Hawkins, though something of a martinet, remembered the man's former position, and interceded for him to such good purpose that a sound flogging was substituted for the rope.

So far from being grateful, Larkin rose from his bed of pain filled with hatred of the man who had interfered to save his worthless neck, and though, when in course of time the Major took him back into his service, his demeanour was invariably subdued and respectful, his mind was made up to a bitter revenge.

From the day of his flogging he thought but of two things, revenge and flight, and his scheming brain began to revolve plan after plan of escape.

It was no ordinary plot which he conceived at length. To escape for a time, or to meet in the bush with a worse fate than he left behind, formed no part of his plan, which, briefly put, was to watch his opportunity, seize a ship and set sail with a picked gang for the China seas. But his plan included more than this: he had no desire to be followed; at any cost, therefore, when the seizure was made, attention must be distracted from those who made it.

His methods were characteristic. One Adams, who had been a sailor, and four-and-twenty carefully chosen men, he took into his confidence, and they set to work to make a boat. As may be

supposed, this was not done off-hand; but done at
last it was, plank after plank as it was finished
being stowed away in a secret place. It must be
remembered that assigned convicts enjoyed considerable liberty so long as they behaved themselves.
While this was going on, Larkin went about among
the convicts who were employed in clearing the bush
to the north of Parramatta, whispering treason and
inciting them to rise against their oppressors and
sweep the Settlement clean. None knew better than
he how impossible of execution was such a scheme,
but his fiendish design was that, while the misguided
mob rushed upon certain death, he and his chosen
few should escape in the confusion.

The boat had been put together in one of the
numerous inlets of the middle harbour, and as time
went on was laden with muskets, powder and ball,
pikes, and whatever else might be of use, while the
general body of convicts on their part busied themselves in collecting arms when and wherever they
could, and stowing them in a common hiding-place.
At last, eight months after the idea of the rising
had been broached to the wretched men, during all
which time they had loyally held their peace, all
was ready. It needed only the arrival of a suitable
ship, and the signal would be given.

Then came the fracas with Anthony, and for a
fortnight Larkin nursed his sores and his wrath
together. But at the end of that time the goal
towards which he had toiled hove in sight, and he
rose to the occasion.

A whaling brig of some four hundred tons put
into Port Jackson for provisions and water, and to

B

ship, if possible, fresh hands; for, owing to an unfortunate encounter with a whale, the original crew had been reduced to fourteen. Some provisions she got and plenty of water; but men, no, they were not obtainable. Nothing could better have suited the designs of the conspirators.

Word was quickly passed round among the ruthless twenty-four, and Larkin, after an anxious debate with Adams, decided upon adding three more to their number. The day appointed for the departure of the brig was ascertained, the hour for the insurrection fixed, and a rendezvous at Broken Bay arranged with Adams, who with nineteen men was to cut out the brig.

Fortune favoured the bold rascal Larkin, and on the appointed morning, trusting that the brig had fallen into the hands of Adams on the previous night, he led the insurgents, five hundred in number, against Parramatta. Cheered by the hope of freedom, the poor men went on blithely; but towards evening, just as a collision with the military became inevitable, their trusted leader and his lieutenants disappeared, and they were speedily attacked, routed with heavy loss, and many of them slain.

Flushed with his own success, and heedless of the misery of those whom he had so cruelly betrayed, Larkin paused a moment in his flight to attack the homestead of Major Hawkins and glut his revenge; but finding the house strongly guarded, he swallowed his disappointment and hastened to the rendezvous, which he reached some four-and-twenty hours later.

CHAPTER II.

KIDNAPPED.

'HURRAH!' shouted Jerry, capering on top of a pinnacled rock, whence he looked out afar upon the blue, dimpling ocean. 'Watch her dancing over the waves. I wonder what she is. There she goes on the other tack. Hurrah! Isn't she a beauty? Hurrah!'

'How beautiful is the enthusiasm of youth. It is quite a pleasure to watch your activity after a hard day's march, Jerry, boy,' drawled Anthony, who was lying reposefully on his back with his feet towards the smouldering logs of the camp fire.

'Don't you be after settin' up for my grandfather,' retorted Jerry, prancing upon his airy perch. 'Wough! you old lazybones, by the time I am your age '——

'You will be wiser, let us hope,' put in Guy, laughing up at him.

'An' is it you now, Guy Trimball, givin' yourself airs over me,' replied the irrepressible Jerry. 'I won't have it. Do you hear? I won't have it. I'm as good a man as any of you when I'm camping out, if I am a boy when I'm at home.'

'Ho! ho! ho! ho! ha! ha! ha! ha! ho! ha! ho! ha! ha a ah!' burst suddenly from among the branches.

'A man!' chuckled Anthony. 'Why, even the laughing jackass can't restrain himself at the idea.'

'Och, the crachur!' cried Jerry. 'I'll tache him to laugh at a man.'

'And a brother,' supplemented Guy.

'The critter has got your measure, Jerry,' laughed Eli, as the bird, disdaining to dodge the piece of biscuit Jerry hurled at it, broke into another hilarious cackle. 'Say, what's the racket? What hev you struck?'

'It's a brig,' announced Jerry, scrambling down to join the party by the fire. 'She's tacking about, first on one tack and then on the other, in the strangest way. I can't make her out. P'raps she's a pirate.'

'Then you had better signal her and offer to take command,' suggested Guy. 'Such a billet would suit you famously. Pipe good, Eli?'

'I believe you!' answered the Virginian, puffing away with quiet satisfaction. 'You don't know the consolation thar is in a pipe o' terbaccer. Jest ez well, too. Ef you two had took to it ez airly ez I did, you wouldn't hev growed to the size you are now.'

'It doesn't seem to have interfered with your growth, Eli,' said Jerry saucily. 'Let me have a draw.'

'My land! Jest don't you le' me ketch ye tryin' it on, you outrajus imp you,' cried Eli. 'I lay I'll skelp you ef I do. Give you a draw! He, he! My land! Give you a draw!'

'Father will be here to-morrow,' said Jerry. 'Of course I shall be glad to see him, but I wish we hadn't to go home just yet.'

'I don't know ez I'm sorry,' remarked Eli. 'Lookin' after the lot o' you is a terrible responsibility. I'll be glad enough to git you safe back to the Settlement. Your ma said '——

'Whose ma?' interrupted Jerry. 'I thought you were talking to the lot of us.'

'So I am,' drawled Eli. 'Your mas—your collective mas, that is, speakin' ez one ma, they said : "Eli, look after them boys, an' ef thar's any skelpin' to be done, lay it into Jerry, for it'll do him a heap o' good."'

'If you lay a finger upon me, I'll hand you over to yonder pirate,' threatened Jerry in mock wrath. 'Really, though, I wonder what she is doing out there.'

'The brig you mean,' said Eli. 'Tryin' to beat up to Port Jackson, I should say. Take her all her time, too, I 'magine.'

'Well, pirate or no pirate, I'm going to sleep,' said Anthony drowsily, 'so you had better make the most of the light while it lasts if there's to be any reading to-night, parson Guy.'

He sat up as he spoke. Eli knocked the ashes from his pipe, and Jerry pulled the muscles of his face into as grave an expression as their stubborn inclination towards comicality would allow, while Guy, taking from his pocket a small testament, read out a short passage. Then they knelt for a few moments, opening their hearts to God in the grand cathedral of His own building.

For already the night had fallen, and a full-orbed moon was climbing over the horizon to join the myriads of stars that shone and twinkled in the clear, dark-blue sky. All around were long dark aisles of forest trees, stretching from the water's edge into the illimitable gloom of the great bush, and the breeze that rustled gently through them came heavily laden with fragrant, delicious odours. Almost at their feet the smooth waters of the cove lapped in slumberous fashion upon the beach, while around the point came ever a musical, booming bass, as the long Pacific swell flung snowy-crested wave after wave upon the scarred and giant rocks.

And with no thought, no foreboding of the evil that was coming upon them, the four comrades cast themselves down beside the smouldering logs, and peacefully slept.

Some two hours after midnight Jerry awoke with a start. He had been dreaming that he was imprisoned in a burning house, and now, as he sat up and rubbed his eyes, his dream appeared to have had a certain foundation, for a hundred yards away, upon the opposite shore of the cove, there blazed an enormous fire.

'Now, who lit that?' mused Jerry, assuring himself by a glance that his companions were still in their places. 'There was no one there at sundown, and I don't see any one there now. I'll go and find out.'

No doubt he should have aroused Eli, but the spirit of adventure was strong in the boy, and he went alone, moving cautiously, as a bushman should, and making no noise as he dodged from trunk to

trunk until he stood just outside the irregular circle
of light. There he stopped short, catching back his
breath lest even that faint sound should betray his
presence. And no wonder. Behind the fire, upon
the shoreward side, stood a group of men. It did
not need a second glance to tell the boy what they
were. Besides, he recognised some of their villainous
faces.

'Convicts!' he said within himself. 'They're
making a bolt of it. What's the fire for? What's
that? It's a boat.'

Far away out upon the water he could hear the
regular dip and plash of oars, and his quick wits led
him at once to the right conclusion.

'A boat from that brig, I do believe,' he thought.
'Where else could it be from? That fire is a signal.
I must get out of this, and wake the others.'

But even as he turned to go, a hand was clapped
roughly over his mouth, another grasped his shoulder,
and as he was half pushed, half dragged into the
light, a voice muttered in his ear: 'Keep quiet, or I'll
knock your brains out. Now then, who are you?
Phew! this is a piece of luck. So it is you, young
Jerry Blake. Well, well, doth not a meeting like
this make amends? I knew that you and your
cousins were away from the Settlement, but I own I
did not look for a piece of good fortune like this.
Where are they, boy?'

'You let me go, Larkin,' answered Jerry fearlessly
as he recognised his captor. 'I see you're making a
bolt of it. We won't try and stop you. You're too
many for us.'

Larkin's low, soft laugh was not pleasant to hear.

With one hand he swung Jerry round into the grasp
of a man who stood near. 'Hold him, Johnson,' he
said. 'Knock him on the head if he makes the
faintest noise.—Oh, mates,' he went on, 'who could
have thought of this ?   What a chance to pay off old
scores !   See, there is their camp fire, burning low on
that spit yonder.   They are all asleep.   Lads, I have
done much for you.   I will do more—anything, anything—if you will only do this for me—take them
alive.   I want them for a little, only for a little;
afterwards you may work your will upon them.   But
give them to me now.—Parsons, away to the beach
and meet the boat.   Follow with the men to the
spit there.—The rest of you with me.   Quick !
quick !'

Jerry's hair stiffened upon his head, and his flesh
crept.   Everything depended upon him.   If he played
the coward now, Eli, Anthony, Guy—oh !   A great
sob rose in his throat, because for the first time he
stood face to face with death, and his strong young
body, warm with life, recoiled from the grim spectre.
It was but for an instant, and the brave spirit con-
quered.   Writhing out of the grip of the man who
held him, he bounded to one side, shouting at the top
of his voice, 'Convicts, convicts !   Eli, Anthony, take
care, take care !'

Then he dropped limply among the ferns, stunned
by a furious blow.

And after all, the warning came too late; for ere
Eli had fairly grasped the situation, or Anthony and
Guy shaken the sleep from their heavy eyelids, three
or four men fell upon each of them, and held them
fast.

'Good!' chuckled Larkin, when the capture had been effected. 'That was cleverly managed.—Now, now, Mr Hawkins,' as Anthony struggled desperately to shake himself free, 'all that is quite useless; even your phenomenal strength cannot help you now. —To the boat with them, lads.—Johnson, bring the boy.—Some of you clear out their camp, and scatter the fire. Be careful not to leave anything behind.'

'Quiet, Anthony,' advised Eli. 'They're five to one now, and you don't know how many there may be behind 'em.—Whar's the little boy?' he added to Larkin. 'Fetch him here. Thar's no sense in frightenin' him.'

'Jem,' said Larkin to Johnson, who just then came up, 'where is the boy?'

'In the bushes somewhere,' returned Johnson. 'You told me to knock him on the head if he yelped. Well, he did yelp; didn't ye hear him?'

'So you knocked him on the head,' said Larkin pleasantly. 'Quite right.'

A cry of bitter wrath broke from Anthony, and so furiously did he struggle to get at Larkin that even the three men had work enough to restrain him. At last a fourth approached, and between them he was cast violently to the ground and firmly held.

'Such a fuss about so little,' said Larkin. 'Here comes your cousin.'

'Thank God!' exclaimed Guy, as Johnson, who at a hint from Larkin had withdrawn once more, now reappeared, holding Jerry by the arm.

The boy walked with uncertain steps and staggered every now and then, for he was still faint and dizzy from the effect of the cruel blow. He stared about

him in a bewildered fashion as he reached the group,
and then recognising how matters stood, broke from
Johnson's grasp and ran to Anthony's side with a low
cry of dismay.

'Oh, Anthony,' he said, 'I'm so sorry; I did my
best, but he hit me, and I think I must have fainted.
Oh! there's Eli. I'm so glad.'

'You brute!' exclaimed Anthony, lifting his head
to glare at Johnson. 'I'll punish you for this.'

'Why?' asked Larkin lightly. 'The man was
only obeying orders, Mr Hawkins, and as a soldier's
son, I am sure you will admit the propriety of that.
You seem to forget, too, my young friend, that our
positions are reversed. We are up now and you are
down.'

'Don't anger him, Anthony,' urged Guy as the
former made a hot retort.—'Eli, be quiet. Can't you
see that we are quite helpless?—Come, Larkin, there
has been enough of this. Call off your men and go
your way; we can't do anything to stop you.'

'Onless you like ter stop an' go back with us in the
Hornet at sunrise,' put in Eli. 'That'd save a heap
o' trouble all round.'

Again Larkin laughed that unpleasant laugh of his.
'You don't suppose, my young parson,' he said, addressing Guy, 'that I'm going to turn you loose just
as the Fates have been kind enough to deliver you
into my hands.'

'Why, what can you do with us?' demanded
Guy. 'You can't take us with you into the bush,
and as I've been told you were a gentleman once,
I don't suppose you'd allow us to be murdered in
cold blood.'

He spoke in a tone of easy superiority. The young fellows had been so long used to absolute and unquestioning obedience on the part of the wretched men, cowed as the latter were by fear of lash and rope, that they were actually slow to realise the danger in which they stood, now that the tables were turned.

'It does not matter what I was once,' answered Larkin in a grating voice. 'What I am now, your father and his'—pointing to Anthony—'have helped to make me. As to murdering you in cold blood, as you put it, I would do it without compunction if it suited my plans. Fortunately for you it does not—at present; so after all, I must trouble you to go with me.'

'Oh, very well,' said Guy almost carelessly. 'Of course you will do as you choose. I suppose you think that by holding us you will be able to make terms with the authorities. It's rather clever of you.'

'You don't understand, Guy,' cried Jerry. 'They've got a boat, and I shouldn't wonder if that brig we saw this afternoon were waiting for them.'

'Oh!' ejaculated Guy weakly. This was news indeed.

'Yes,' said Larkin; 'the boy is right. We have a ship out there; and much as I regret the necessity, I am going to ask you all to take a cruise with me.'

'Better knock 'em on the head and have done with it,' suggested one of the convicts.

'When I want your advice I will ask for it, Ben Danby,' said Larkin sharply. Then as some murmuring arose among the men, he hastened to add: 'Can't you see, lads, that to finish them off and leave them

here would give a clue to the way we had gone?
Their friends know that they are hereabouts, of
course, and you heard what the American said as to
the vessel which is to call for them in the morning.
Were they found here dead, the matter would at once
be laid at our door. Having thus traced us to the
coast, the authorities would certainly conclude that
we had found some means to quit the country, and a
ship would be despatched to scour the seas in search
of us. So long as we are supposed to have gone inland, we are safe from that, whatever happens. You
shall have ample opportunity to pay off old scores by-
and-by, I promise you.'

'Bravo! Well argued! That's the ticket! We
can drop 'em overboard in blue water!' exclaimed the
convicts as Larkin paused.

'Go then, some of you, gather up their belongings,
and scatter the camp fire,' went on the leader. 'It
must be supposed that they have gone inland or that
the blacks have carried them off. In fact, it doesn't
matter what is supposed so long as attention is drawn
from us. Be careful to leave nothing behind. To
the boats, now. March, you three.'

'We will not stir a foot,' cried Anthony.

'Mr Hawkins,' said Larkin impressively, 'but that
I have a particular reason for wishing to take you
aboard alive, I would not stop to argue with you. It
is different with your cousin here.' He drew Jerry
towards him. 'I'd as soon ship him dead as alive;
but I leave the responsibility with you. At the first
sign of any further struggle on your part I will put
a ball through young Blake's head and carry you off
just the same. Choose.'

Anthony cast one despairing glance around which showed him the madness of resistance, and with a muttered execration marched towards the beach and followed his companions aboard the boat.

As soon as Larkin had taken his place the men shoved off, and in a few moments the little brig, now lying almost becalmed, hove in sight, looking like a fairy picture in the moonlight.

'Brig ahoy!' shouted Larkin. 'Are you there, Tom Adams?'

'Ay, ay!' came the prompt reply. 'Well, well, Bill, it's been long adoing, but done it is at last. What kep' you so long?'

'A mere trifle,' answered Larkin. 'I've got four prisoners in the boat with me—young Hawkins, his cousins, and the American.'

Adams swore a broad oath. 'Hand 'em up,' he said when he had sufficiently recovered from his surprise to be able to express himself in plain English. 'Hand 'em up. There's a land breeze coming off the shore. I'll hear your story and tell you mine when once we're on blue water.—Hook that boat on, and run her up to the davits!' he shouted at the men. 'Smart, you lubbers!—Luff up, you there!' to the man at the wheel; and the brig coming up to the wind, checked her way and gave the fellows who were hauling at the boat a chance.

'Now then, lads,' went on Adams as soon as the boat was up, 'make sail! We'll give her the canvas while we've got the breeze.' And soon under a press of sail the brig stood out of the bay on a north-easterly course.

'Keep her at that,' ordered Adams. 'She'll stand

all this and more, though she does be manned by a
lot o' land-lubbers. No matter. Who cares ?—Now
Bill,' he said, coming up to Larkin and extending a
brown, hairy paw. 'I wasn't going to lose this
breeze, not for any man ; but now we 're off and away,
give us a grip, old hunks. Here we are, and here
you are, and right glad I am to see us all.'

'So am I,' answered Larkin, shaking hands heartily.
'Now, lads, three cheers for Captain Tom and his
merry men, and three more for freedom and a jolly
life.'

'Hurrah ! hurrah !' shouted the convicts joyously ;
and when the cheering ceased, Larkin turned again
to Adams.

'Where can you stow the prisoners until I have
decided where to put them ?' he inquired.

'Bundle 'em down in the hold the while,' replied
Adams.

'Along with the crew of the brig, I suppose,' said
Larkin.

'The crew o' the brig !' echoed Adams. 'Why,
Bill, ye don't suppose we took this here craft by
squirting gruel along her decks. The crew o' the
brig ! That's a good un. They 'll have to go a good
bit deeper than the hold if they want to bring up
alongside the crew o' the brig. Ho ! ho ! ho !'

'What do you mean ?' demanded Larkin.

'Arsk Davy Jones,' grinned Adams.

Larkin turned upon him in a flash. 'Why, you
blundering idiot,' he cried wrathfully, 'you don't
mean to say that you have made away with them.
You clumsy rascal, how are we to navigate the
brig ?'

'Don't you be so free with your tongue, Bill Larkin,' answered Adams sullenly. 'You ought to have thought o' that afore. You don't suppose we took the brig without some little trouble. I've got three o' 'em under hatches. The others was killed or wounded at the first rush. We sailed east a bit and dropped 'em overboard, and then put about to look for you. I don't see as we could have done aught else.'

'No; of course not,' assented Larkin. 'I spoke hastily. But how do we stand for men ?'

'Well, there's me and Abel Dobbs, and Bob Hunt, and Luke Rogers, we've all been to sea one time or another,' answered Adams, ticking off upon his fingers. 'Then there's the mate and two men belonging to the brig—that's seven—and then there's the American, he's a sailor, and them two lads as knows more about a ship, so I've heard tell, than many as has been to sea. That's ten.'

'You take a good deal for granted, you rascals. You will get no help from any of us,' cried Anthony defiantly.

Larkin took no notice of him. 'Ten serviceable men,' he said to Adams, 'and a score or so more who are willing to learn. Come, we shan't do so badly after all. It's not quite what I had decided upon with regard to one of them at least,' with a malevolent glance at Anthony; 'but no doubt before long we shall be able to dispense with the services of the impressed men. Meantime, take them down below, some of you. All but the youngster; he can stay with me.'

'What are you going to do with him,' demanded

Anthony, struggling fiercely with the men who held him.

'That depends entirely upon your behaviour, as I have already told you,' answered Larkin. 'If you persist in giving exhibitions of your brute strength, I won't answer for what may happen.'

'You cur,' shouted Anthony, shaking and trembling with rage. 'I'll teach you such a lesson some day as shall make you sorry that my father begged you off when the rope was round your worthless neck.'

'Shet your head, Anthony'—'Hush!' exclaimed Eli and Guy in a breath, while the former added in a sharp whisper: 'Don't make things wuss'n they are already. Thar's no sense in that.'

'I don't forget my debt to your father, Mr Hawkins,' said Larkin stonily.—'Get rid of them, Tom.'

Anthony recovered his self-command. 'Jerry, lad,' he called out as he suffered the men to lead him away, 'we can't help you without harming you just now. But keep a good heart; it will all come right.'

'I'm not afraid, Anthony,' replied the boy stoutly, smiling back at Guy, who laid a hand gently on his shoulder as he passed by.

'Right, boys; don't let him skeer you,' cried Eli. 'Bill Larkin holds all the cards jest now; but thar's many a deal in the game o' life, and we'll have a fresh one by-an'-by.'

CHAPTER III

MAKING THE BEST OF IT.

ARKIN stood with Adams on the poop of the *Swallow*. The stars were paling, and along the eastern horizon a pink glow edged the dark border of the sea. In a few moments the soft and lovely colour flushed a sudden red, and long lines of crimson climbed into the purple sky. Another pause, and a broad blaze of golden light came rippling over the white-tipped waves to the side of the brig; up went fiery shaft after fiery shaft, shooting higher and higher, and, as with a bound the mighty sun sprang from his bed, Night spread her wings and fled away.

'How beautiful!' exclaimed Larkin, expanding his chest and inhaling the delicious morning air.

> '"Morn,
> Waked by the circling hours, with rosy hand
> Unbarred the gates of light."

'I think I quote it aright, though it's a long time since I've seen the book. Was ever so bright a sun? Was ever so glorious a world?' And it is all ours, Tom—all ours to do as we will with. For we are free, Tom Adams; we are free! Think of it, man.'

c

He brought his hand down with a slap upon the other's broad back. 'Ha, ha! It was worth working and waiting for so long.'

'It were, Bill, it were,' agreed Tom; 'though I think as you might have said it plainer.'

'Can you look at that and not recognise the beauty and the glory of it?' said Larkin, pointing to the sun. 'What a blaze! what a splendour! I can well believe that certain races worship it. I declare it makes a new creature of me. I've been in darkness all these years. I've been a beast, a brute; but now I'm a man again, for I'm free! I'm free!'

Tom Adams glanced queerly at him. 'I don't rightly understand you, Bill,' he said soothingly. 'I 'spect this has been a bit too much for you, coming so suddent like at the end. But there, you'll get used to it in time.'

Larkin laughed. 'Well, never mind me,' he said. 'I see Bennet carrying breakfast into the cabin, and I for one am quite ready for it. First of all though, let us have up the prisoners and give them a little straight talk. You were serious, I suppose, when you said that we should need their services?'

'Oh, perfec'ly,' answered Adams. 'Let's keep 'em till we get some of our own lubbers brushed up a bit.'

'Very good,' assented Larkin, adding with a sinister emphasis, 'I can wait.'

'You've got a big grudge agen the Major, Bill, I know,' said Adams; 'but I should say as you've pretty well paid for it by walking off with his son, which o' course you won't let him go home agen. But you'll be a bigger fool than I take you for if you do him any harm. Why, he 's as good as three men.'

Larkin jerked his hand over his shoulder and tapped his back. 'For every scar his father and he laid upon my back I will lay two upon his. I swear it,' he said.

'The boy ain't his father,' protested Adams. 'Seems to me you 've got your fill o' the old man without going no further.'

'The son is in my hands; the father is not,' said Larkin emphatically.

'Well, leave him be till I give the word,' grumbled Adams. 'We 're short-handed enough as it is. Look at them land-lubbers,' he added contemptuously, jerking his thumb towards the convicts, most of whom were lying about the deck in the agonies of sea-sickness. 'If you want to chuck any one overboard, begin with two or three o' them. They 'll be better food for the sharks than young Hawkins and his mates.'

'I won't touch him till you 've drilled them into shape,' Larkin promised. 'Now fetch them on deck.'

Adams uncovered the hatchway and thrust in his head. 'Below there,' he shouted. 'Come up on deck. Tumble up, sharp, now !—You, Dobbs, fetch aft the brig's crew—what 's left of 'em.'

'Extraordinary talk these sailors indulge in,' muttered Larkin. 'Tumble up! If it were tumble down now.—Ah, Mr Hawkins,' as Anthony stepped on deck, 'you look a trifle pale. Have you found the hold unpleasant, or are you afraid of what I may be going to do to you ?'

Anthony's sole answer was a fierce scowl, at which

Larkin laughed. 'Come along, Mr Trimball,' he went on to Guy. 'You look rather the worse for wear too. Feeling ill?'

'No, thank you,' answered Guy pleasantly, 'but I'm much obliged to you for letting us out. I couldn't have stood the air of the hold much longer.'

'A lesson in manners for you, Mr Hawkins,' said Larkin with a nod towards Anthony. 'You will find before I've done with you that politeness pays.' Then observing that Guy looked anxiously about the deck, he added, 'Your cousin is asleep in the cuddy, Mr Trimball.'

'Thank you,' said Guy again, and whispered to Anthony, 'Do be civil to him. Everything depends upon our behaviour.'

'How can you truckle to the brute?' answered Anthony disgustedly, in a low voice.

'Hello! Shiver my timbers! What's this?' exclaimed Adams, as Eli, the picture of distress, staggered upon deck. 'Why, I thought you was a sailor, Eli Banks.'

'So I am, and a heap better'n you at that,' quavered Eli. 'You can't jedge a man by his stummick; not by a long sight, I tell you. I'm always like this for a bit when first I leave port; but I'm 'most better now, fer I've had the worst o' the wrastle out, thank you.'

He too seemed determined to make the best of matters and to keep a smiling face, and he cast a glance at Anthony, who still stood frowning haughtily, as if imploring him to do the same.

'Now, listen to me,' said Larkin, turning to the survivors of the crew of the brig. 'I understand from Captain Adams here, that we are unfortunately very short-handed. You probably guessed that. Well, we must have your help. Will you give it willingly?'

'No?' answered the men with one voice, whereat Anthony cried out exultantly, 'Of course they won't. They are honest British tars; not murdering pirates like you.'

'I'll deal with you presently,' said Larkin. 'Meantime, hold your tongue.—Very good,' he resumed to the men; 'I will put the matter differently. You have had your chance, and you must not suppose we cannot get on without you.—Three or four of you there, throw that short fellow into the sea.'

'Mercy!' shrieked the man, falling upon his knees.

But Whitson, the mate, took a step forward.

'Belay, there!' he exclaimed. 'If you'd put it that way before, we'd have answered different. We'll work the ship for what we're worth, and there's an end on't. But we'll do nothing else.'

'I ask no more of you,' answered Larkin shortly, waving back the advancing convicts.—'Now, you others, you have heard and seen. Will you do seamen's duty along with these fellows here?'

'We will,' answered Guy quickly.

'We will not!' roared Anthony.—'Guy, how dare you say such a thing? You may all go to the bottom of the sea before I will do a hand's turn to prevent it. You—I'——— He stammered, stopped, and let his clenched fists fall to his sides, for just then Jerry stepped from the companion-hatch. Larkin,

too, observed the boy; but though he smiled, he made
no remark.

'Will you give us a moment together?' asked
Guy, taking Jerry's hand as he ran up to them.

'Certainly,' acquiesced Larkin, and at once retreated a few paces, taking Adams with him.

'Eli, tell Anthony that I am right,' urged Guy
earnestly. 'I am sure we ought to agree. It is
most providential that we all know something about
a ship, otherwise I believe he would have dropped
us overboard without thinking twice about it. For
Jerry's sake we must obey him.——Oh! Anthony,
do be patient. Those sailors are honest men, and
perhaps by-and-by'——

'By George! I never thought of that,' interrupted
Anthony, his face brightening. 'Of course if we can
teach them not to be afraid of that brute, Larkin,
we shall win the game. Guy, old fellow, I wish I
had your head.'

'You've a good enough one o' your own, ef only
you'd use it,' said Eli. 'You'll be the death o' us
all ef you don't rein back that temper. Guy's got ez
much spunk ez you hev, an' a heap more sense.——Go
on, Guy, tell Larkin we agree.'

Anthony reddened and bit his lip. 'You are right,
Eli,' he said with an effort.——'Go ahead, Guy. You
won't have any more trouble from me.'

'Tell him that I'll be cabin-boy an' do anythin'
to sarve him, if only he'll give me somethin' to ate
just now; for it's starvin' I am entoirely,' said
Jerry in his broadest brogue, though his eyes
were swimming in tears. Whereat they all broke
out laughing.

Larkin advanced, his face plainly showing the surprise he felt.

'Something amuses you, gentlemen,' he said. 'I am glad to find that you take your troubles so lightly. May I ask if you have decided?'

'Yes,' answered Guy; 'we agree.'

CHAPTER IV.

'ANTHONY, you've done splendidly,' said Guy a few minutes later, as they sat in a group apart, discussing the breakfast which Bennet had brought them. 'I know what the struggle must have cost you.'

'You do not,' snapped Anthony, savagely bolting his food. 'You can't possibly know. You—you—you have no spirit. If it hadn't been for Jerry, I'd have jumped into the sea before I'd have given in.'

Guy looked hurt. 'I meant that,' he said gently. 'I know you were not thinking of yourself.'

'Ah, never mind me,' said Jerry. 'I'll do the best I can, if you'll show me how. I suppose he'll make a cabin-boy of me. I—I—I'—— He choked, flung his tin plate with a clatter upon the deck, and, rising hastily, walked aft and sprang into the main shrouds, where he hung on, gazing in the direction of his home.

'Pore little boy!' said Eli. 'He feels pretty badly jest now, an' I don't wonder, thinkin' o' his ma and all.'

Guy swallowed something that sounded suspiciously like a sob, and Anthony, as quick to atone as to offend, grasped him warmly by the hand.

'But Jerry is young,' went on Eli, 'an' his trouble won't seem so sharp after a while goes by; that is, provided we do the best we can fer him an' help him to fergit. An' I 'low, Anthony, much depends on you. I'm the oldest man among you, an' you mustn't mind me speakin' straight, fer I reckon to stand in the place o' your pas an' mas, as it were; an' more 'n that, you know 'thout tellin' that whatever Eli Banks kin do to serve any one o' you won't be lackin'. So I'll jest say one word an' be done. Keep that red-hot temper o' yours fer them ez deserves it, an' wait till the proper time comes before ye show it even to them; that is, ef you ever want to see your home agen, ez I jedge you do. But ef you 're goin' to fly down Guy's throat ez you did jest now every time he opens his mouth to talk sense, an' ef you 're goin' to make Jerry discontented with what he 's got to bear, an' with what he 'll larn to bear right enough ef you set him a good example, why then you 're not the boy I 've took you fer all through these last three years. Now I 've done, an' I hope you 'll not git riled, fer I mean no offence.'

'Not I, Eli,' answered Anthony frankly. 'I deserve all you have said and more.—Guy, forgive me.'

'Dear old fellow,' said Guy, smiling affectionately at him.

'Waal, ef you want more, hyar it is,' said Eli. 'I reckon ef Larkin had meant to get rid o' us he 'd

hev done it at the start. Sence he's shipped us,
I 'magine ez soon ez he gits his rascals in hand he'll
set us ashore somewhar. An' it don't matter whar,
for anywhar's better'n this, an' we'll find our
way home somehow. But ef you don't rein back
that temper, you'll be the death o' us all; an' jest
you remember it.'

'I will,' answered Anthony. 'You will have
no more trouble of my making. But if Larkin—
you forget the cause he has to feel vengeful against
me'—— he broke off. 'I hope you may be right as
regards his intentions.'

'No, I don't fergit,' said Eli; 'an' ef I'm not
right, waal, thar's no sense in meetin' trouble
half-way. Don't you give him an excuse more'n
what he's got; that's all I ask.—Hello, boy;
got back?'

'Yes,' answered Jerry, walking up and nestling
against him. 'What are you talking about?'

Eli threw a protecting arm about him. 'We
were sayin',' he replied, 'ez thar never was a night
so dark ez the day didn't dawn at the end o' it.
—So now, boys, hands round, an' with the help o'
God we'll make the best o' our bad-luck, an' hope
fer better times.'

He grasped their hands one by one and held
them for a moment firmly in his own. Then he
walked quickly away, for his own emotion was
deeper than he chose that they should see.

But, as was only to be expected, the excitement
which had at first sustained the boys was succeeded
by a violent reaction. Their spirits, elastic as they
were, refused to rise, and a feeling of despair took

possession of them. It was not so much upon
their own account, for they were quick to realise
that they were in no immediate danger, but the
thought of their parents waiting and watching for
their home-coming, ignorant of the fate which had
befallen them, searching in the wrong direction, and
finally abandoning all hope of ever seeing them
again, filled them with anguish. In those dark
days of trial Eli was father, mother, elder brother,
and friend, all in one, to them. In turn he soothed
Jerry, calmed Anthony, and encouraged Guy, adapt-
ing himself with wonderful sympathy to the mood
of each of them, and striving by every means in
his power to lighten their load of sorrow.

But time tempers all things well, and as the
brig held her course over smooth seas and under
bright blue skies, the lads began to accommodate
themselves to their altered positions. Though
there were hours when their hearts were sad, yet
hope returned to buoy them up; and faithful to
their agreement to make the best of the situation,
their faces were always bright and cheerful, and
they did their work with a thoroughness and goodwill which excited the admiration of not a few
of the rough rascals by whom they were surrounded.
Whatever Larkin's faults were, he had a genius for
administration, and with the aid of Adams, who
was appointed skipper, the state of confusion pre-
vailing on board the brig was very quickly reduced
to order, the spirit-room locked, and every weapon
that could be found aboard passed aft and secured
in the cabin. It was enough, Larkin declared,
that he and Skipper Adams should carry arms;

they had not come aboard to cut one another's
throats, and all disputes were to be referred to
him for settlement. To keep the fellows in good
humour after this first show of authority he divided
amongst them the clothes of the late crew, reserving
the captain's effects for his own use, and served
out a tot of grog all round. With the help of Eli
and Timothy Whitson, the mate of the brig, the
crew were divided into watches, and carefully
instructed in their various duties. Every day they
were drilled, taught the names and uses of the
various ropes and spars, and sent aloft for a few
minutes at a time until gradually they grew accustomed to the novel sensation. Half-a-dozen useless
members were soon weeded out and set to other
work, while before they had been three weeks out,
the remainder had at least learned to hand a reef
and to know the difference between a sheet and a
halyard. The actual navigation of the brig was
entrusted to Whitson, whilst Eli, Adams, and the
experienced seamen took charge of the wheel in
turn.

While he treated his prisoners with civility, and
Jerry with some approach to consideration, Larkin's
behaviour to Anthony was very different. The
lad's lot was harder by far than that of any one
on board; he was set to the most menial duties,
and by every method which cold malignity could
devise, Larkin sought to inflame his temper and
provoke him to retort. In this, however, the
convict was unsuccessful, for Anthony, burning
with wrath though he was, and desiring nothing
more fervently than a chance to turn upon his

tormentor, was mindful of Eli's advice, and kept his temper splendidly under control.

But Larkin possessed an extraordinary fund of patience and was content to bide his time. He saw clearly enough the effect produced upon some of his men by the cheerful submission of the boys, and he was by no means sure that any act of unreasonable tyranny might not be resented by that section of the crew. Could he but excite Anthony to a display of insubordination, his course would be clear, and to this end he worked and schemed.

'I suppose our fellows are becoming fairly expert at their duties now,' he remarked to Adams one evening when they had been about a month at sea.

'Oh, well, I've known better,' answered Adams, turning the quid in his cheek; 'but the lubbers has larned something, I'll admit.'

'And you would trust them to handle the ship under your direction?' went on Larkin, leaning over the taffrail and gazing at the sparkling water as though not particularly interested in the answer.

'Oh, well, I dessay,' replied Adams carelessly.

Larkin nodded and walked forward, thinking deeply. Presently he encountered Guy, who was staggering along towards the galley bearing a pile of greasy plates. A moment later Jerry's fresh young voice rose in a merry song on the forecastle. Larkin leant against the bulwarks and listened with evident pleasure. His artistic sense was stirred, and a dreamy far-away look came into his eyes as his foot mechanically beat time to Jerry's song. As he stood there, clad in the late captain's best suit of blue pilot cloth, his cravat neatly tied, and the cruel lines of his mouth half hidden under his rapidly growing moustache and beard, he did not even faintly suggest the desperate convict of a few weeks ago, who had coolly plotted the death of so many for his own benefit. His manner, too, was invariably smooth and refined; nor, even when he had occasion to assert his authority over his lawless companions, was his language ever foul or violent. The wickedness of this man lay far below the surface, and was all the more dangerous.

'What an exquisite voice that youngster has,' he said to himself, 'and how well he bears his troubles for so young a lad. Upon my word, to judge by the behaviour of all four of them, one might suppose them to be out for a pleasure cruise instead of prisoners who hold their lives at my disposal. It's all in the breeding, I suppose. Good blood can't lie it is said. Can't it? What was I? What am I?' His face became overcast, and he sank into a gloomy reverie.

The loud clapping and shouts of applause that greeted the conclusion of Jerry's song roused him.

'If this goes on, my influence will be undermined to a certain extent,' he mused. Then as a sudden thought struck him his blue eyes flashed, a sinister smile curled his lip, and he brought the clenched right hand down with a slap into the palm of his left. 'By George!' he muttered. 'The very thing; I wonder I did not think of that before. Now I think I have you, Mr Hawkins. Hullo! there, Mr Trimball, I want you,' he hailed Guy, who just then stepped out of the galley.

'Yes,' said Guy in his usual quiet voice as he came up. 'What is it?'

'Your cousin has an exquisite voice, Mr Trimball,' began Larkin, 'but he uses it rather too freely. There must be less of his singing.'

'There won't be much difficulty about that,' answered Guy. 'I 'll tell him.'

'Understand me; I don't refer to the class of song that he was singing just now,' went on Larkin. 'I am aware that the men in a measure force him to pipe to them, though I dare say that like a bird in captivity he takes some pleasure out of his own song. But at night as a general rule I hear his voice raised in something which I take to be a hymn, to which, I grieve to say, some of the men appear to listen with close attention.'

'We do not ask the men to listen,' said Guy. 'If they choose to do so, that is their affair.'

'No,' answered Larkin; 'it is my affair. As an educated man yourself, Mr Trimball, you must be aware that ignorant men are usually superstitious, and I can't allow you to make milksops of my crew with your rubbish. The example is a very bad one. I am sure that you are the chief mover in things of this sort, and I look to you to stop it. There must be no more of this psalm-singing non-sense; and I should like you to clearly understand that if there should be, I shall hold you responsible, and the consequences will be serious—very serious indeed—for you. Now you may go.' Guy turned away in silence; but Larkin stopped him. 'What are you smiling at, Mr Trimball?'

'I wasn't smiling,' answered Guy.

'Yes, you were, Mr Trimball, or, at least, you had your tongue in your cheek as you turned away.'

'That is not true,' said Guy with slight heat. 'I see how it is, Larkin. You are trying to find some excuse for making trouble.'

'Very astute of you,' sneered Larkin, though his eyes glittered. 'You are not so polite as usual. This is my ship, and I mean to be treated with respect by all on board of her. I don't permit you to address me in that off-hand way. As a punishment, be good enough to ascend the mainmast, take your seat on the what d'ye call it, and scrape the paint off the what's its name—you probably know what I mean much better than I do myself. Up with you, and stay there until I call you down.'

This time Guy smiled broadly, but he made no answer as he ran rapidly up the rigging to the main-topmast-head, and began to scrape the *grease*, not the paint, off the cap. The swift and sudden darkness of the tropics fell long before he had finished, and he began to wonder if Larkin had forgotten all about him, since the order had been given with a sort of mock seriousness. It certainly never occurred to him that so simple an action as skying him to the mast-head covered a deep design. All at once, Jerry's sweet voice floated up to him, and he listened apprehensively, expecting a hasty interruption. But none came, and as the last notes of the hymn died away Larkin hailed him from below: 'Come down on deck, Mr Trimball.' Guy hastened down, supposing that he should find Larkin waiting for him, but encountering no one, he made his way to the forecastle, where he got his supper before turning in.

The convict dropped senseless to the deck.

PAGE 47.

'I'll tell Jerry about Larkin's order in the morning,' he thought as he climbed into his hammock; for Jerry, his mouth wide open, and emitting the most tremendous snores, was sleeping soundly.

But when he awoke, his cousins were still asleep, so again postponing the announcement, he slipped on deck, stripped off his shirt, and prepared to take his usual morning towelling at a bucket of salt water.

While he was drying himself he was roughly seized, dragged along the deck, and before he could realise what the men were about, was securely tied up to a grating.

'What is this for?' demanded Guy indignantly; 'what have I done?'

'You have disobeyed my express orders,' said Larkin, who had been directing the scene, which had evidently been carefully rehearsed. 'I told you that if there was any more of that caterwauling the consequences would be serious for you. You can't say I didn't warn you.'

'But I never had a chance to tell Jerry,' protested Guy. 'You mastheaded me.'

'I called you down in good time,' answered Larkin.

'You did not,' cried Guy. 'Oh, I see it all. You have laid a trap for me. Larkin, you are not going to flog me?'

For at that moment Hunt, the boatswain, stepped forward with a cat-o'-nine-tails in his hand, and ran the lashes lovingly through his fingers.

'Oh no, I wouldn't call it flogging,' answered Larkin. 'Just a few light strokes to convince you that I mean to be obeyed.'

He did not look at Guy; his whole attention was

D

fixed upon the fore-hatch. He appeared to be expecting some one.

'Anthony! Eli!' shouted Guy at the top of his
voice. 'Help! help!'

With a bound Anthony sprang on deck. For a
moment he looked about him bewildered, and then as
his eyes fell upon the figure at the grating, sprang
forward with a shout of rage. But everything had
been carefully prepared, and as Anthony leaped to the
relief of his cousin, Dobbs tripped him up, and he
fell heavily to the deck. At the same time Eli, who
had come up the hatchway with Jerry at his heels,
was seized and firmly held.

The Virginian recognised the position of affairs
instantly. His quick eye noted that for the first
time some two or three of the convicts were armed,
and further, that the mate and the two sailors belonging to the brig were not upon deck. As a matter of
fact, they had been battened under hatches when they
went below at the conclusion of their watch. Adams
was at the wheel, viewing the scene with apparent
indifference.

'It's a plant,' thought Eli. 'He don't want to
flog Guy. It's Anthony he's after. Lord! if the
boy gits loose thar'll be murder done.'

'Quiet, Mr Hawkins,' ordered Larkin. 'What do
you mean by making such a commotion?'

'You brute!' panted Anthony, struggling to his
knees. 'If you lay a finger upon him, I'll'——

'Silence!' vociferated Larkin. 'I'll have no insubordination aboard this ship. Keep quiet if you
value your own skin,' whereat Anthony only
struggled the more.

'Why, what's the young 'un done?' inquired Luke Rogers, stepping forward a pace.

'He has been disobedient,' snapped Larkin, turning swiftly upon the man. 'Do you mean to dispute my authority?'

'No, not me,' said Rogers, recoiling as he saw Larkin's fingers playing with the butt of a pistol.

'You had better not,' said Larkin grimly. 'It is just as well that you should all realise that there is but one master here.—Hunt, do your duty.'

Guy's face was deadly pale: He was brave, but his heart sank and his spirit quailed at the horrid prospect: His lips moved slightly as he glanced at Anthony, and then with a weary hopeless sigh, he turned his face to the grating, and closed his eyes.

Hunt stepped back a pace, and raised his arm. A scream of horror burst from Jerry, who flung himself sobbing upon the deck, but ere the blow could fall, Anthony, mad with fury, broke from the men who held him, and with a growl like that of an enraged mastiff, ran right at Hunt. Like lightning his fist shot straight out from the shoulder, and the convict, caught squarely between the eyes, dropped the cat, flung his hands above his head with a hoarse cry, and dropped senseless to the deck.

'Seize him!' roared Larkin. He had no time to say more, for without an instant's pause Anthony wheeled and rushed at him. The convict sprang aside to dodge the furious blow aimed at his head, but before he could draw his pistol the young giant's arms were wound about him, and he found enough to do to keep his feet.

'Hold on to him!' shouted Eli, springing from between his captors; but one of them struck him smartly on the head with a belaying pin, and down he went like a log.

Meanwhile the furious struggle raged between Larkin and Anthony. The convict was a strong man, but, as he soon began to realise, no match for his antagonist, whose terrible embrace crushed in his ribs until he fairly gasped for breath.

Suddenly Anthony shifted his grip. The great muscles of his arms stood out like thick ropes, and with a mighty heave he swung Larkin off his feet, and heedless of a rain of blows upon his face and head, staggered with his heavy burden to the side of the ship.

'Help!' screeched Larkin. 'Rush him, you curs!'

But the convicts, amazed, or perhaps actuated by the Englishman's love of fair-play, stood still and made no attempt to interfere.

In another moment their leader would have been hurled into the sea, but Adams with a twist of the wheel brought the brig sharply up to the wind, and as she pitched violently, Anthony, unable to retain his footing, fell heavily against the gunwale. Instantly half-a-dozen men flung themselves upon him, and though he fought desperately, he was speedily overcome.

'Take the helm, Dobbs,' shouted Adams. 'Keep her away.' As soon as he had been relieved he hurried forward. 'Where are Whitson and them other skulkers?' he demanded. 'Go below and fetch 'em up,' he vociferated as some one in-

formed him. 'Turn them lads loose, and be sharp
about it.'

What do you mean?' panted Larkin, livid with
wrath.

'Turn 'em loose !' roared Adams again ; and as the
men looked hesitatingly at Larkin, he sprang to the
grating, and with a few slashes of his knife cut the
cords which bound Guy.

'Do you know that I command aboard this ship,
Mr Adams ?' hissed Larkin, advancing, pistol in hand.
'If'——

'Yah !' snorted Adams. 'Put up that popgun, or
I 'll brain you.—Away aloft there, lads, and reef
topsails. Away there, Whitson, with your men. By
all that 's blue, we shall catch it hot before we can
get snug.—Curse you for a fool,' he stormed at
Larkin. 'Do you see what you 've done ? There 's
two good seamen knocked out o' time all along o'
you and your tantrums. Didn't you promise me to
put off this flogging humbug till I gave the word ?
Do you think I 'm going to have my crew cut into
strips to please you ?—Up there, you lubbers ! Up,
and do what ye can, though it ain't much. Up there,
sharp !'

As Adams continued to rave, Larkin recovered his
self-command. He saw that something unusual was
about to occur, though being no sailor, he could form
no idea of what it might be, for the brig was bowl-
ing merrily along, and his inexperienced eye could
discern no cause for alarm. So taking advantage
of a break in the skipper's flow of profanity, he
inquired in the smoothest of voices what was the
matter.

'Matter!' howled Adams. 'Matter! why you, this, that, and the other thing swab of a land-lubber, as don't know a backstay from a gridiron, there's a hurricane tearing down on top o' us at sixty miles an hour, and that's what's the matter!'

CHAPTER V.

BREAKERS AHEAD!

THOUGH it was certainly true that in his desire for revenge Larkin had acted without consulting Adams, yet, as certainly, the skipper would not have interfered had not his trained eye detected the first sign of an advancing storm, when his indifference instantly vanished in concern for his own safety. But wroth though he was at the temporary loss of two of his best seamen, there was scant time for recrimination, for already the breeze was freshening and the horizon to windward darkening ominously; every moment was of importance if the ship was to be made snug before the squall struck her. Anthony and Guy, forgetful of their immediate wrongs in the presence of the greater danger, found no opportunity to exchange congratulations until they laid out upon the fore-topsail yard, whence they could see that Eli was sitting up and comforting Jerry, who had been hanging over him in the greatest distress.

Adams ran hither and thither, working like a horse and bellowing directions to the more ignorant

members of the crew. At last all was done, the courses
hauled up, the small sails furled and stowed, and the
Swallow raced along under double-reefed topsails, the
white sea-dust flying before her, and the water churning at her bows and running aft in silver streaks.
All was snug for the present, and as the boys swung
down and hastened to Eli, Adams, his anxiety allayed,
turned to see how Hunt was faring.

'Dear old Eli,' cried impetuous Anthony, 'I'm so
glad you are not much hurt. It seemed such a
shame to leave you ; but we had to go aloft.'

'Eli understands,' said Guy, who, while his cousin
had been speaking, had despatched Jerry to dip a
handkerchief in water, and was now holding the cool
pad over the lump on Eli's scalp. 'Cheer up, Eli ;
there's nothing wrong with the bone.'

'Ain't thar ?' said Eli slowly. 'They've sorter
shook up my thinkin' appyratus though. My ! that's
grateful.'

'I was afraid he was dead,' sniffed Jerry, the tears
running down his face. 'I never thought of the wet
pad. Guy, you know everything—I'll go and get
another.'

'Bring the bucket, an' I'll stick my head into
it, called Eli.—'You're a pertic'ler kind of a fool ;
ain't you ?' he added witheringly to Adams, who had
just come up. 'Don't you know any better'n to
knock a good sailor endways in the face o' a risin'
gale ?'

''Twasn't none o' my doin',' returned Adams
gloomily. ''Twas that long-jawed son of a gun
there,' scowling in the direction of Larkin. 'I'll
give him what for, if he don't mind his eye.'

'Faith! he'll have enough to do to moind his eye for awhoile, judging by the illigant colour of it,' put in Jerry in an undertone.

'You're a rummy lot, I must say,' declared Adams, with reluctant admiration. 'Two o' you nigh being flogged, and Banks there with a lick on the head, and yet there you go, cracking your jokes and larfing as if you was sailing into Port Jackson. I says blow me if I can understand you; that's what I says.'

'A very sensible frame of mind, and one requiring more delicacy of comprehension than you possess,' said Larkin, drawing near with his continual sneering smile. 'Make the best of everything — eh, Mr Hawkins? The stars fight for you; but of course you understand that the settlement of our little account is only delayed until a more convenient opportunity, and '——

Adams turned upon him in sudden fury. ''Vast heaving there, you lantern-jawed swab,' he roared. 'Leave the lad be; if you try to stop him adoing of the work he's able and willing for to do, I'll—I'll turn him loose on you.'

Larkin was quite unabashed. 'I must remind you, Skipper Adams,' he replied airily, though there was an evil sparkle in his eyes, 'that such language to the commander of this expedition will be entirely subversive of discipline.'

'Why, you blundering land-rat,' cried Adams wrathfully, 'what are you trying to come over me with your jaw-breakers for? I tell you I'm the cap'n o' this brig, and so long as I've got to sail her I'll have my own way. Come, Bill,' he went on, dropping his bullying tone, 'don't let you and me fall out. Once

we 're in port you shall have it all your own way;
but I know better what 's wanted aboard just now.
Come, Bill, wait till we gets out o' blue water.   Don't
bear malice.'

At this Eli and the boys exchanged glances, which,
Adams observing, said hurriedly to Anthony. in a
gruff undertone: 'Don't you take no 'count o' what I
says to Bill.   I won't let him touch you.'

'Not till it suits your convenience, thank you.   I
can take care of myself,' answered Anthony loudly
with fine scorn.   Larkin walked away smiling.

'Ef you 'll be guided by me, you 'll take another
reef or two in them topsails,' said Eli.   'She won't
carry what she 's got much longer, to my thinkin'.'

'You 're right, mate,' answered Adams.   'Can you
lend a hand ?'

'I 'd rayther not,' said Eli; 'for I 'm a bit giddy.
But ef you 'll lay aloft, I 'll take charge here, an'
show the lubbers what to do.'

'Right !' agreed Adams; and with a shout of
'Away aloft there, lads ! reef topsails !' he sprang
into the main rigging, while Anthony and Guy
swarmed up the fore.

Eli waited for a few minutes, and then made his
way to Whitson, who was now in charge of the
wheel.   'A chance for honest men when rogues
begin to fall out, mate,' he said in a low voice, at
the same time slightly opening his jacket and showing
the butt of a small pistol.

'Ah !' said Whitson with a responsive grin.   'How
many 's that ?'

'One apiece.   I got another yesterday and put it
in the cask.   I begin to see the end o' this game, ef

things go on ez they're goin'. Don't talk; you never
know whar that snake may be. Wharabouts are we
d'ye reckon?'

'I don't rightly know,' answered Whitson; 'but it
ain't the pleasantest latitude to run races in. We
must be getting near where the sea is full of coral
reefs. Otherwise I wouldn't care, for the brig is
sound enough.'

'I guess it won't last long this time o' the
year,' remarked Eli to Whitson.

'May be not; but it'll be warm enough while it
does last,' answered Whitson grimly.

And it was. For the next fourteen hours the
Swallow raced before the wind under close-reefed
topsails, and only escaped being pooped by the great
curling waves, that lifted her stern and threatened to
break on board, by the most careful attention on
the part of the men at the wheel. And so the long
day and longer night wore to an end.

'I'll tell you what it is,' said Whitson at dawn
next morning. 'I don't rightly know where we are,
but I should say we can't be far off some of the
islands that are hereabouts; and the next thing we
know we'll run smack on to one or another of 'em;
that is, if she don't get the bottom knocked out of
her on a reef, which she may do any moment.'

'What'll we do, then?' asked Adams.

'Lay her to, ef we kin manage it, while we've
got the sea-room,' said Eli. 'It'll be a tough job;
but ef the mate's right—an' I reckon he is—it's our
only chance.'

'Take the wheel then, you two,' cried Adams. 'I'll
set 'em at it. Lee braces, lads! Haul aft starboard

staysail sheet!' he roared, hollowing his hands before
his mouth.

The yards were braced forward, Eli and Whitson
keeping sharp eyes for a 'smooth,' and to the relief
of all, the little brig was brought up to the wind
without shipping a sea, and lay with her helm almost
a-lee, riding over the huge waves, and no longer
rolling and lurching as if the very masts would be
pitched out of her.

But the real force of the hurricane had only now
begun, and Eli's expression was grave and anxious as
he cast his eyes to windward and then aloft at the
straining spars and sails.

'Will she weather it?' asked Anthony, noting the
trouble in his face.

'Ef we kin hold on,' was the answer; 'but let
masts or sails give out now, an'—— Good land!
thar goes the foretopmast.'

A squall more furious than all that had preceded
it struck the ship, and with a loud crash the foretopmast went short off at the cap, the broken spar
hanging by the lanyards of the lee rigging, and
threatening death to any one who came within reach
of the tangled mass, as with every roll of the ship it
crashed backwards and forwards against the lee bulwarks. There was not a moment to be lost.

'Aloft there, and cut away!' shouted Adams; but
not a soul moved. 'Aloft there, and cut them spars
adrift!' he roared in dismay. Still no one stirred;
the danger was too great.

Then with a loud shout of 'Follow me!' Anthony
seized an axe and clambered into the foretop with
Guy close behind him.

With starting eyes Eli, who dared not leave the wheel, watched the brave lads as they delivered stroke after stroke with their keen axes at the lee lanyards, which the heavy lurches of the ship assisted to carry away and so free the wrecked spar with sail and yard still hanging to it.

'Well done!' yelled Adams.

'Thank God!' breathed Eli, as with the last stroke of Anthony's axe the whole mass fell clear away to leeward, and down slid the venturesome boys to the deck.

Foiled for the moment, the hurricane seemed to pause and take breath, as if considering where and how it should strike them next. But a yet more terrible danger was before them, and Whitson's quick eye, roving to leeward in search of what he had been dreading all the time, caught sight of the fearsome thing.

'Breakers!' he shouted. 'God help us! Breakers!'

It was but too true. There, just off the lee bow, was a churning, leaping mass of water, danger-signal of the destroying reef. There was just one chance; but oh! how slender, that they might clear it.

'Hard up!' roared Adams. 'Haul aft port staysail sheet! Round in after-yards!'

Away rushed the crew to their stations. But it was too late. Crash! A shiver shook the brig from stem to stern, there was a horrid grating sound, a howl of dismay from the crew, and for one instant the ship appeared to be brought up. Then a mighty wave lifted her clear off the reef and sent her once more into deep water.

'She's cl'ar agen!' cried Eli. 'Lord grant she ain't much hurt. We'll weather it yet.'

Breakers ahead!   Breakers on port bow!
Breakers on starboard bow!   Breakers all along
the line!

A dismal cry went up from the convicts, who so
far had done their best and really worked well, considering how ignorant they were. But in this dire
extremity their wits deserted them and they gave
way. Some flung themselves down and grovelled
in their terror, others ran blindly hither and thither,
stumbling and falling over ropes and wreckage, and
a gang of half-a-dozen dashed towards the spirit-
room, intent only upon stupefying themselves before
the death that stared them in the face overwhelmed
them.

'Take my place at the wheel, Adams,' shouted Eli;
and as Adams obeyed he sprang forward. 'Anthony!
Guy! Jerry! Form line to pass the word aft.'

The boys hurried to their places, Anthony with
his fair hair blown all about his face, looking like a
young viking, Guy serene as usual, and Jerry, pale
but firm, clinging to a ring-bolt with all his might.

Eli leaned over the bow and gazed intently at the
terrible snowy line. 'Steady!' he called, and Larkin
who was next to him took up the word.

'Steady! Steady!' went down the line, and
'Steady!' echoed Whitson and Adams at the
wheel.

Nearer and nearer the *Swallow* drew to her dreadful end, and faster and faster beat the hearts of the
anxious watchers, whose eyes were fixed not upon
the breakers, but upon the crouching figure of Eli in
the bows.

Suddenly the Virginian straightened his tall form.

'A passage on the port bow!' he shouted. 'Starboard! Starboard hard!'

'Starboard hard it is!' The wheel spun swiftly round, a wall of foam rose towering above the brig, and fell, drenching her decks; and then as a mighty wave rolled after her, and lifted her upon its curling crest, the *Swallow* slid down the steep incline, swept through the passage like a bird indeed, and as the breakers roared and lashed in disappointed wrath behind her, glided with all her way upon her over the waters of a sea which, by comparison with that which she had left behind, was as smooth as a millpond.

For a few moments no word was spoken. The sudden and entirely unexpected escape from a frightful death, the swift transition from the raging, tossing ocean to this peaceful haven awed every one into silence. Even the convicts in the spirit-room hushed their drunken ravings as they noted, without comprehending, the cessation of the violent motion of the brig. But at last Guy broke the stillness with a fervent 'Praise be to God!'

'Amen!' said Eli devoutly. 'But for Him we'd never hev weathered that.'

Silence fell upon all once more. The friends drew together and clasped hands; Adams, strangely moved, staggered against the taffrail, hiding his face in his shaking hands; Larkin, who, pale and with tremulously moving lips, had been leaning against the mainmast, started as a fresh burst of laughter ascended from the spirit-room, and plucking a pistol from his belt, hurried below.

Meanwhile the *Swallow* glided on unchecked,

when suddenly Eli awoke to the situation, and springing into the fore-chains, began to heave the lead.

'Deep twelve!' he cried. 'Stand by, boys, to cast
anchor! Deep eleven!'

Whitson and the boys, with such of the men as
remained on deck, rushed to their places.

'Mark ten!' sang out Eli. 'Deep nine! Shorten
sail! Hands by both anchors!'

Smartly came the response to each order, and as
the anchors plunged into the quiet sea, the brig
swung round once more to the wind.

'By time, that's good!' exclaimed Eli, pulling out
his pipe and preparing to soothe his strained nerves.
I never thought we'd be hyar to talk about it.
Whar air we, mate, d'ye reckon?'

'Blest if I know,' answered Whitson. 'We can't
see anything for this mist that's all round us, and
we can't hear anything; but we must be close against
land of some sort.'

'Hadn't you best go below and see what the damage
is, Adams?' suggested Eli. 'Take Whitson with you;
he knows her better'n what I do.'

'Come on then,' assented Adams, still greatly
shaken. 'But I must have a tot of grog first; I'm
all on the jump.'

Eli waited till the deck was clear, and then diving
down the fore-hatch, reappeared almost immediately
with three small pistols in his hands.

'Take 'em and stow 'em out of sight, quick!' he
whispered. 'You may want 'em any minute. Ye
can't trust this pizen. I've found a way to git into
their armoury. No; ye can't trust 'em. They've
got a shake jest now; but it won't be long before

'My land, William. I've got the drop on you.'

they pull themselves together, an' then—hush! Ah, it's Whitson.—Well, mate?'

'Lost her false keel, I'll warrant,' said Whitson, who was looking remarkably perturbed.

'That's not what's given you sech a twist though,' said Eli, regarding him keenly.

'No, it isn't,' assented Whitson with a glance at Jerry. 'The sooner we can quit this ship the better.'

'Why?' asked Eli; but his eyes said plainly to the boys, 'I told you so.'

'Would you believe it?' answered Whitson. 'Would you believe it after all we have done? That scoundrel Larkin is plying Adams with rum, and asking him not to interfere. I only heard a word or two; but I heard enough. Your business is to be finished off first, Mr Hawkins, and for the rest'—he drew his finger significantly across his throat.

They were brave; but the blood left their faces and went back with a rush to their hearts.

'He wouldn't dare,' Guy got out with an effort.

'Why wouldn't he?' said Eli. 'He has got the will, an' he has got the power, an' ef thar's any soft hearts among his crowd o' rascals, they'll agree to anythin' once he fills 'em full enough o' rum.'

'Let us try and retake the brig,' said Anthony. 'Why should we not, since you can lay hands upon their arms and ammunition?'

'Too risky,' answered Whitson. 'I can't trust my men; Larkin has more than half won them over to his side already, so there'd be more than five to one against us. We mustn't count Jerry in.'

'Why not? I could shoot,' affirmed Jerry stoutly.

E

'An' be shot,' added Eli drily. 'No; thar's no sense in that. Fer one thing, every man agin us'd be fightin' with a rope round his neck, an' don't you go for to 'magine he'd fergit it when it came to the nip. Fer another, we couldn't git much good out o' the brig till she'd been beached an' overhauled.'

'But what are we to do?' asked Guy. 'Have you any plan? The storm is abating. Can we seize a boat and put to sea?'

Whitson shook his head with a mournful smile. 'If that fog would only clear away and show us where we are!' he said, staring with troubled eyes into the thickness.

'It is lifting now,' cried Jerry. 'And oh! What's that?'

From out of the mist came a curious sound. 'Rub! Rub-a-dub! Rub-a-dub-dub! Rub-a-dub!' many times repeated.

'It sounds like a drum,' said Guy.

'A drum!' echoed Eli. 'I've heard many a drum; but never one that made me feel skeery like that one. It don't sound nice. My land! Listen!'

A yell! Another! A chorus of them! Then, high above all, a long, ear-piercing howl of agony.

The five stared at one another in dismay. Was that the land to which they must flee? More yells and shrieks! And all the time the great drum sounded, 'Rub-a-dub! Rub-a-dub-dub!'

Larkin came rushing upon deck, followed by Adams and the convicts, most of them half-drunk, and just able to stagger along.

'Whatever is that?' cried Larkin, looking into the white scared faces in front of him.

'It's devil's work somewhar,' answered Eli. 'We shall soon know.'

And as he spoke, the mist rose slowly, rolling upwards upon itself like the curtain in a theatre, and there, upon the stage on which they were presently to play their parts, a scene, at once strange and terrible, was being enacted.

CHAPTER VI.

THE LIFTING OF THE MIST.

HE setting of the scene was exquisite indeed. The brig lay in a wide bay, belted upon two sides by a lovely shore, where, in native luxuriance, tall coco-nut palms waved above the stately bread-fruit and the broad-leaved banana. From the rank and tangled undergrowth gigantic tree-ferns raised their heads, whose graceful feathery fronds swept up and down and to and fro in the brisk breeze that formed the tail of the hurricane now sweeping northward. Inland, clumps of noble forest trees alternated with patches of cultivated ground, while, farther still, low rolling hills stretched away to a magnificent background of lofty mountains, darkly blue in the dim distance. To the north a low reef of coral jutted out for a mile or so from the mainland—if mainland it really were—till it became lost in a small island, opposite to which the brig rode at anchor. Along the shore-line and, save on the very summit, dotting the hill that composed the island, were houses of peculiar build, with thatched roofs, and arranged in irregular streets. Beyond, farther to the north, the calm water stretched, a

sapphire sheet with here and there a tiny emerald
flashing on its surface; while, more distant still,
the great sea, scarcely yet recovered from its battle
with the gale, flung swelling, snowy-crested rollers
thundering against the outer encircling reef. But
the people on the brig paid small attention to this
beautiful panorama, for their eyes were fascinated by
a very different scene. Upon the hillside stood a
building whose curious architecture and prominent,
projecting ridge-poles distinguished it from the ordinary dwelling-houses. Behind and to one side a
clump of graceful trees formed a grove, and the whole
was enclosed within a neat lattice fence. In front
of the temple, for such it was, could be discerned the
figure of a man, who beat vigorously upon the sides
of a great wooden drum, which at every stroke gave
forth that appalling 'rub-a-dub-dub;' while outside
the fence a crowd of almost naked savages danced
and leaped and yelled furiously together. On the
beach another crowd, running at full speed towards
their comrades on the hill, dragged behind them, face
downwards, the dead bodies of three men. Lending
their yells to swell the horrid din, on they rushed
into the compound, and with fearful violence dashed
the heads of the corpses against a great flat stone
set slopingly before the temple wall.

Then with a suddenness, startling in itself, the
booming drum stopped its noisy clamour, and the
frantic yelling ceased. For the lifting of the mist
had disclosed another side to the picture, and for
the first time in their lives the startled eyes of king
and priest and people rested upon the great canoe of
the white man.

For a few moments terror and astonishment held
every man rooted to his place, and then, as a great
cry went up, a sudden confusion and scuffling arose
in the midst of a group of natives who had stopped,
fascinated, upon the beach, and out from among
them burst a man who fled for his life towards the
long reef.

The tide was falling, and in some parts the coral
pathway was bare, in others covered; but the man,
who was of lighter colour than the half dozen tall
savages who followed at his heels, raced along it,
sometimes running, sometimes wading, sometimes
swimming, until he came abreast of the brig, when
he plunged into the sea and, rising after a long dive,
made for her with swift, powerful strokes.

There was some slight hesitation, and then, as
crowds of natives poured down the hill towards the
beach, a dozen men sprang into a canoe and dashed
to intercept the swimmer, who, with his brown body
thrown half out of the water at every desperate
stroke, drew rapidly near the brig, where the drunken
convicts were shouting themselves hoarse, and offering
bets in a maudlin fashion upon the result of the
race.

'The poor wretch will be caught,' cried Anthony,
springing into the shrouds. 'Stop that canoe, some
of you, if you are men at all. Heave a rope over
the taffrail, Guy.'

A furious spurt carried the brown man to within
fifty yards of the brig; but the canoe was well up,
and as he cast a despairing glance over his shoulder,
he saw that three men stood with their short clubs
poised, ready to throw. A few more strokes, and the

contest would be over. Stopping short he drew a quick breath and shouted with all the force of his remaining wind, 'Help! help! shoot!' Then, as the clubs flew through the air, alighting, as it seemed, as one weapon upon his head, he threw up his arms and sank like a stone.

A quick shock of surprise thrilled the watchers on the brig, silencing the noisy convicts, as with a shout Guy sprang over the taffrail into the sea; and Anthony, acting upon the impulse of the moment, swooped swiftly upon the man nearest him, wrested a musket from his hands, and fired at the canoe.

So suddenly had it all happened that the hands of the throwers were still raised aloft, their bodies slightly bent, and their heads craned forwards to see if the fugitive would reappear. The ball pierced the hand of the foremost of them, and with a resounding yell of pain and surprise he leaped high into the air, then with a convulsive twist of his body flung himself clear of the canoe and struck out madly for the shore.

But the others! For an instant amazement held them silent, and then they opened their mouths and screamed shrill screams of deadly, helpless terror. Some cast themselves down and beat their foreheads upon the deck until the blood flowed; others followed the example of the stricken man and sought refuge in the sea, while the scullers, lashing the water into foam in their anxiety to escape, drove their light vessel shore-wards at a tremendous rate. It was the same on the island, where the crowded masses of people added their frantic howling to the screams of their comrades, and either flung themselves flat on the earth where

they stood, or fled, deviously darting hither and thither
through the low doorways of the houses like frightened
rabbits into their burrows.

With shouts of derisive laughter, the convicts,
spurred by the example of Anthony, levelled their
muskets and fired at the retreating canoe; and as the
shower of balls fell sputtering ahead of, behind, and
all around it, the miserable savages, none of whom,
fortunately, were hit, tumbled headlong into the water,
and dived out of sight with resounding 'whoos!'

Meantime the swimmer had come to the surface
again close to the brig, and catching sight of Guy,
who had also risen, swam towards his would-be rescuer.

'Hullo!' panted Guy. 'They didn't hit you then.
Up with you.'

'No hit Faatu,' replied the brown man, with an
expansive grin. 'Faatu dife too quick. Up wif you,'
he went on, repeating Guy's words. 'Up wif you.
Plenty shark here.'

After that Guy wasted no more time in argument,
but very quickly swung himself aboard, where he
was met by Anthony. The brown man followed
instantly, and no sooner had he touched the deck
than he flung himself down before the boys, em-
bracing their knees and pouring forth his gratitude
in voluble queer-sounding speech.

'By time, he's a real nigger after all!' exclaimed
Eli, pushing through the ring of convicts. 'I 'lowed
he was a white man dyed brown. Say, nig, you're
different from them ez was after you. Whar are you
from? What war they goin' to do when you up 'n
legged it?'

The brown man stared, as well he might. Evidently his English did not go as far as this. So he made no answer, but only looked helplessly at Guy.

'You are quite safe, poor fellow,' said the latter soothingly. 'What is your name? Where do you come from?'

'Name Faatu,' answered the brown man. 'Come from Tonga-tabu. Am you missinary ship?'

A burst of uproarious laughter convinced poor Faatu of his mistake; and as Larkin advanced, he shrank back against Anthony trembling with fear.

'Don't you be afraid, Faatu,' said the lad; 'he's not going to hurt you.'

The tone conveyed more than the words, and really meant 'He'd better not.' Larkin was angered at Anthony's somewhat tactless assumption of superiority, but he controlled himself, and said, with his usual cold sneer:

'If my geographical knowledge serve me, Tonga is classed under the Friendly Isles. This Faatu, or whatever his outlandish name is, seems to have good reason to cry 'Save me from my friends, that is, if that small island be Tonga. Is that Tonga?' he asked Faatu, waving his hand towards the island.

'Not Tonga,' answered Faatu. 'Um name Mbau.' Then nodding towards the larger land, 'Um name Fiji Levu.'*

'Fiji! Fiji!' echoed Whitson. 'Fiji: Heaven help us!'

'Why?' inquired Larkin, staring into the man's white face.

'The bloodiest race of cannibals alive,' muttered Whitson. 'I've heard tell as even the missionary

* Tongan mispronunciation of Viti Levu—*i.e.* Great Fiji.

ship *Duff* durstn't go nigh them.—Banks,' he added
rapidly in a whisper, ' we can't land there.'

Larkin shot a keen glance at him ; but otherwise
gave no sign that he had heard the words. ' So that
is Fiji ?' he said to the Tongan.

'Yes,' answered Faatu. ' Fiji mans want eat me
cause shipwrecked on reef.'

'Shipwrecked on the reef were you ? Why should
they want to eat you ?'

'*Va Fiji*' (Fiji fashion), returned Faatu. ' Me
come from Rewa in canoe. Plenty Tongan at Rewa.
Shipwrecked on reef. When man shipwrecked, Fiji
man eat um if can catch um. *Va Fiji.*'

'Oh, do they?' said Larkin with a grimace.
'Then lads, it is just as well we did not run upon
that reef, or even aground on the island.'

'For which you may thank those whom you have
injured,' cried impetuous Anthony. 'Try and remember that next time you meanly plot to cut their
throats.'

Eli shot a look of vexation at the fiery youth, and
Larkin bit his lip as a low murmur of applause came
from somewhere among the men. He swung round
in the direction of the sound, and for a moment seemed
about to speak. He altered his mind, however, and
turning again to Anthony, said quietly enough :

'Patience ; you shall not find me unmindful of
past obligations, I assure you, Mr Hawkins.'

As he spoke, his eyes rested for one moment upon
the island, noticing which, Guy shivered slightly,
though he would have found it difficult to explain his
emotion. Faatu, who was holding his hand, looked
at him wonderingly. He scented trouble, and was

quick to trace it to its source. Nestling up to Anthony, he gazed into the young fellow's flushed face for an instant, and then exclaimed emphatically : 'You am good man ! Am um pirate ?'

Some of the crew guffawed at this, but Larkin, not liking the invidious distinction, called sharply for silence.

'Have the men of Fiji never heard a musket fired before ?' he inquired of Faatu.

'No,' was the answer. 'White mans nefer here. Come to Tonga. Missinaries come, too. T'en white mans say kill missinaries. So Tonga mans kill um. White mans in Tonga now. Me learn um spik *papalangi* (foreign) talk.'

'Then you are a Christian, Faatu ?' said Guy gently.

'No ; me no *lotu*. Me *lotu* for you, hey ?' answered Faatu with a genial grin.

Larkin mused for a moment. 'What injury has the brig sustained ?' he demanded of Whitson, who briefly informed him.

'So then we are likely to be detained here for some little time,' said Larkin. 'It is fortunate, perhaps, that we have already scared these cannibals with our muskets ; for now they will hesitate to attack us.'

'Will they though ?' cried Jerry, who had climbed again into the shrouds. 'Look ! Here they come, a dozen canoes full of them.'

* Traditions differ as to whether firearms were introduced into Fiji by the convicts in 1804, or by the crew of the shipwrecked brig *Eliza* in 1809.

CHAPTER VII.

NA ULIVOU, NA VU-NI-VALU.

IT was true. A dozen great canoes, each crowded with men, had already traversed half of the short distance that divided the brig from the island. The rowers and most of the warriors, the latter armed with spears and clubs, were naked, save for a strip of cloth adjusted in a T-shaped bandage round the loins, and knotted in a loose bow behind; but many on board, who appeared to be chiefs, or at least persons of distinction, wore in addition a snowy gauze-like turban, which covered, without entirely concealing, their enormous heads of fantastically dressed hair. Their loin-cloths, too, were of ampler proportions than those of the rank and file, passing higher up the body, and with long flowing ends trailing on the deck behind them.

Amid perfect silence the canoes drew near, and there was something in the stillness, broken only by the monotonous click of the rocking sculls, more menacing than the loudest shout of battle.

On came the grim line, the scullers standing up and throwing their weight from side to side upon the vertical oars and raising each foot alternately as

though walking, till but fifty yards or so separated
the two parties. It was an imposing sight, but
calculated just then to inspire fear rather than
admiration.

At the first alarm Adams dived below, returning
almost immediately with an armful of muskets and
a supply of ammunition, which he hastily divided
among the prisoners. The meaning of this sudden
solicitude was so obvious that Anthony broke into a
scornful laugh.

'So,' he cried, 'we are to fight for you as well as
sail your ship.'

Larkin, who was running up and down, busily
engaged in encouraging his men, shot a malevolent
glance at him, while Eli silently bewailed his young
comrade's all too ready tongue.

'Steady, men!' cried Larkin, who certainly did
not lack courage. 'Steady! Be ready now, and
when I give the word, fire a crashing volley. Then
load again before they have time to recover.'

Suddenly the scullers in the leading canoe sank
upon their haunches, paddling with short and feeble
strokes. As if at a signal for which they had been
waiting, the oarsmen in the other canoes imitated
their example, while from five hundred throats pealed
a long-sustained cry, ' *Ndua! Wo! Ndua! Wo!*'

'Fire!' roared Larkin, not unnaturally supposing
this to be a shout of defiance; but before a trigger
could be drawn, Faatu rushed down the line, vocifer-
ating loudly, 'Not shoot! The *tama!* * It am
peace! Peace!'

* The shout of respect or submission uttered by an inferior in
presence of a superior.

'Don't shoot!' echoed Larkin. 'It is better not
to come into collision with them if it can be avoided.
Faatu, speak to them, and say that if they come any
nearer we shall fire.'

His aid thus invoked, Faatu sprang into the shrouds
and shouted his message aloud. The scullers immediately rested on their oars and an imposing person in
the leading canoe delivered a voluble answer.

'What does he say?' demanded Larkin.

'Him say him want come talk wif white chiefs,'
answered Faatu, translating according to the best of
his ability. Him bring pig and *yangona*.* Him
want know how you make death out of nofing.
You got whales' toofs?' he broke off abruptly.

'Yes, there are some aboard,' answered Larkin.
'Why?'

'Let um come,' advised Faatu. 'Gif um whales'
toofs and um lofe you. Not let um come, um come
some time by-'n-by all a same.'

'Good advice,' said Larkin. 'Tom, run down and
fetch up some whales' teeth.—Faatu, tell them to lay
the leading canoe alongside. Six people may come
aboard; no more. The other canoes must return to
the island. Unless they agree to this, I shall give the
word to fire.'

Again Faatu interpreted, and after some consultation
on the part of the chiefs, the big canoe approached
the brig, while the others slowly retreated to the
island.

'Let down the ladder,' ordered Larkin; 'and
remember, lads, they are still three to one. Be
watchful.'

* The Kava root, producing *Piper methysticum*.

But the occupants of the canoe had no treacherous design, for no sooner had their vessel touched the side of the brig than the imposing chief who had conducted the conversation scrambled on board, closely followed by four other men, scarcely less distinguished-looking than himself, and all five immediately squatted on the deck.* The chief who brought up the rear, and who after a haughty and comprehensive glance around remained standing, outshone all his companions in the grandeur of his build and the stateliness of his demeanour. He was quite six feet in height, and splendidly proportioned, the great muscles swelling out under his smooth skin, which was painted a shining black. He wore an enormous quantity of white *masi*, or native cloth, wound about him, the end trailing upon the deck behind him, while those of his ample turban fell gracefully down his back from the roots of his gracefully arranged hair. Around his neck was a collar of red whales' teeth, and in his strong right hand he grasped a small but beautifully carved club, inlaid with tortoiseshell and mother-of-pearl. In his left he carried a root of *yangona*. His face, handsome in spite of its coating of black, wore a remarkably intelligent expression, and it was easy to see from the loftiness of his bearing and the respect paid to him by his attendant chiefs that he was lord of them all.

Larkin was quick to apprehend this, and turning to Faatu inquired, 'Who is that?'

'Na Ulivou, Tui Mbau' (king of Mbau), replied Faatu. 'Him fery big man.'

* Fijian etiquette does not permit an inferior to stand upright in the presence of a superior.

'So he seems, indeed,' said Larkin. 'Ask him once more if he comes in peace.'

Faatu put the question not to Na Ulivou, but to the *Mata-ni-vanua*,* who had conducted the conversation from the beginning, and the latter in turn rendered it to the king, who, although he had of course understood Faatu perfectly, was much too exalted a personage to converse directly with a common man. So, too, his answer passed from the *Mata* to the Tongan, and thence to Larkin.

'Tell the lord of the clubs that speak with fiery mouths that I am king of Mbau,' said Na Ulivou. 'Mbau is a little place, but its king is mighty and its people are many. They have but to kneel upon the shore and open their mouths and they will swallow up the sea and the ship of the *papalangis* (foreigners), and I, Na Ulivou, am the greatest of them all, for I am Na Vu-ni-Valu, the Root of War. But let not the pale chief be afraid, for I would love him. Let him take the *yangona* root I bring, and fear nothing; for Na Ulivou comes in peace.'

'Say to him,' answered Larkin when this long-winded oration had been translated, greatly to its disadvantage, by Faatu, 'Say to him that I do not fear him, Root of War though he be. I have but to raise my hand and ere the sea could fail by so much as a drop, he and his swallowers would fall dead.' As he spoke he pointed his musket full at the king's broad chest. Na Ulivou endeavoured to smile incredulously; but his eyes wandered hither and thither, and his breath came and went rapidly.

* Literally 'Eyes or Face of the Land'—*i.e.* Controllers of public affairs. Here Master of Ceremonies, or Herald.

'It is an idle boast,' he said unsteadily. 'The white chief cannot harm one who is *ngali thuva ki langi* (subject only to heaven). But it is not meet that he should threaten one who comes in peace, bearing a gift. Yet I fear him not. As well might he hope to harm the bird that floats under the sun as injure Na Ulivou.'

For answer Larkin brought his musket to bear upon a large gull, poised with outspread wings high above the mainmast. An instant later the report rang out, the snowy wings were folded suddenly, and whirling over and over in its descent, the gull fell heavily almost at the feet of the astounded Na Ulivou, who, with considerably more haste than befitted his regal dignity, dodged behind the mainmast, while his still more badly scared followers fell flat upon their faces, screaming and beating their foreheads upon the deck.

'The king is safe; but let him take heed,' said Larkin with a superior smile. 'Stand forth, O Na Ulivou, and let there be peace between us.'

Shivering with dread, Na Ulivou advanced and crouching at Larkin's feet, humbly proffered the *yangona* root, which being graciously received at a hint from Faatu, the king clapped his hands softly together in token of respect. Then still crouching, he issued an order to the grovelling *Mata*, who crept along the deck and repeated it to the men in the canoe. These in their turn passed up a couple of baskets containing two pigs, a quantity of bread-fruit and cocoa-nuts, and a supply of *ndalo* (taro) and yams. Three trembling natives followed, who bore the baskets forward and set them down in front of Larkin.

'This will be an agreeable change of diet,' said
Larkin, waving aside the convicts, who crowded round
to view the good things. 'Keep back, mates. Don't
crush these dark-skinned gentry; their nerves are
still rather shaken.—What is he saying now, Faatu?'

'Him say if you want um man,' answered the
accomplished Faatu with a grin. 'Me tell um no.'

'Tell him yes,' corrected Larkin, and Faatu, looking exceedingly surprised, obeyed.

Na Ulivou rose from the deck, and taking a firm
grip of his club, beckoned to one of the slaves who
had carried the basket. The poor wretch crawled
upon his hands and knees to the feet of the king,
and after one upward, supplicating glance, bowed
his head in meek submission.

With the utmost unconcern Na Ulivou raised
his club, poised it an instant, and then smote
heavily downwards. But ere the blow could fall,
Anthony burst through the convicts, and catching the
king's sinewy wrist in his left hand, held it in an
iron grip.

The king glanced admiringly at the proportions of
his stalwart antagonist as with a twist of his supple
body he wrenched himself free, exclaiming: 'What
is this, O Tongan? Which is the chief? Who is
the liar?'

Taken aback at this direct address, Faatu became
confused and bluntly informed Larkin, 'Him say
you great big liar. You say you want man. Now
you not want him. Me tell him again you want
eat man all along a pig?'

'Eat him!' ejaculated Larkin, aghast. 'What do
you mean?'

'King gif you yam and taro and pig. Him put man on top for chief to eat,' exclaimed Faatu.

'Faugh !' ejaculated Larkin in disgust. 'I meant as a hostage. Tell him to leave the man alone. Step back, Mr Hawkins, and give me your musket. Your hot blood will be getting us into trouble.'

'It is well,' said Na Ulivou, motioning to the slave to return to the boat, which the miserable man lost no time in doing.

'Now,' resumed Larkin, 'ask the king if he will supply us with food and treat us well so long as we remain here. Tell him that if he refuses, we will come ashore with our fiery bolts as he calls them, and kill him and all his people.'

The roundabout process was resumed, and the king having listened attentively to the words of the *Mata*, who threw in a little advice on his own account, replied :

'Will the white chief show his power once more to Na Ulivou ?'

'Certainly,' acquiesced Larkin, and taking aim with Anthony's musket, which had been reloaded, he brought down another gull.

'It is true,' said Na Ulivou, 'the white chief is very great. Now will he let Na Ulivou hold the fire-stick and see if he can kill something ?'

Larkin considered for a moment, and then with a grim smile handed the chief the empty musket, cocking it, and explaining by signs how the trigger was to be pulled.

Na Ulivou took the weapon gingerly enough, but recovering confidence as it did not offer to harm him,

he stepped forward, and with a sudden movement
presented the musket at Larkin's head.

Larkin smiled again, and folding his arms across
his chest, calmly nodded to the king to pull the
trigger. Na Ulivou did so, and, of course, there was
no report.

'Na Ulivou is a fool,' said the convict lightly. 'He
has no power over the white man's thunder. See.'
He snatched a loaded musket from the man next to
him and fired over the king's head. As the bullet
sang past his ears, Na Ulivou once more dropped
abjectly to the deck; but finding that he was un-
harmed he rose, and drawing himself up proudly, said:

'It is well. The white chief is great, but he
cannot harm the Root of War, and the Root of War
cannot harm him. Now, listen. Na Ulivou would
be friends with the white chief. Let him come to
Mbau with his followers, and teach Na Ulivou how
to deal unto his enemies the death that comes from
nowhere and goes up to the sky and down to the
sea. If the white men will fight for Na Ulivou and
teach him this, he will give them houses and wives,
and I will give him and them who follow him food
in plenty, pigs, and fowls, and turtle; yes, and man,
when they have learned to like him; for baked man
is better than pig. Land will I give them as much
as they will, and slaves to plant it for them. Houses
shall they have, and wives to minister unto them,
and they shall sit with the king at the brewing of
yangona, and drink of the cup next after the king.
Behold, I, Na Ulivou, Na Vu-ni-Valu, have said it!'

'Hurrah!' yelled the convicts as this fascinating
prospect opened before them.

'I think we might do worse than give it a trial, lads,' said Larkin looking round at them. 'It's a choice between piracy in the China Seas and a quiet life here. Shall we say yes ?'

'Ay, ay! Stay!' chorused the convicts, to whom Na Ulivou's lavish promises conjured up visions of a terrestrial paradise.

'I believe you are right,' said Larkin briefly.— 'Now, you two,' he added, addressing Tirrel and Jenkins, the survivors of the crew of the brig, 'make your final choice. Will you throw in your lot with me, or will you not ?'

'We will,' answered the men, casting at the same time a sheepish look at Whitson.

'Oh, keep your eyes off me,' exclaimed the sturdy mate wrathfully. 'I wish you joy of your bargain. A set of lubberly, hang-dog cut-throats.'

'Silence!' vociferated Larkin.—'Faatu, tell the king that we agree.'

The Tongan obeyed, shrewdly inserting a clause on his own account to the effect that his life should be spared, for he had 'salt water in his eyes,' and by the custom of the land stood condemned to die. His cleverness met with its reward, for Na Ulivou at once commanded the *Mata* to see to it that it was proclaimed that the Tongan was *tambu* in Mbau.

'Then,' said Faatu, 'the white chief accepts your offer.'

'*Vinaka! Vinaka!*' (Good! Good!) cried Na Uli vou, and his courtiers echoed the sonorous exclamation.

'Let this clinch the bargain,' said Larkin, stepping forward with his hands full of whales' teeth, while

one of the men followed with an unloaded musket.
'Permit me to offer your majesty these trifles.—Tom,
give the *Mata* a musket; he deserves it for his
trouble.'

Na Ulivou's eyes glistened, but he was careful not
to show too much enthusiasm as he grasped the
coveted gifts. Bowing courteously, he exclaimed,
'*Mole saka mole!*' (Thanks, sir, thanks) while his
inferiors softly clapped their hands.

'Faatu, ask the king to withdraw now and arrange
for our reception ashore,' said Larkin. 'Later in
the day we will visit him.'

Na Ulivou was disappointed, for he had hoped to
have been shown over the ship; but his native
courtesy came to his aid, and advancing, he placed
his hands upon Larkin's shoulders, drew the convict's
face towards his own, and sniffed strongly first at
one cheek and then at the other, the Fijian method
of taking farewell of an equal. Not to be outdone
in politeness, Larkin returned the salute, whereupon
Na Ulivou, with a smile of pleasure, presented him
with his own handsome club, a mark of no ordinary
favour. The *Mata*, and after him the subordinate
chiefs, then paid their respects to Adams, the convict
captain, by sniffing strongly at his hands, while he,
much to his embarrassment, was compelled to submit
his hairy face to their salute. This done, the visitors
withdrew, the convicts sprang into the shrouds and
cheered lustily, and amidst much laughter and shouting, the royal banner with its bars of black and white
was hoisted again, and the brown-skinned rowers
rapidly sculled the canoe toward the shore.

'Bravo! We are well out of that difficulty,' cried

Larkin. 'Now, lads, you have earned a holiday,
and you shall have one. If I have held any authority
over you on board ship, I lay it down now. There
is the happy land. Go in and enjoy yourselves,
every one after his own fashion. Food in plenty,
houses, land, and everything that the heart of man
could desire! Three cheers for his dusky majesty,
the King of the Cannibal Islands!'

'Hurrah!' roared the convicts, mad with joy at
the rosy prospect before them, when all of a sudden,
—*Rub-a-dub! Rub-a-dub-dub!*—the great drum
sounded sonorously from the temple on the hill.

'*Mbakolo!*'* cried Faatu. 'They goin' to cook
mans now. Haf um ready for you by-'n-by.'

Silence fell upon the shouting crowd, and every
man looked at his neighbour, not caring to put the
thought that possessed him into words.

Perhaps there might prove to be a thorn or two
along the rose-strewn pathway before all was done.

Eli stepped forward. 'See hyar, Mr Larkin,' he
said, 'you are countin' on havin' a good time among
yourselves, an' I reckon you can ez fur ez we're
consarned. But we don't jest happen to share
your views. You may take it ez a fact that we
don't want no houses, nor lands, nor any brown
heathen's wigwam. So ef it wouldn't trouble you
too much when you've sech a heap on your mind
already, may be you'd indicate what's to become o'
us.'

Rub-a-dub! Rub-a-dub-dub! Larkin's glance
wandered towards the temple on the hill and back
again to Eli. There was a sinister smile on his lips,

* Term applied to bodies devoted to the oven.

and an evil glitter in his eyes as he answered : ' Your case shall have every consideration, my good Banks. Meantime, you and your companions will descend into the hold and consider yourselves under close arrest.—You have no further need for their services at present, Tom ?'

' No,' answered Adams sullenly, and looking considerably ashamed of himself ; ' I can get along without 'em.'

' Ah !' said Larkin significantly.   ' So can I.'

CHAPTER VIII.

SCYLLA AND CHARYBDIS.

RESISTANCE being out of the question, the five prisoners descended into the hold, the cover of which was immediately clapped on and battened down, and through the clatter of feet, as the convicts separated this way and that about the deck, they could hear Larkin's low peal of mocking laughter.

'You were right,' exclaimed Anthony; 'the brute means mischief, though what particular form it will take it is hard to say. Yes; we must get out of this as soon as possible.'

'I don't see that it is possible now,' said Whitson gloomily. 'I believe he overheard what I said to Banks about going ashore, and he don't mean to give us the opportunity. Not that I'd care to take it now if he did.'

'Why not?' put in Jerry. 'Those chiefs were splendid-looking men, and Na Ulivou himself was a grand fellow. 'I believe we'd be safer there than here.'

'What, among cannibals!' said Whitson with a shudder.

'Jerry is right, to my thinking,' said Guy. 'I am for getting away if it can be managed. The influence Larkin possesses over the men is something extraordinary. He is plausibility itself, and seems able to persuade them to anything. Look at Adams. A few hours ago he was vowing we should come to no harm, and yet after half an hour alone with Larkin, he '——

'Has the grace to feel ashamed of himself,' interrupted Anthony. 'Didn't you see his face?'

'I did; but all the same I don't think we can count upon him for any real help. The fact is we are in their way, and it is to their interest to get rid of us. We are no longer at sea, and consequently no longer of use.'

'What harm can we do them here?' said Anthony bitterly. 'They won't be in a hurry to leave the island, and we *can't* leave it, while we may live all our lives out here before any one will come to look for us. It's just our luck that the brig should have been injured. Otherwise we might have had a try for her.'

'Aisy there, Anthony,' put in Jerry cheerily. 'Isn't there such a thing as a boat on board?'

'A boat!' echoed Anthony sarcastically. 'Oh yes, several. Do you propose to navigate the Pacific in an open boat?'

'Why not?' said Guy. 'It was done not so very long ago. Don't you remember how we heard that Captain Bligh of the *Bounty* was set adrift with certain others by his mutinous crew somewhere near

the Friendly Islands and reached Timor in safety after
a voyage of nearly four thousand miles? So it's been
done once at any rate.'

'By George, yes!' cried Anthony, brightening up,
as he always did when Guy took him in hand. 'I'd
forgotten that. And now you mention the Friendly
Islands, that's where Faatu comes from. He must
have made the voyage in a canoe.'

'Precisely,' said Guy. 'There's another instance,
and I've no doubt we could find a good many more.
I'd rather trust to the savages than to Larkin, but
I confess I'd rather risk the voyage than trust to
either.'

'I'm with you there,' agreed Whitson; 'if we can
seize a boat, let's be off and chance it. I wouldn't
wonder if Bill Larkin had it in his mind to finish
that bit of business the storm put a stop to. He's
got a terrible grudge against Anthony.'

'By heaven!' flashed Anthony, 'if he should try
that on again, I'll shoot him where he stands, be the
consequences what they may. The circumstances are
slightly different now. He shan't have it all his own
way next time.'

'He didn't get it all exactly his own way last time,'
said Whitson with a chuckle at the recollection of the
struggle, which Eli had described to him.

'No; and he's not likely to forget it. We must
be ready for him,' said Jerry valorously.

'Don't talk so lightly, Jerry,' said Guy, drawing
the younger boy towards him. 'It must be a horrible
thing to shed blood even in self-defence. Let us hope
it will never come to that.'

'Why not?' demanded Anthony wrathfully. 'I

declare, Guy, I have no patience with you sometimes.
It is all very well to be meek, and—look here, do
you mean to say you would have any hesitation in
ridding the world of a brute like Larkin ?'

'I should indeed—a very considerable hesitation,'
answered Guy. 'I am not his judge.'

'He has been tried and condemned twice already,'
said Anthony with passion. 'I'd take on myself the
office of executioner with the greatest satisfaction.
The pity of it is that shooting is too good for the
rascal.'

'Anthony, Anthony, don't talk like that,' implored
Guy in great distress. 'You know we did not bring
this upon ourselves. It will all come right in time,
and if not'——

'If not,' interrupted Anthony hotly. 'I know
what you are going to say, "It's God's will." I don't
believe it. How can it be God's will that we should
submit to whatever these ruffians choose to do to us
without an effort in our own behalf ? That is a
monstrous idea. However,' he finished rather rudely,
'you do the praying, and I'll do the fighting.'

Guy laid his hand upon his cousin's shoulder.
'Come, Anthony, old fellow,' he said, 'you don't mean
that. Surely we are not going to quarrel now—now
of all times.'

'I should say not!' cried Anthony impulsively,
catching hold of Guy's hand and wringing it warmly.
'Forgive me, dear old Guy. I am behaving like a
brute and a fool. But I'm at my wits' end about
Jerry. It isn't so much for myself. It isn't really.'

'Ah, then, never mind about me,' struck in Jerry,
anxious to create a diversion. 'I'll stand by you

through thick an' thin.   Never fear that I 'll desert
you.   Has it occurred to any of you to wonder where
Eli is all this time ?' he concluded, as Anthony
laughingly rumpled his hair.

'He 's fallen asleep I expect,' said Whitson; 'and
if he 's as tired as I am, I 'm sure I don't wonder at
it.   Talk low, boys, so as not to disturb him.'

'Asleep! Not much I ain't,' chuckled Eli, his voice
coming out of the gloom of the after part of the hold.
While you 've been talking I 've been doing, that 's all.
Step right hyar an' see for yourselves.   Watch now.'

They heard a faint rattling sound, and as Eli stepped
aside, a beam of light shot through from a smaller
hold or cabin behind him.   'That's the armoury,'
announced Eli with satisfaction.   'I tell't ye I knowed
a way o' gittin' thar.   Now when Mr Larkin makes
a start fer the shore, which I reckon he 'll do soon,
we 'll have a leetle entertainment on our own account,
jest to keep us from bein' lonesome.   Beyond that
again is the after-cabin.'

But it was some time before Larkin made any move
to leave the brig; and, meantime Eli replaced the
board and they waited patiently, conversing in low
tones and talking hopefully of their chance of escape
and the delight of home-coming after all they had
been through.

'Thar he goes, I reckon,' said Eli an hour later, as
the trampling of feet was once more heard overhead.
'Hold on awhile, though.   We can't be too careful.'

But no one disturbed them, and after the commotion
died away Eli once more withdrew the board, and
squeezing through into the armoury, made for a door
opposite, which communicated with the after-cabin.

'Open!' he said, turning the handle cautiously. 'Watch now lest any one uncovers the hold. I'm goin' to take a squint out o' the starn windows and see how many are gone.'

Presently he returned. 'Thar's five left aboard,' he said. 'That's all right. Now we kin git to work.'

'What do you propose to do?' inquired Guy, as, leaving Jerry in the hold to give the alarm if necessary, they joined Eli in the armoury.

'It's ez cl'ar ez noonday,' began Eli, that the five ez is left aboard won't be long before starting in to drink, an' seein' ez thar's no one to stop 'em, it won't be long either before they fill 'emselves full. That bein' so, we'll provision a boat, lower away, an' be off before Master William an' his rascals can git back. Meantime, lest they come before we're ready, we'll take the liberty o' helpin' ourselves to a musket apiece, an' an extry lock or two in case of necessity.'

He opened his clasp-knife, and using the strong blade as a screw-driver, rapidly detached the locks from a couple of muskets, while his companions, seeing his drift, each manipulated one in similar fashion.

'Ye never know what'll happen,' remarked Eli sententiously, as he stowed the detached locks carefully in his pocket. 'We're all right now if anything should go wrong with our guns.'

'Are you going to shoot sea-gulls on the way home?' inquired Jerry, poking his head through the hole in the partition.

'Git,' replied Eli laconically. 'Or, say, Jerry, see ef you kin find any old canvas lyin' around the hold.'

'It's so dark,' said Jerry, and added after awhile, 'No, I can't find any.'

'Waal, no matter,' said Eli. 'Come through hyar. —Hark,' as the noise of a volley rolled from the direction of the shore. 'Mr Larkin is showin' the pore benighted heathens what he kin do in the way of makin' a row. I judge they'd be a leetle more keerful o' their ammunition ef they knew what was goin' on hyar. Hello, thar's another. Ho, ho! the silly critters. Come hyar, Jerry. You're only a leetle one. Jest you squirm up the cuddy-ladder and see what them fellows is doin'.'

Delighted to be employed on active service, Jerry passed through the door into the after-cabin, ascended the companion-stairs, and was back again in no time with the information that the men were lying down and apparently fast asleep.

'Hogs,' was Eli's comment. 'I judged it wouldn't be long before they stoopified the leetle brains they've got among 'em. Now, Jerry an' Guy, cut away an' find some canvas, suthin' we kin make bags of. Be keerful they don't see you from the shore.'

This time Jerry was not long in discovering what he had been sent in search of, and his quicker wits readily grasping the situation, he helped himself at the same time to several strong needles, some twine, and a small hatchet.

'What's this for?' inquired Eli as the boy handed him the last mentioned-article.

Jerry cocked his eye in the direction of a small keg of powder. 'I thought you'd want to stave in the head of that barrel,' he answered.

'Good boy,' said Eli approvingly; 'and it'll come

in handy besides.——Now, Guy,' as the lad entered
with his bundle, 'cut and snip hyar, and help dress
this canvas into bags, haversacks you know, sech as
we kin wear on our shoulders.'

'These two kegs don't represent the total supply
of powder,' observed Whitson. 'I wonder where
they 've stowed the rest.'

'It don't matter,' said Eli. 'We haven't got time
to look for it. What we don't take o' this we 'll heave
through the porthole. No use leavin' it fer them,
I should say. A bag o' powder and a bag o' bullets
apiece, and some extra flints, an' we 're right. Mate,
take Guy, and go an' see about pervisionin' the boat
fer the trip.'

In an hour all was ready, and with a great deal
of subdued laughter, Jerry began to fling the powder
out of the porthole. When the kegs had been
thoroughly emptied, and the spare balls and lead been
sent to join the powder, Eli heaved a sigh of satisfaction.

'Thar,' he said, 'that 's done. I reckon, Squire
Larkin, we stand on better terms with you than we
did at sunrise this mornin'.'

'So much better,' agreed Anthony, 'that I don't
see why we shouldn't take possession of the brig after
all. In fact, she is ours as we stand.'

'Much good she 'll do us,' grinned Eli. 'Hold on,
Anthony, you always gallop when you orter walk.
Fust thing, you don't s'pose Larkin an' Company 's
goin' to set on their heels an' watch us sailin' off
with their ship. Why, they 'd be down on us with
a thousand o' their nigger friends before we could
weigh anchor. Second, ez I said before, seein' the

knockin' about the brig has had, she 'll not be much good fer anybody till she 's been overhauled. Leastways, I wouldn't care to sail her outside the bar.—What say, Whitson ?'

'No,' agreed the mate ; 'we 'll be safer in a boat by a long sight.'

'I said so.—Waal, Anthony, ef you 're achin' fer a job, go an' bring me the muskets o' them five on deck. Take a look round while you 're thar, but mind they don't see you from the shore. We 're not quite ready fer 'em yet.'

'All 's well,' declared Anthony, returning with the muskets a moment later. 'There is a great crowd on the island, but there is no sign of the return of our worthy commander so far.'

'That 's all right. I don't want him pryin' into this leetle job too soon.—Away thar, Jerry, while I fix these muskets, an' fetch me some laths and big screws from the carpenter's bench.—Whitson, you go with them other boys an' lift the cover off the hatch.'

'But that will set Larkin on the scent, and show him that we must have come out this way,' objected the mate.

'Not it,' said Eli. 'He 'll blame his sleepin' beauties on deck, an' they 're so drunk they won't know whether they took it off or whether they didn't.'

'But our arms,' went on Whitson, who was somewhat slow of comprehension. 'He is bound to know that we got them from the armoury.'

'Shucks !' exclaimed Eli. 'Won't he s'pose that we took 'em from the sentries ? Up on deck and

G

lend a hand to stow whatever you think 'll be wanted
in the boat.——He's a good sort,' he remarked, when
left alone with Jerry; 'but he ain't smart; my land
no, he ain't smart!'

He closed the door of the armoury, locked it, and
threw the key out of the porthole. Then stepping
back into the hold with Jerry, he rapidly replaced
the board he had removed, screwed it firmly in its
place, and piled some empty cases against it to conceal
any trace of interference.

'Larkin can break into the armoury easily enough
if he wants to,' said Jerry, watching the performance.

'Course he can, honey; but he'll have a hunt fer
the key first, 'lowin' ez he's mislaid it, an' that'll
keep him back a bit. I want us to git a bit o' a
start before he does find it out. It be a sweet surprise
for William,' he chuckled. 'He'll be ez mad ez he
can stick. My land! I'd like to see his face.'

'You'll have your wish before long then,' Anthony
called down. 'The boats are just putting off from
the island.'

'You don't say so!' exclaimed Eli, springing on
deck. 'By time, that's too bad. I 'lowed we'd git
off before he came back. Same time we're ready fer
him. I reckoned thar was an off chance he'd be
hyar to head us off. That's why I was so keerful
settin' things straight below. What about the boat,
Whitson?'

'She's not the one I would have chosen,' answered
the mate; 'but she's the only one left. There's a
mast and a sail and a pair of oars.'

'Waal, I wouldn't ask more,' said Eli cheerily.

'Who slung her out?' For the boat had already been lowered half-way to the water.

'They did, I suppose,' replied Whitson, 'and then changed their minds and took another. I wish they'd changed back again.'

'Oh, she'll do,' said Eli, glancing into the boat. 'Got some rations aboard?'

'Yes; but not enough.'

'They've got to be. Stand by now. Hyar they come.—Now, Anthony, you shut your head, an' let me do the talkin'. We'll git out o' the muss 'thout ary a fuss, which is po'try; but ef you let loose on Larkin, you'll spile all.'

'I'll be silent,' promised Anthony; 'but if he tries to stop us '——

'He won't,' interrupted Eli; 'he's too careful o' his skin. Don't you see, boyee, we've got the drop on him. Quiet now; we'll larn him.'

It was late afternoon, and the islands lay in a haze of sunshine, purple patches in a golden sea. On the beach of Mbau stood the convicts, drawn up in long line and ready to give a parting salvo to their entertainers, who crowded down by hundreds to see them off. Crash! the long volley rolled over the quiet sea, and as the savages, now more accustomed to the strange and horrible noise, answered with a loud shout, the white men embarked and pulled rapidly for the brig.

'That's another down to us,' chuckled Eli from the security of the companion-hatch, to which they had withdrawn. It's all Verginny to a cob o' corn they won't have the sense to load at once. Look to your primin', boys. Let 'em git well aboard, an' then step right out upon 'em.'

There was silence for a space, then the lap of oars
under the brig, Larkin's voice hailing the men who
snored upon the deck in blissful ignorance of what
was going on, and then the convict captain stepped
aboard, followed hard by Adams and the rest of the
crew.

'Parsons! Gorman! Danby! Why didn't you
answer?' called Larkin imperatively. 'Faugh!
You drunken brutes,' as his eye fell upon the
prostrate men, 'is this the way you keep
watch?'——

'Cover's off the hatch, Cap'n,' cried Adams springing towards the hold. 'The birds have flown.'

'What? Impossible!' exclaimed Larkin. 'The
boat—Ah! Trapped!'

He stepped backwards so suddenly as almost to
overset Adams, for, as he turned, he found himself
looking down the barrels of five muskets, every one
of which covered him.

'Hold up, William,' said Eli cheerily. 'I tellt
you way back yonder to Broken Bay ez thar was
bound to be a fresh deal some day. Waal, this
is it.'

'Fire on them, some of you,' gasped Larkin, whose
own musket was unloaded.

'Shucks!' jeered Eli. 'I don't b'lieve thar's a
loaded piece among you. You shouldn't hev been so
free with your salute over thar. Say, you thar,' his
voice taking on a stern, harsh ring, as one of the
convicts began furtively to raise his musket; 'drap
it, smart on the deck right thar.'

The man let his piece fall clattering to the deck,
and the others, who, as Eli rightly surmised, had not

a loaded musket among them, huddled together like frightened sheep.

'Now, Larkin,' went on Eli, 'I ain't given to makin' speeches, but I'll trouble you to listen to a few words before I've done with you. You can rush us ef you like, and, seein' ez you're four to one, like 'nuff you'll git the best o' us. But'——he made a significant pause—'if you should elect to play that card, thar's five o' you'll go down before you well start, an' you'll be the first, William, my honey. You'll be the very first.'

'What do you want?' asked Larkin, whose face, either from rage or fear was white as chalk.

'All we want is to be let go in peace,' answered Eli, adding, as Larkin gave a start of surprise, 'Oh yes, I dessay you find that hard to swaller, but it's so. Mind, I'm not sayin' that ef things were different we wouldn't try a rally with you and bundle you into the hold, what was left o' you. But seein' the brig is ez she is, an' we can't make nothin' o' her, we've elected to take this yer boat and try our luck. It's for you to say whether you'll stop us or not. Same time, I warn you ef you try it on, it'll be your last act any way, whatever becomes o' us. Now then, our minds are made up. What do you say?'

'Let 'em go,' murmured most of the convicts; but there were some who growled, 'And split on us when they get back to Sydney. No, no; rush 'em.' But there was none who ventured to act on this advice, for they knew well that the first man to advance would be the first to fall.

'We ain't back to Sydney yet,' said Eli, overhear-

ing the growl; 'but s'posin' we were, I reckon ef you
elect to cast in your lot along with man-eatin' niggers,
you can do it ez fur ez we're concerned. Folks has
too much to do these days 'thout huntin' down a
pack o' coyotes like you. I wouldn't wonder but
what your new friends 'll take a hankerin' to try the
taste o' you before long. Not ez I grudge 'em. Say,
Larkin, what's it to be? Peace or war? Answer
straight, an' remember it's all up with William
Larkin ef he says war.'

The colour had returned to Larkin's face, and there
was a smile on his lip as he glanced at Adams, who
throughout the colloquy had remained somewhat
apart, shuffling uneasily from one foot to the other.

'My dear Banks,' began the convict'——

'Now see hyar,' interrupted Eli; 'I ain't your dear
Banks, an' more 'n that, I don't want to be. Can't
you answer a straight question? Will you stand by
an' let us go, or will you make a fuss? My land,
William, I've got the drop on you, an' I don't know
what henders me from pullin' trigger.'

Larkin waved his hand airily, and his smile
broadened as he glanced again at Adams. 'Because
you are far too humane a man to shed blood unnecessarily,' he answered. 'Now, would it surprise you
very much to learn that I had already arrived at the
conclusion that the best thing to do would be to let
you go?'

'None o' that,' grunted Eli. 'Talk straight.'

'I am talking straight. This very afternoon before
we went ashore, I said to my friend Skipper Adams
here, 'We have no further use for those gentlemen
whom we have been compelled to bring with us so

far. Let us put them into a boat and send them off with our blessing.—Didn't I, Tom ?'

'Yes, ye did,' mumbled Adams, the picture of shamefacedness.

Eli glanced keenly from one to the other.

'It's a fact, though you do not believe it,' went on Larkin, noting the glance; 'so you have only anticipated my plan. By all means go. You are quite at liberty to depart, and I wash my hands of all responsibility.'

'That's real kind o' you,' said Eli. 'So kind that I'm half inclined not to take your permission. Says somewhar " The tender mercies o' the wicked is cruel." ——However, in with you, boys. Whitson an' I'll lower away.'

The lads took their places, but as Eli and the mate caught hold of the ropes, two men stepped from the ranks of the convicts. They were Tirrell and Jenkin, the two sailors who had apparently cast in their lot with Larkin.

'We'll go with ye, mate,' said Tirrel, looking, to be sure, very awkward as he said it.

'Will you ?' returned Eli, looking over his shoulder. 'No you won't though, not ef I know it. You turned your backs on us when we wanted your help, an' now we don't want your comp'ny. Quit !'

'Let them come, Eli,' pleaded Guy from the boat. 'It is enough if they see that they have done wrong and are sorry.'

'Come on then,' growled Eli. 'It's more than you deserve; but, ez Guy's fond o' sayin', I ain't your jedge. Catch hold hyar. Whitson an' I'll git in, an' you can foller.'

The sailors grasped the ropes, and at a sign from Larkin three or four of the convicts—no less surprised than relieved by the quiet termination of the affair—sprang to their assistance, and in a few seconds the boat rested lightly on the surface of the water.

Larkin approached the side of the brig and looked over.

'Good-bye, gentlemen,' he said, as Tirrel and Jenkin swung down and took their places. 'Since you seem to have helped yourselves, I need not inquire if there is anything I can do to further your comfort. We have had one or two little differences on the voyage, but that is all over now; so I trust that we part friends.'

The stupendous impudence of this remark produced a shout of mocking laughter from those in the boat. Otherwise it went unanswered.

Larkin kept his place, and seemed to be watching the proceedings with considerable interest. Presently Adams joined him. The skipper's face was drawn and ghastly, and he looked with haggard eyes at the serene countenance of his associate. Larkin met the look, and laughed that low, unpleasant, mirthless laugh of his.

At this the skipper groaned aloud, and fixed his eyes upon the boat as if fascinated.

The tide was running strongly inshore, and the little craft had already drifted some distance towards the island before her crew were fairly settled in their places. At last Eli seized an oar.

'She's pretty wet,' he remarked. 'Hyar, Jerry, take that tin dish and bale her out a bit. Run out

the other oar, Anthony.—Port, mate,' to Whitson, who
had the tiller. 'Bring her nose round.'

Out went the oars, the two strong backs were bent,
straightened and—away went Eli and Anthony into
the bottom of the boat, their feet in the air and the
stumps of the oars in their hands, while the blades
danced gaily off on the rippling waves.

'What pesky luck,' grumbled Eli, scrambling up.
'Them oars were rotten ez touchwood.—Step the
mast, Tirrel and Jenkin. Be spry, now. The tide's
runnin' in hard. Thar's no wind. No matter, up
with her; it'll help us some. My land! Jerry, why
don't you bale?'

'I am baling; but it seems to me that the water
is rushing in faster than I throw it out!'

'The oars were not rotten! They have been sawn
through!'

These exclamations were almost simultaneous.
There was one instant of horrified silence, and then
with a bitter cry Eli fell upon his knees, and
wrenched up the planking from the bottom of the
boat.

Through a dozen large auger holes along her whole
length the water was pouring in. The boat was
settling fast.

Eli muttered one furious word. 'Bale all!' he
shouted. 'Let her drift in. Bale! Bale for your
lives!'

Rub-a-dub! Rub-a-dub-dub! Rub-a-dub!

A scream of horror broke from Jerry. From all
directions the islanders were crowding to the beach,
brandishing clubs and spears, and filling the air with
horrid yells.

'Look at them!' raved the boy.   'And, oh! don't
you remember what Faatu said, that every one who
was wrecked would be eaten.   Oh! oh! oh!'

The blood rushed to Eli's face, and for a moment
it seemed as if he would fall forward in a fit.   Then
as a low laugh floated over the water from the brig,
he seized his musket and, straightening swiftly up,
fired.

Well was it for Larkin that the rocking of the
boat disturbed the Virginian's aim.   As it was, the
convict's cap flew from his head, and with a shout of
terror, he staggered back and dropped behind the
bulwarks for safety.

Instantly Eli's coolness returned to him.   'Bale!'
he shouted, as he rapidly recharged his piece.   'Bale
for all you 're worth.   Keep her afloat, and we 'll be
all right yet.   Look!   The shot has scared the
niggers already.   They 're falling back.   Hold up,
Jerry.'

But Jerry, ashamed of the spasm of terror which
had suddenly seized him, had flung himself down on
his knees and was baling away for dear life.

Splash! splash!   Tirrel and Jenkin, mad with
fear, flung themselves into the sea and began to
swim towards the brig.   Eli threw one contemptuous
glance after them.

'Good riddance,' he muttered.   'And it lightens
the boat, too.—Oh, good land!'

A swirl and commotion in the quiet water, a
furious rushing to and fro of lithe black forms,
two ear-piercing screams of wildest agony, and Tirrel
and Jenkin, traitors alike to friend and foe, disappeared for ever.

'Bale!' said Eli sternly. 'God help us if we sink before we get into shallow water with those brutes around!' he muttered under his breath.

With white set faces the four continued to bale, while Eli, his musket thrown across his knee, grimly watched the shore, now but fifty yards away. And spite of all they could do, the water crept up to the thwarts of the boat.

Forty yards, and still the boat laboured on. Thirty! Eli cast an apprehensive glance at the sea. He loved his life as much as any man, and a shudder crossed him at the recollection of the fate of Tirrel and Jenkin. Still, if the boat were lightened she would float a little longer, and—there was Jerry.

He gathered himself together for a spring, but just as he was about to launch himself into the air, Anthony's strong fingers closed upon the back of his neck and held him motionless.

'Sit still, Eli,' said the young man firmly. 'We can't allow that. If we must die, we will die together. In two minutes more we shall be in shallow water.'

'Two minutes!' groaned Eli, not daring to move, lest in his struggles he should make matters worse than they were. 'Two minutes! It's an eternity. Will she last so long?'

'She will,' said Anthony firmly; 'and then we must make a rush altogether. It's pretty well hopeless; but it's our only chance.'

'Right then,' acquiesced Eli. 'Bale away once more, and take your time from me. When I give the word, jump all together.—Jerry, honey, you keep in the rear.'

Once again they set to work, baling furiously, the boat nearing the shore by inches at a time with every heave of the waves. A moment more and they would reach the shallows. But what then ? In front of them, some twenty paces from the beach, was a living wall of islanders, silent now, but watching intently, each man with spear or throwing club poised in his hand. Evidently they were keen observers. The lessons of the day had not been thrown away upon them, and they understood that the death-dealing tubes must be fed after each discharge. Five might fall. Well, let them ; men must die some day. Five must fall and then those who had salt water in their eyes should fall in their turn. Meantime they waited.

'Be ready,' warned Eli. 'Don't fire unless they rush, and then fire only one at a time. Likely each shot 'll check 'em at first. Ready ? Jump, and God help us !'

With an echoing shout the four sprang after him waist-deep into the water as the boat sank under them, and rushed up the beach, where they halted, their muskets thrust threateningly forward.

For an instant the great line of islanders gave way. Then once more it formed, and from a hundred throats arose the plaintive chant,

'A mata na rawarawa !
Me bula-na ka ni hava ?

'Death is easy. What use is life ?'

And so singing, the savages swept down upon their victims. There was no help for it. With a muttered prayer upon his lips, and black despair in his heart, Eli raised his musket, covering the heart of a tall chief who strode proudly in advance.

In another moment the ball would have sped, when high up on the hill sounded the loud blast of a conch shell, and a sonorous voice called in commanding accents,

'*Tambu!*'

And at the word, the chant was hushed, the lifted arms fell limply to the sides and the dusky host stood still.

CHAPTER IX

A NIGHT ALARM.

ROM his house upon the hill, Na Ulivou, King of Mbau and Root of War, had been a keenly interested spectator of all that had passed. His first idea on seeing the boat put off from the brig had been that the white chief was about to send him a message, perhaps even another present; but this idea had been very swiftly dispelled by what followed, and he had held his judgment in suspense. Meantime, the case evidently presented but one aspect to his subjects: a boat was on the point of being cast away; then by unalterable custom the occupants must be clubbed and eaten. Very simple.

But the astute Vu-ni-Valu saw farther than this. It became clear to him at once that what he had suspected on board the brig was true, that there were dissensions among the white men, and he immediately determined to discover how far his own ends might be served in consequence. At the same time he was puzzled, for not being in the secret of the auger holes, and the sawn mast and oars, he could not understand why the crew of the boat had stepped

into her apparently of their own accord and allowed
themselves to drift to their doom. Then as they
ran ashore and he recognised Anthony's stalwart
form, a still more violent curiosity took possession of
him, and, determining to probe the strange affair to
the bottom, he assumed his prerogative and laid a
tambu upon the intended victims. Gathering up
with one hand two or three spears tipped with the
spines of the stinging-ray, and taking a highly ornamented club in the other, Na Ulivou addressed the
Mata, who with certain other chiefs sat respectfully
at a little distance from him.

'Where is the Tongan ?' inquired Na Ulivou.

'If my lord the king pleases, he is awake; otherwise he is asleep,' replied the *Mata*.

What this actually meant was that Faatu, worn
out with the excitement of the day, was fast asleep
in some corner. The *Mata*, however, was far too
ceremonious to state the simple fact so bluntly.

'Let him be fetched, and follow me,' said Na
Ulivou, striding down the hill towards the beach.

Meanwhile, the five whites stood still, facing the
crowd. They knew not how long this respite might
last, and their fingers rested lightly on the triggers
of their muskets, while their watchful eyes roved to
and fro along the line of dark faces. But as no
further attack was offered, and they saw the splendid
figure of Na Ulivou advancing in stately fashion
along the path that wound under the coco-nut
palms, they took heart of grace.

'Hyar comes the king,' said Eli; 'and from the
look o' him I think he means us well. But, look
out.'

With his club loosely shouldered, Na Ulivou drew near, each of the numerous spectators lowering arms and crouching respectfully at the outside of the path until his majesty had passed by. But when he came within a few paces of the warriors on the beach, as one man they sank to the ground with the deep-throated acclamation, '*Ndua! Wo! Ndua! Wo!*' while the women on the hillside and at the doors of their houses screamed their *tama*, '*Ma-i-na-va-ka-ndu-a!*' long-drawn-out and shrill.

'Down with you, boys!' cried Eli. 'He's king hyar, and you bet he's goin' to have his own way, too. Down with you! Don't let him 'magine we defy him.'

Quick to follow this sensible advice, they crouched down in imitation of the Fijians, and though their hands still grasped their muskets tightly, from their lips came the humble saluation, '*Ndua! Wo! Ndua! Wo!*'

Na Ulivou stopped short in surprise, and then a smile of pleasure rippled over his strong face. Whatever the faults of the early Fijians, a lack of good manners could not be numbered amongst them. Politeness in Fiji was as the breath of a man's life, the most rigid forms of etiquette existed and were carefully and scrupulously observed in all ranks and classes of society; and anything like boorishness of behaviour among equals, or refusal of an inferior to show proper respect to an admitted superior, would have excited as much surprise and disgust as though a man should raise a scene in an English drawing-room, or refuse to salute his sovereign as she passed by. Politeness has been said to be the natural out-

come of a kind heart; but there are those who have
averred that it prevailed in Fiji rather because rudeness would have been promptly corrected with a club,
though at the same time the instinctive kindliness
of the people is not disputed. Whatever the cause,
the politeness was there, and it leavened the whole
mass of the people.

Though Larkin had certainly comported himself
with some dignity during his visit to the chief, yet
in his secret soul Na Ulivou had been grievously
shocked and offended at the gross and vulgar behaviour of the convicts, who had rioted over the
land, and committed the most flagrant breaches of
decorum, not so much from want of knowledge of
the customs of the country—which they could not
be expected to possess—as from the promptings of
their own brutal and unrefined natures. Now, however, as Na Ulivou considered the supplicants before
him, and noted their bright, open countenances, their
trim, well set-up figures, and the readiness with which
they observed the ceremoniousness which was due
to his rank, he needed no prompting to know that
he was dealing with men in all respects superior to
those from whom he had recently parted. So, after
the first moment of surprise passed, he smiled.

'That fetched him,' said Eli in an undertone.
'Give him another. Dunno what it means; but it
works.'

With grave faces the little company saluted once
more, '*Ndua Wo! Ndua Wo!*' and murmurs of
applause, mingled with a good deal of suppressed
giggling, broke from the listening crowd, for Jerry
in his excitement, or perhaps thinking to give

H

variety to his performance, had imitated as closely
as possible the *tama* of the women, which was, of
course, utterly wrong.

Na Ulivou smiled again, and acknowledging the
salutation with a courteous wave of the hand, exclaimed, '*Sa loloma !*' *

'What does that mean, I wonder,' muttered Eli.
'Sounds pretty, anyway. Hello! Now we're all
right.'

For at that moment Faatu, who had been hurrying
down the hill, intent upon obeying the instructions
of the *Mata*, recognised Anthony and Guy, and
regardless of the presence of the king, rushed forward and flung himself at their feet with a cry of
joy.

As Faatu sped past him, omitting the customary
obeisance, the smile faded from Na Ulivou's haughty
lip, and his brows contracted in a heavy frown, while
his fingers twitched nervously upon the handle of
his club. Quick to read the signs of the gathering
storm, Eli thrust out the butt of his musket and
prodded the ribs of the grovelling Tongan.

'Turn round, you brown sinner,' he said in a low
voice; 'turn round an' do your dooty by the king.
Never mind us. Sharp now! I declar' old Oliver
looks ez though he'd start in an' eat you right
away.'

Faatu caught but two words, 'eat you,' but they
were enough. Executing a rapid *volte face*, he flung
himself at the feet of the king, imploring pardon
and pouring out a voluble explanation of his apparent

* Equivalent to 'How do you do?' 'My love to you!' or 'Peace
be with you.'

disrespect, to which Na Ulivou listened with manifest
impatience.

'Enough,' he interrupted at last, addressing the
Mata. 'Inquire of the Tongan what these men are
doing here. Is there war between the white men?
Has Lakini (Larkin) sent them to me in his anger;
or have they fled from his wrath to my protection?'

'See hyar, Faatu,' said Eli, when the Tongan had
rendered this in his own peculiar English, 'say to
his majesty that Larkin an' his crew ain't chiefs at
all, but only a gang o' thievin' murderous rascals.
Tell him we're the chiefs, only that Larkin has been
a leetle too soon fer us, an' got us in the door, so to
speak. But if the king, old Oliver thar, knows
what's good fer him, he'll hold on to us an' give
them skunks on the brig the toe o' his boot, which
is o' course a figger o' speech, seein' he don't wear
boots, nor yet even moccasins. Tell him that ef he
does the squar' thing by us, he'll never be sorry fer
it; while ef he 'lects to stand by Larkin, he'll find
hisse'f in the wrong box sooner or later.'

Faatu's expression at the conclusion of this speech
was such a whimsical mixture of comprehension and
bewilderment, that in spite of the danger in which
they stood, Jerry gave way and burst into a ringing
peal of laughter. Na Ulivou turned sharply upon
him, but the sight of the boy's wide mouth, open to
its fullest extent, the flushed face, and the mop of
red hair caught him so suddenly, that his kingly
muscles relaxed and he gave vent to a most unregal
cackle of merriment. The *Mata* and adjacent chiefs
followed suit, as in duty bound; and as the Fijian is
naturally prone to laughter, the whole assembly took

up the chorus, and in less time than it takes to tell it, every man of them was holding his sides and shouting hilariously at a joke the existence of which he did not even dimly perceive.

Na Ulivou held up his hand, and the laughter died away as suddenly as it had begun. Then Faatu, turning to Guy for help with the difficult passages, explained the position of affairs to the king with more detail than had been furnished by Eli.

Na Ulivou listened thoughtfully, his eyes now and again straying towards the brig, whence the convicts, crowded in the bows, were eagerly watching the proceedings on shore. Finally, he said :

'The day comes to an end and the night is at hand. Let the *papalangis* be brought to the *Mbure ni sa* (stranger's house) and let food be given to them. To-morrow I will hear their story. Meantime, let them give me the long clubs that know how to spit death from the little end, and let them trust the word of the king that no harm shall befall them.'

'Boys,' said Eli, when he heard this, 'I don't see ez we can say no. It's cl'ar that Oliver's the sort o' high an' mighty customer ez has only to say "do this, or do that," an' it'll be done. Ef he tells 'em to rush us, why, rush us they will, an' though we kin account fer a few, we're bound to go under in the long run, an' not so long at that. Give up the muskets, I say; we've got our pistols, which he don't know nothin' about, an' it'll astonish him consider'ble ef we have occasion to pull 'em out. My advice is, let things slide, an' trust in Providence. What say?'

'Agreed!' they all cried, while Jerry added,

'Stick to the powder and shot, Eli; the muskets won't be of any use to him without.'

'Right, boyee,' answered Eli with a quiet grin; 'an' p'raps we 'll find a way to git 'em back before long. We must let 'em off first though, or they 'll be shootin' themselves or us by accident. It 'ud be mighty hard fer us to explain matters either way ef that happened.' He turned to Faatu and went on, 'Say to the king that we have faith in his word, and will give him the clubs that spit death from the little end; but first we must make them safe or they will kill him who touches them.'

An intelligent gleam came into Faatu's eyes, and with a very long face he translated Eli's speech to the king, who replied:

'It is well. Let them take the sting of death from the long clubs.'

'Good!' exclaimed Eli with a soft chuckle. 'Now, boys, we 'll arrange a leetle surprise for our friends the enemy aboard the brig. Face round when I give the word an' all fire together. We are too far off to do any harm, but I guess we 'll skeer 'em some. —Faatu, say to the king that the very best way for him to make sure the muskets won't hurt him once he gits 'em is fer him an' every man in the crowd to raise his club in his right hand, shake it over his head, an' roar at the top o' his voice the moment we fire. Mind now, they 're all to stand firm an' not to run away. We won't hurt 'em. Tell him the clubs are goin' to spit death out o' the land.'

'*E mana ndina!* So be it,' said Na Ulivou, and the *Mata* conveyed the order down the line.

Eli rose to his feet, and saluting the king, swung

round facing the brig, his comrades drawing up in line on his right.

'Brig ahoy!' he hailed loudly.

'Ahoy! On shore there!' shouted Adams in reply.

'Tell that skunk Larkin ez he's caught in his own trap, an' ef he comes ashore we'll larn him it's so,' roared Eli.—'Fire, boys, fire!'

A rattling volley followed the order, and simultaneously the savages, though shaking with fear, brandished their clubs and yelled furiously, while the terrified women and children, scurrying like frightened rabbits into their houses, added their high-pitched screams to the din.

Of course the balls fell far short, but no answering shout, no responsive volley came from the brig. Only in sullen silence the convicts drew together on the forecastle, and prepared to resist the attack they felt sure would follow.

'Ef that ain't the biter bit, I dunno' what is,' observed Eli, with grim satisfaction. 'Moreover, ef that little trick don't give Mr Larkin the idee that the heathen has elected to stand by us, I'm a Dutchman.—Now, Faatu, tell the king he can have the clubs, ez he calls 'em, whenever he wants 'em.'

But Na Ulivou, with fear in his eyes, made no effort to take the muskets. Striving to maintain a calm demeanour, he said in a low voice: 'Let them take the roaring death clubs to the *Mbure ni Kalou* (temple of the gods), and let them be hung up as an offering to *Ndengei*.* See that it is done.' And shouldering his club, the king walked off to his house, his subjects crouching and uttering the *tama* as he went.

* The chief deity of the Fijians.

The sun sank behind Viti Levu as Na Ulivou turned away, and in the gathering darkness the *Mata* approached the group of whites.

'Come,' he said through Faatu; 'I will show you where to go.'

'Right you are, matey,' answered Eli. 'Heave ahead.—All the better fer us, boys. When Bill Larkin sees us walkin' off with our muskets on our shoulders his bamboozlement 'll be all the bigger. He! he! I reckon he didn't look fer this when he set us afloat in that pesky boat.'

'Larkin is not the man to sit quietly down under a reverse though,' said Anthony, as they followed the *Mata* up the slope, the savages giving place and eyeing them curiously as they moved along. 'He is sure to make an effort to come to terms with the king, and if we are to be cooped up here defence-less'——

'Waal, he won't do it to-night,' interrupted Eli, with some impatience; 'he 'll be too skeert, and he 'll be busy makin' things snug against a possible attack. He ain't no fool; but he can't see no farther through a stone wall than any other man.'

'But to-morrow he will try,' persisted Anthony. 'We did wrong to give up our muskets.'

'Sufficient unto the day is the evil thereof,' put in Guy. 'We have been wonderfully preserved so far, Anthony, and I do not think that we shall be deserted now.'

Anthony made no reply. His blood was up, and such bitter hatred and resentment filled him that he felt only a wild desire to feel his fingers about Larkin's throat. Guy's cheerful submission angered him. While things went smoothly with them, and life moved on in its old groove, he would have echoed his cousin's sentiments, thoughtlessly perhaps. Now, in his present mood, he could not understand it, and it made him furious. However, he had self-control enough to hold his tongue, and presently they came opposite to the door of the chief temple, *Na Mbure ni na Vata ni Tawaka.*

'Ah, now by this and by that, did any one ever see the like of that little man?' giggled Jerry, as a short, round, and enormously fat priest appeared at the door of the *Mbure*, stepping carefully over the carcases of several freshly killed and cooked pigs. 'Bedad! I don't think the poor gods will get much of the porkers while he is about.'

'Hush, Jerry, he may hear you,' warned Guy.

'Arrah! he won't understand me if he does, and it's getting too dark for him to see me,' said Jerry, with another giggle.

The priest listened attentively to what the *Mata* had to say, and then receiving the muskets, not without unwillingness, retired into the gloom of the *Mbure*.

The *Mata* turned to Eli.

'*Sa lakki mothe. Sa mbongi Saka,*' he said politely in his musical tongue. 'Go to sleep. It is night, sir.'

'I believe ye, matey,' answered Eli impressively, though of course he understood not a word of what had been said. 'Where the mischief is that Faatu?'

Faatu, however, was not at hand, having been summoned quietly to the *vale*, or house of the king. The *Mata*, therefore, having repeated his observation, smiled, nodded, blinked his eyes, yawned heavily, stretched his arms above his head, and went through an admirable pantomime of a man with difficulty keeping himself awake.

'I think he means to convey that we ought to go to bed,' suggested Guy.

'Is that so?' said Eli. 'Waal, I b'lieve you're right.—But say, matey, see hyar, you're not goin' to drive us to roost 'thout any supper. Hi, look!' He stooped down, poked the fat side of one of the pigs, and pointed to his mouth.

'*Vinaka!*' responded the *Mata*, smiling again, and without attempting any further explanation, turned and strode towards another building that stood faintly outlined in the increasing darkness.

'They keep early hours here,' said Jerry, 'and it seems they go to bed in the dark. However, as they've got no clothes to take off, I suppose that doesn't matter.'

'That's all very well,' grumbled Eli; 'but seein' ez things is ez they is, I ain't goin' into any place in the dark. Keep a grip o' your pistols, boys. Say, matey, can't ye raise a light?'

The question received a practical answer, for almost as Eli finished speaking, there was a sudden flare in front of them, and half-a-dozen dusky figures, holding aloft as many blazing bamboo torches, were seen lining the pathway that led up to the stranger's house.

'That's decidedly better,' said Anthony, who was recovering his good-humour; 'and see, there is a light inside the house too.'

'They're lighting up everywhere,' said Jerry, as

twinkling points appeared in all directions. 'May be it's an illumination in our honour.'

Encouraged by a wave of the hand on the part of the *Mata*, who stepped to one side with a polite bow, they passed through the low doorway and entered the *Mbure*, which was really a large hall about fifty feet long and twenty wide, with no ceiling, and having a spar of beautiful native wood, ornamented with gleaming white shells, as a central rafter. Along the sides were sleeping-places, covered with mats of plain and variegated native cloth, or *masi*, and overhung with a mosquito screen of the bark of the paper mulberry. Between each sleeping apartment, to call it so, was an open fireplace, above which was stored a quantity of firewood, and in two or three of these a fire was burning. A quantity of loose grass covered the centre of the floor, or rather, ground, for flooring there was none, and this, along with some wooden pillows for the head, foot-rests, a large wooden bowl, and some bamboo vessels, completed the furniture of the apartment, which, save for the refugees, was untenanted, the *Mata* having remained outside.

'Waal, I won't say ez I haven't slept in a worse place,' began Eli, walking about and examining everything with great curiosity; 'an' I won't say ez I haven't seen better. My!' he broke off, smacking his lips with infinite gusto, as the mats which formed the door were gently raised, 'old Oliver don't mean to starve us, boys, at any rate. I declar' that's good.'

Through the doorway stalked the *Mata*, and following him, submissively crouching, came half-a-dozen women, dressed only in the *liku*, an em-

broidered girdle of hibiscus fibre, and each bearing
provisions in her hands. One carried a small baked
pig, another a basket of yams, a third a pot of fish,
while the others were laden with plantains, bananas,
fresh coco-nuts, and bread-fruit pudding. They
piled the viands upon banana-leaves, in front of one
of the fireplaces, and the *Mata*, having by a courteous
gesture invited the guests to fall to, withdrew, and
left them to their own devices.

'By time, ain't that wonderful?' exclaimed Eli,
watching one of the women as she rapidly cut up the
pig with a knife of bamboo sharpened to an edge.
'I'm obleeged t' you, young woman,' he went on,
awkwardly, as the girl, smiling and showing her
beautifully white teeth, dexterously skewered a slice
and held it up to him. 'Thank you, my dear,' as
another peeled a yam and laid it down beside him.
—'Pitch in, boys; this is Liberty Hall, I guess.
Make yourselves at home.'

'And don't you wish you were there,' added Jerry,
as, with a broad grin, which was instantly responded
to by his dusky attendant, he accepted a share of the
pig.

'Well, I don't know,' said Anthony, whose wants
were also being supplied. 'I think this is the first
moment that I have felt comfortable since we left
Broken Bay. To breathe an atmosphere apart from
those ruffians on board the brig is a delight in itself.
That's quite a pretty girl who is feeding you, Eli.'

'I can't say as much for your Hebe,' laughed Guy.
—'Look at poor Whitson; he's really too bashful to
eat.'

'Not me,' said Whitson, making a grab at a coco-

nut, and in his confusion endeavouring to bite a piece
out of it. 'Well,' he added, throwing down the nut
and joining in the laugh against himself, 'it is rather
—rather'——

'Embarrassing,' supplied Jerry. 'Not a bit of it
when you're used to it. This pudding's good; try
some, Guy. I wonder where Faatu is?'

'Oh,' said Eli carelessly, 'he can take care of
himself, I guess. Thar he is now.'

'No,' corrected Anthony, as the mats were lifted
and a dark face peered in; 'that is one of the natives.
I have noticed several of them taking peeps at us
from time to time. Curiosity, I suppose.'

'Never seen a white man before, you know,' said
Eli. 'I wish Faatu'd turn up, fer I'm a bit curious
myself, an' thar's a heap o' questions I'd like to ask
these young women. I reckon the Tongan is havin'
a blow out on his own account. He'll turn up in
the mornin'.'

But Eli would scarcely have spoken so lightly had
he known the business that Faatu was about, and
how the Tongan had been forbidden, upon pain of
death, to hold any communication with the white men
in the *Mbure ni sa*. Fortunately for their chances of
repose, of which they stood sorely in need, the
prisoners, for such they really were, knew nothing of
what was going forward.

'Only seven o'clock,' said Anthony, drawing out
his watch and consulting it, to the unbounded amazement of the women. 'How soon it grows dark here.'

'We're not so far off the equator as we were,' said
Whitson. 'I expect it's pretty nearly always dark by
six o'clock or thereabouts in these parts. It's not too

early to turn in though, to my thinking, considering
how little sleep we've had in the last two or three
days. Look at young Jerry; he's over already. But
before we follow his example, Mr Trimball, won't you
read us a little out of the good Book. I'm sure I
can't get it out of my mind how much we have to be
thankful for.'

'With pleasure,' answered Guy; 'I was about to
suggest it myself.' He liked Whitson. There was a
sturdiness and simplicity about the man which, in
spite of his somewhat dull wit, was very admirable.
'Don't wake Jerry; he's quite worn out, poor boy,'
said Guy, and after a short pause, he repeated the
twenty-third psalm. His voice trembled a little as he
came to the words, 'Though I walk through the
valley of the shadow of death, I will fear no evil, for
thou art with me,' and his glance fell for a moment
upon the sleeping Jerry. Eli caught the look, and,
with a smothered sigh, rapidly brushed his hand
across his eyes. The psalm finished, Guy drew his
Testament from his pocket, and began the fourteenth
chapter of St John. He went on bravely enough until
he came to the line, ' I will not leave you comfortless :
I will come to you.' And then, as a harsh dry sob
shook him, he dropped the book and buried his face
in his hands.

Anthony moved quickly, and, kneeling beside his
cousin, flung a strong protecting arm around his
shoulders. Eli and Whitson knelt also, and in deep
silence the four bruised hearts poured out their sup-
plications to God.

Meanwhile the women withdrew somewhat apart,
and sat watching the group and staring with rounded

eyes at the book, the significance of which they could by no means understand. Now and then they murmured '*Kalou*' (belonging to a god) and nodded mysteriously; but for the most part they sat in affrighted silence, waiting for the strange ceremony to come to an end. At last Eli rose, and as the others looked up, said :

'It'll not do fer all of us to go to sleep at once. I'll take the first watch, and, Whitson, you can take the next. I'll call you at midnight.'

'That's too long,' answered Whitson. 'Make it eleven;' and Anthony and Guy also put in a protest.

'Eleven be it, then,' agreed Eli. 'Don't lose time argyin'. Why, it's ez much ez ye can do to sit straight now. Turn in.'

He lifted Jerry gently in his arms, and laid the boy upon a pile of mats. The others flung themselves wearily down beside him, and in a very few moments all four had forgotten their troubles in peaceful sleep.

'Now, my pretty dears,' said Eli, moving softly over to the women, 'quit, and go ez quiet ez you can. We're obliged t' you fer all you've done, an' we'll be proud to hev your comp'ny at breakfast in the mornin'.'

The women smiled up at him, and one or two of them giggled faintly as he pointed to the door, but none of them made any show of going.

'Waal, ef you won't you won't,' observed Eli philosophically, as he cast himself down upon a mat, and taking his pipe from his pocket, proceeded to cut up some tobacco and fill it. The women watched him with growing astonishment, but when he calmly drew

a glowing chip from the fire, and laying it on the
bowl of his pipe, puffed out huge volumes of smoke,
their fortitude gave way, and, rising to their feet,
they scuttled out of the *Mbure* with low cries of
terror.

'That fetched 'em,' chuckled Eli, puffing away
with great satisfaction. 'Never see sech a thing in
all their lives before, I bet. Pore ignorant critters,
they 've a lot to learn. Hello! what do you want?'
For the mats at the door were again lifted, and three
or four dark faces cautiously intruded, their owners
staring at him in absolute bewilderment.

He soon grew used to this, however, for during
the next hour relay after relay of the natives paid
him a visit, gazing in upon him for a moment, and
then retreating precipitately, muttering ' *Whoo*,' and
' *Kalou*.' By-and-by these visits grew less frequent,
and finally, about half-past nine, ceased entirely.
The faint noises outside died away, and the deep
hush of night brooded over everything.

The minutes wore on and grew to hours. Eleven
o'clock came and went, and still Eli smoked on, not
choosing to disturb Whitson.

'I 'll give him till twelve,' he said to himself.
'He 'll be all the better fo' the extry hour.'

Midnight! Eli rose, and, knocking the ashes from
his pipe, placed it carefully in his pocket, and moved
quietly across the room to where Whitson lay asleep.
As he passed the door he thought that through a
chink in the hanging mats he caught the gleam of a
fire somewhere outside. He paid no attention to this,
but stooping over Whitson, laid a hand upon his
shoulder. Suddenly, startling the silence, rang out

a strange and terrible cry, and then the frightful
banging of the great wooden drum.

'Wake!' shouted Eli. But the warning cry was
unneeded, for the sleepers sprang to their feet, and
stood gazing at one another with looks of terror.

Eli leapt to the door, and wrenched away the
hanging mats. 'Pistols out, boys!' he cried. 'Oh,
my good land, look at that!'

They crowded round him in the doorway, and a
horrible sight met their eyes.

Within the ironwood fence that surrounded the
great temple a huge fire was blazing, and circling
round it in a wild rhythmic dance were numbers of
women, chanting in shrill tones to the accompaniment of bamboo drums and clapping hands. Somewhat apart crouched the men, while in a group by
themselves sat the *matas* and superior chiefs, Na
Ulivou standing erect in the midst of them, his
tall form clearly defined in the strong light of the
fire.

And the eyes of all were fixed upon three or four
great holes in the ground, whence arose clouds of
steam.

Faster and faster whirled the dancers, shriller and
shriller pealed the unholy chant, till at last, at the
very moment when it seemed that their limbs must
give way under the strain, they stopped suddenly
with a long-drawn scream, ' *Wa-oo!* ' With a nod of
satisfaction, Na Ulivou cast himself down upon a
mat, and uttered some command. The fat priest
waddled from the temple, and stood waiting.

From out the crowd crawled a man, and approached one of the pits from which the steam had

ceased to rise. Thrusting in his hand, he brought out something wrapped in leaves, and still crawling, made his way to the priest. Shaking off the covering, he presented his offering.

It was the arm of a man!

With low, gurgling cries of horror, the watchers reeled back from the doorway, and stood shivering with dread in the middle of the *Mbure.**

* These midnight feasts were not uncommon in the old heathen days.

CHAPTER X.

THE HAUNTED GROVE.

RESUMPTION of the shouting roused them, and Anthony and Whitson, fearful of a rush in the direction of the *Mbure*, sprang to the door with their pistols in their hands.

'They are not thinking of us,' reported Anthony, returning. 'Na Ulivou is taking his share of the feast, and the butcher is cutting up the bodies and distributing the pieces. Some bits are being packed with leaves in baskets, perhaps to be sent away.'

'Ugh! don't,' groaned Jerry; 'it's horrible.'

'It is marvellous to think of,' said Guy. 'Here are these fellows, perfect specimens of high-bred gentlemen, and kindly too. I am sure the *Mata* was kindness itself both in voice and manner, and yet there he is, and the rest of them, eating'—— A strong shiver shook him.

'Don't talk of it,' said Eli. 'What we've got to think of is the best way to quit this yer island before these high-bred gentlemen take a fancy for a change o' diet.'

'Quit the island!' echoed Anthony. 'Pray, how

is that to be done ? Even could we reach the shore
unobserved, we have no boat.'

'I dunno,' returned Eli stolidly. 'All the same, it
has got to be done. Let's figger the thing out a
minnit.'

'Could we not make some use of that bar, or
reef, or shoal, or whatever it is, that connects Mbau
with Viti Levu ?' suggested Guy. 'It appeared to
be fordable at low-tide. It may even be so when
the tide is high.'

'By time, boyee, I b'lieve you've struck it,' said
Eli. 'We orter try it, to my thinking.'

'Maybe we shall only walk from the arms of the
savages here into those of the savages there,' said
Anthony gloomily.

'I ain't carin' so much about their arms s'long ez
we kin steer cl'ar o' their stummicks,' said Eli with a
dry grin. 'Ef we kin only git hold o' our muskets
agen, I'm willin' to take the chance ef you are.
Let's see, the tide orter be slack somewhar about four
o'clock. Ef the heathens go to roost agen presently,
an' I jedge they will, we might make a grab fer the
guns, an' light out for the reef. Oh, I know it's
desp'rit; but we've got to risk suthin', an' to my
thinkin' we risk less by goin' than by stayin'.'

'Yes,' acquiesced Anthony, 'you are right. If we
stay we shall have to face both savages and convicts,
while if we go we shall only have the former to deal
with.'

'Surely Larkin will not attempt to carry his vin-
dictiveness any further,' said Guy, always pacifically
inclined.

'Won't he ? I wouldn't trust him,' remarked Eli.

'Wait till he finds out the trick we've played him over the guns an' powder—ef he han't found it out already.'

Anthony walked to the door again. 'They are dispersing quietly, each man carrying his share with him,' he said, returning. 'The priest has disappeared, and the great fire is burning down.'

'Right!' exclaimed Eli. 'We'll give 'em an hour or so, an' then, ef all goes well, we'll make another break for freedom.'

'Faith, I hope it will be luckier than the first one,' murmured Jerry, helping himself to what remained of the *vakalolo* or native pudding, an appetising compound of split bananas, stuffed with grated coco-nut and sugar-cane. 'There's nothing wrong with this at all events,' he added, smacking his lips.

'Why, you little glutton,' said Guy, smiling at him indulgently, 'you ate more at supper than any of us.'

'Well, I don't know when I'll get breakfast,' returned Jerry, 'so it's best to be on the safe side. I'——

'St!' ejaculated Eli. 'What's that?'

'It's a rat, I think,' said Whitson, as a faint scratching was heard at the far end of the *Mbure*, opposite to the door.

'It's more than that,' whispered Eli. 'There's another door down there we didn't notice before. Watch!'

The scratching continued for a moment or two, and then the mats were gently stirred, and in the dim light they saw a dark figure crawl in, and make for the obscurity at the end of the *Mbure*.

'It's a man,' breathed Eli, clutching his pistol; and their nerves tingled expectantly as out of the gloom came, low-voiced but distinct, the single word, 'Faatu !'

'It's the Tongan,' muttered Eli. 'To the doors, boys, and watch lest any one else comes in.—Guy, you go and talk to the brown heathen; you can make him understand better 'n any of us.'

Guy obeyed, and as the others stood on guard at the doors, they could hear the rapid muttering of low-pitched conversation, Faatu talking eloquently in his broken fashion, and Guy every now and then throwing in an exclamation of astonishment or assent. It was fully ten minutes before he returned to the fireplace, and as his comrades crowded round him they saw that his face was very pale.

'What is it ?' asked Anthony eagerly.

'We are in a trap,' answered Guy, struggling to speak calmly. 'Na Ulivou has determined upon the death of all of us.'

'So much for his great kindness,' said Eli sarcastically, as exclamations of dismay escaped the rest. 'Tell us the worst o' it.'

'Shortly after nightfall, presumably while we were enjoying our supper,' resumed Guy, 'the king and leading chiefs held a council, in which they debated whether they would get most good by protecting us or supporting Larkin. There was considerable argument, for it appears that some thought that we were made of better stuff than Larkin's gang; but others declared that he had more in his power, and would, moreover, reward them richly with whales' teeth and muskets if we were given up, while we, of course,

had nothing to offer. Finally, Na Ulivou cast his
vote against us, and the upshot of it was that Faatu
and others were sent off with a present of a pig and
vegetables to Larkin, and an invitation that he should
come with all his men to a council to-morrow—to-
day, that is. On their arrival we are to be brought
out, and Na Ulivou will make pretence of hearing
both sides of the case. But the end is predetermined.
Larkin will be asked whether he will make certain
concessions; of course he will agree, and at a given
signal we are to be suddenly clubbed, and afterwards'——

He made a significant pause, and a shudder shook
his hearers.

'I wonder he didn't club us to-night and be done
with it,' said Eli at last.

'No doubt he wishes to preserve an appearance of
justice,' answered Guy. 'It will seem as though he
were doing the best for himself and his people, as I
suppose he persuades himself that he is.'

'Gosh l' exclaimed Eli. 'He must be powerful
good at s'posin' ef he reckons we don't hev no voice
in the matter. Boys, thar 's no help for it; we must
try the reef.'

'No,' said Guy; 'Faatu says that won't do at all.
On the opposite shore is a tribe friendly to Mbau, and
as news of us has spread, they would be certain to
intercept, if not to kill us.'

'Well, but what is to be done ?' demanded
Anthony. 'Surely we are not to wait here to be
killed like rats.'

'Faatu has a plan,' answered Guy; 'but the
chance it offers is so slender that I hardly like to

suggest it. Faatu, however, says he is sure that it offers the best, the only way of escape.'

'Why then, let's have it by all means,' said Eli.

'It seems that some months ago a great chief died,' went on Guy, 'and just before his death he informed his attendants that his spirit would pass into a grove of bananas, which is higher up the hill behind the great temple.* In consequence, since the death of the chief, this grove has been rigorously *tambu*, the superstitious natives refusing to gather the fruit and, indeed, not venturing to approach the haunted spot. Faatu suggests that if we can escape to that we shall be safe, for in the first place no one would think of looking for us there, and in the second no one would venture to attack us if we happened to be discovered.'

'So far good,' said Anthony as Guy paused; 'but we can't stay there for ever.'

'No,' proceeded Guy; 'but meantime Faatu is going to steal a canoe, load it with provisions and hide it in a sheltered cove he knows of. In the morning the canoe will be missed, and it will be supposed that we have escaped in it; but at night Faatu will come for us, and with God's help we shall escape in good earnest.'

'Waal,' commented Eli, 'it does seem a pretty desp'rit venture; but ez it's the only thing to be done, I jedge we've got to try it. Ef we could only git our guns.'

'We can, if we are lucky,' said Guy. 'Faatu says the priest does not sleep in the temple, and our guns

* This particular tambu was actually laid by a chief upon his death-bed.

are hung up there as an offering to the gods. We
can get them as we go by.'

'Then I 'm for making the attempt,' said Anthony.
'When are we to start ?'

'Now. Faatu is waiting to guide us. He is
horribly afraid of the grove himself, but he will show
us the way. At the same time he is enlightened
enough to believe that our God is stronger than the
Fijian deities, who will not be able to hurt us.'

'We 'll try a tussle with 'em an' welcome,' chuckled
Eli. 'Come, let 's be movin'. Take ez much fruit
an' vegetables ez you kin carry comfortably; ef
thar 's any fightin', it 'll be better done on a full
stomach.'

They moved to the door, where Faatu, who was
waiting, gave them each a silent, but none the less
fervent, greeting, and then one by one they passed
out into the open air, and throwing themselves upon
their hands and knees, crawled as noiselessly as possible towards the great temple.

'Mu'kets in t'ere,' mumbled Faatu, who was shaking with fright by the time they reached the precincts
of the sacred *Mbure.* 'Me not go in. Me frightened
of god.'

'I 'll go,' whispered Guy. 'We mustn't expect too
much of poor Faatu.'

He glided away, followed by Eli, who did not
choose to allow him to go alone, and together they
ascended the thick notched plank which led to the
door of the temple, some six feet above the level of
the ground.

'It 's dark as pitch,' whispered Eli. 'Hold on till
I strike a light.'

'Is it safe?' asked Guy, as the other fumbled for his flint and steel.

'I reckon if any one sees the spark he'll take it fer a god o' some sort.'

Which was precisely what poor Faatu did, and only Anthony's iron grasp upon his neck prevented him from taking to his heels.

'Hyar you are,' said Eli, returning with his arms full of the precious muskets. 'Ketch hold.—Smart now, Faatu. On with ye;' and they resumed their cautious march, Faatu leading; but presently the Tongan halted, with a low-voiced exclamation of terror.

'What's up now?' inquired Eli, peering right and left, for they had passed the line of houses, and not a sound was to be heard to account for Faatu's fright.

The Tongan sank to the ground, his teeth chattering and his whole body trembling and shivering under the influence of his deadly fear.

'*Hotooa pow! Hotooa pow!*' (goblins) he muttered in his own tongue, and extended a shaking finger in the direction of the clump of bananas, close to which they now stood. The broad leaves waved to and fro with a gentle soughing in the night breeze, and here and there among them went dancing a thousand twinkling points of light.

For a moment or two every one's breath came thick and fast. Was this after all the abode of evil spirits? Then with a smothered laugh Eli ejaculated 'Fireflies!' and, turning, laid his hand upon the shoulder of the grovelling Tongan.

'It's all right, Faatu,' he said. 'They can't hurt

you nor us either. See hyar, boy, away you go an'
borry that canoe. You'll find us hyar, please God,
when ye come back fer us. Quit!' Faatu needed
no second bidding, but rose and sped down the hill,
silent and swift as a lightning streak, while shoulder
to shoulder the white men parted the broad, rustling
leaves, and entered the haunted grove.

CHAPTER XI.

ORNING dawned—the bright beautiful
morning of the tropics—and found them
watching. All trace of the recent storm
had passed away, and the pearly-tinted dawn
touched land and sea till they glowed with radiant
loveliness. From their position upon the flat summit
of the hill, an exquisite panorama unrolled itself
before their eager eyes. Westwards the great land
of Viti Levu with its dreamy horizon of deep blue
mountains, round whose jagged peaks and massive
cones the morning mists swept upwards in fantastic
wreaths. Below them, through a screen wherein the
scarlet blossoms of the hibiscus flashed amid the
tender green of palm and fern, the glittering blue
streak of sea swept onwards, widening out as it
passed the island, and stretching away to where Viwa,
Moturiki, Ovalau, and some few tinier islets marked
the pathway to the north. Westwards, another sheet
of vivid blue, barred from the wide ocean beyond by
a line of radiance unspeakable, shot with tender
colours of every hue, and marking the line of the
coral reef, against which the eternal billows rolled

ceaselessly, marching along in endless procession, sweeping upwards, curling proudly, tumbling downwards with a hollow roar, and rising for the last time a foamy, sparkling shower of rainbow drops.

Below them the village was not yet astir, though here and there a thin stream of smoke, issuing from the doors of the chimneyless houses, seemed to indicate that some active housewife was busy preparing breakfast for her lord. Opposite, the brig with her dilapidated masts swung peacefully at anchor, and dotting her deck could be seen the watch, some stretching their arms and yawning lazily, others hanging over the side and gazing at the island.

'That old chief little thought what a good turn he was doing us when he took possession of this grove,' observed Jerry, pulling a couple of bananas from a great bunch and peeling them.

'No,' agreed Anthony; 'but at the same time I think he might have chosen a more savoury spot. There is a terrible smell hereabouts.'

'Small wonder,' said Eli, peering through the outermost rows of green stems. 'I should say the top of this hill is used as the common rubbish heap of the whole island.' Which, indeed, was the case until, many years later, the missionaries transformed it into a lovely garden.

'Faugh!' said Anthony, with a face of deep disgust. 'And we have to stay here all day. It is enough to make any one sick.—Jerry, you greedy little rascal, nothing seems to spoil your appetite.'

'Why would it?' returned Jerry saucily, taking a pull at the delicious milk of an unripe coco-nut, and smacking his lips. 'Sure, it's always as well to be prepared for the worst. I don't know when I'll get my dinner.'

'Just what he said about his breakfast,' laughed Guy softly.

'Right enough, too,' nodded Whitson, digging out the eyes of another coco-nut and drinking with great satisfaction. 'That's rare good tipple.'

'Isn't it?' said Jerry. 'I wish we could have brought a lot more.'

'Shut your head, Jerry,' warned Eli, shaking a finger and smiling at him. 'We're not out of the wood yet, remember.'

'You don't call this a wood, do you?' returned Jerry, plunging his knife into the soft trunk of a banana tree. 'All the same, I wish we were out of it.'

Eli smiled again indulgently, thinking how elastic were the spirits of the youngster, while deep in his heart he echoed the wish, for though he was careful not to betray it, his own opinion of their situation was gloomy enough.

'They are rousing up down there,' said Guy, peeping through the leafy screen.

'Then let us lie down,' suggested Eli. 'Not ez they're likely to see us; but we can't be too careful jest now. — Jerry, my dear, remember we can't afford to throw away the little chance we've got.'

'I'll remember,' answered Jerry, sobered by Eli's serious face.

'They'll be taking in our breakfast by-and-by,' said Eli as he joined Guy; 'an' then the fat'll be in the fire. I hope Faatu has managed to git the canoe.'

'In the excitement of last night,' said Guy, 'I forgot to tell you that to-day is fixed for a great ceremony. I had it from Faatu that Na Ulivou is to assume the title by which he described himself to Larkin.'

'The Root of War!' exclaimed Anthony. 'Why, I thought he was that already.'

'He certainly styled himself so,' answered Guy; 'but I believe the title has not yet actually been conferred upon him. It seems that the ceremony is always conducted by the men of another island— Ovalau, or Levuka, I think he said—and they are to arrive this morning.'

'By time! Is that so?' cried Eli. 'Then I wouldn't wonder ef that was the reason why Oliver made up his mind so quick to git rid of us. They're sure to hev one o' their beastly feasts, an' he jedged we might ez well serve ez meat.'

'I dare say,' said Guy, with a sickly smile. 'There's a great disappointment in store for him then, if only the ghost of the banana grove plays his part properly.'

'Here come half a dozen canoes,' said Jerry, who had crawled to the other side of the grove. 'These must be the men from Levuka. What a pretty sight.'

'Pretty enough,' muttered Eli, watching the distant canoes with their yellow, triangular sails, and long masthead streamers, as they skimmed lightly over the blue water. 'Same time, I'd sooner see it from a balloon than from the top o' this hill. There's no tellin' though; ef thar's goin' to be a fuss an' fixin', it may take attention off'n us.'

'Some one is going into the *Mbure* in which we slept,' announced Whitson, who, being a practical person with no eye for the beautiful, had remained gazing down the hill.

'Well, now, we may look out for squalls,' said Anthony; and the others crawled swiftly back to Whitson's side.

But the squall did not arise just then, for the visitor, after raising the mats and peering into the *Mbure*, went on his way without remark.

'That's odd,' said Eli. 'Hyar comes another fellow. Let's see what he'll do.'

But number two behaved precisely as number one had done, and so did numbers three and four, and in a word, all the numerous visitors whose curiosity moved them during the next two or three hours to lift the mats and take a peep at the interesting strangers, one of whom, it had been confidently reported, was able to bite burning wood and puff the smoke thereof out of his mouth without taking any harm or hurt.

'A nation of philosophers,' observed Anthony, after a score or two had come and gone. 'They find the birds are flown, and are too wise to make a fuss about what cannot be helped.'

'I don't agree with you,' said Guy shrewdly. 'In my opinion we are supposed to be still sleeping soundly behind the mosquito curtains, and the native politeness of those fellows being stronger than their curiosity will not permit them to disturb us.'

'I jedge that's about the way of it,' Eli agreed. 'They wouldn't be a bad lot ez niggers go, ef they warn't so free with their clubs'——

'And would leave certain articles out of their bill
of fare,' put in Jerry.

'Ah!' grunted Eli. 'You're right.—What's the
time, Guy?'

'Half-past nine,' was the answer. 'It does not
seem as if four hours had passed since sunrise. See
how the people are flocking down to the beach to
meet the canoes. I wonder if the interview with
Larkin has been fixed to take place before or after
the ceremony.'

'Before, I should 'magine,' said Eli; 'fer we were
to come in handy fer the feast afterwards. Thar's
a canoe putting off to the brig now, an' I guess friend
Faatu is in it. We shall soon know what's goin' to
happen.'

The town was now filled with people, some hurrying to the beach to meet the visitors from Levuka,
some moving aimlessly about, others, principally
women, bearing baskets of provisions from one point
to another, and all without exception chattering and
laughing in the greatest good humour. This being
high day and holiday, moreover, every one was
arrayed as sumptuously as his means and position
would allow. Rich and important people wore neck-
laces of whales' teeth, or breast ornaments of orange
cowrie and mother-of-pearl. The *sulus*, or loin-
cloths, were of the softest and whitest *masi*, the *salas*,
covering the carefully arranged heads of hair, of the
gauziest, most snowy *tapa*. Armlets and anklets of
white cowrie shells, or, more simply, of leaves and
flowers; neck-bands of bats' jaws, the backbones of
snakes, or beads of shell; frontlets of parrots' scarlet
feathers (worn only by chiefs and priests); wreaths

and garlands of scarlet hibiscus, scarf fashion over one shoulder—in a word, whatever a light-hearted, colour-loving people could procure in the way of ornament, that they wore this day.

'There goes the *Mata*,' observed Anthony, after they had watched the animated scene for some time. 'Look how the people bow and crouch before him.'

'And see,' said Jerry, 'whenever any one wishes to pass a chief he goes in front of, never behind him.'

'Their ideas of etiquette are certainly very rigid,' remarked Guy. 'There comes the canoe back from the brig.'

'And there is Faatu, talking to the *Mata* on the beach,' said Anthony, as the Tongan landed and delivered his message. 'He will require to be a good actor if he is to keep his face when the moment of discovery arrives.'

'Don't you pester 'bout the Tongan,' said Eli; 'he's got his own skin to think of ez well ez ours. I reckon ef we kin git cl'ar away, that skunk Larkin'll be in a hole 'thout any one to interpret for him.'

'Trust him to wriggle out of a difficulty,' fumed Whitson. 'I wish instead of heaving the powder overboard we had laid a train and blown him and his gang of murderers sky high.'

''Twould hev been as nigh heaven ez he's ever likely to git,' sneered Eli. 'Not but what I think ez him an' Adams put up that job o' the boat between 'em. I don't fancy the crew knew anything about it.'

'They'll be bitter enough, though, once they find about the destruction of their reserve of ammunition,' said Whitson.

J

'Let 'em,' chuckled Eli. ''Twas only tit fer tat, an' it won't matter much what they feel ef we kin on'y show 'em our heels. 'St! Now for it.'

While they had been talking in low tones, though there was no chance of their being overheard, the *Mata* had been slowly pacing towards the *Mbure ni sa* accompanied by several other chiefs and Faatu, who, if he had any shoes, would certainly have been shivering in them. As it was, he could not help glancing apprehensively towards the grove every now and then, wondering within himself whether the spirits, whose eyes he believed he had seen on the previous night, had devoured the rash intruders. 'Hang the critter,' grumbled Eli. 'What does he keep lookin' this way fer? He'll put 'em on the scent before he's done.' Outside the *Mbure* the *Mata* paused, conversing with his fellow chiefs, and occasionally waving his hand towards the house. Then, lowering his heavy club from his shoulder, he pushed aside the hanging mats and went in.

'He's been sayin' we're pretty late sleepers,' grinned Eli, 'an' he's argyin' may be we won't want no breakfast, seein' we're so soon to —— Hello!'

For with a ringing shout that startled the holiday-makers, the *Mata* bounded through the door-way, stood for an instant brandishing his club and gesticulating wildly, and then, all his dignity for the moment cast aside, sped down the hill towards the house of the king.

Frightened out of his wits at the possibility of discovery of his share in the escape of the prisoners, Faatu flung himself down on his face, grovelling with his nose in the ground, and kicking his heels in the air. However, finding that he was not to be clubbed out of hand, he rose at length, and with many backward glances, for which Eli heartily anathematised him, followed the astonished chiefs.

What passed within the king's house of course the watchers could not know, but presently the *Mata* came out again, followed by Na Ulivou, a truly regal figure, his hair frizzed out to a distance of eight or ten inches from his head and pierced by a tortoise-shell hairpin, the end of which projected over his right temple. His forehead and chin were painted a bright red, the rest of his face being covered with a smooth coating of shining black. A scarlet hibiscus blossom decorated the lobe of his left ear; around his neck he wore a massive collar of red whales' teeth, and on his stalwart chest blazed a huge circular disc of mother-of-pearl. Shining wristlets and anklets, and a *sulu* of white figured *masi*, the ends of which swept the ground behind him in a train some yards in length, and a scarf of green vines with shoulder-knot of hibiscus completed his costume; while in his hand he carried a huge war club, covered from knob to handle with elaborate carving, and glittering like an enormous jewel in the sun from its inlaying of tortoiseshell and pearl.

As the imposing figure of the king appeared, the buzz of conversation and the noise of laughter ceased suddenly, and his subjects, prostrating themselves or crouching, according to their rank, reverently intoned the *tama*.

With a peremptory wave of his hand, Na Ulivou acknowledged the courtesy, and turning to the *Mata*

and the chiefs, who had seated themselves respectfully, began an earnest conversation, pointed with
emphatic gestures.

What he said could naturally not be heard by
those on the hill, but it was evident that he was
terribly annoyed. From his point of view, there
was every reason why he should be. Every rule of
custom and courtesy required that at the feast which
was to follow the reception of the guests who had
come from Levuka to do him honour, and confer
upon him the proud title of *Vu-ni-Valu*, a sufficiency
of baked man should be provided. Only two of the
bodies which had been cooked yesterday remained,
and he had counted on the five whites to supply the
deficiency. Jerry, too, fat rollicking Jerry, what a
dainty, appetising dish he would have made to set
before the king. And now they were all gone;
there was no time to send out a foraging party to
Viti Levu; there would not be enough man to go
round, and the king would fall low in the estimation
of his guests. No wonder that Na Ulivou was
angry.

The conversation grew more and more animated,
and presently a man came hurrying up from the
beach, prostrating himself, and crawling humbly to
the feet of the king as he drew near. From his
gestures it was evident that he was telling of the
disappearance of a canoe, and explaining that, in the
opinion of such an earthworm as himself, it was by
the water that the prisoners had escaped.

With an impatient shake of his great shoulders,
Na Ulivou strode forward, and the unfortunate mes-
senger, in endeavouring to get out of his way, raised

himself from the ground, and though it was but for a second of time, committed the enormous breach of decorum of standing erect in the presence of the king. For this, accidental though it evidently was, there could be but one punishment. In the most matter-of-fact way, Na Ulivou raised his club, smote heavily downwards, and the man dropped dead at his feet. One more body had been provided for the feast, but it was unlikely that any one among the grovelling multitude would commit an error which could be turned into an excuse for furnishing another.

'The bloodthirsty wretch!' exclaimed Anthony, nervously fingering his musket as suppressed cries of horror broke from his companions. 'What did he do that for?'

'Quiet, Anthony,' warned Eli. 'Whatever it was for, we can't interfere. Likely he knows his own business.'

'If they have no mercy upon each other, they will have none upon us,' murmured Guy with pale lips. 'I wish it were night.'

'Oliver is in a tearin' rage,' observed Eli. 'See, he 's sending off Faatu fer Larkin.'

'Not likely he 'll trust himself ashore after that,' said Whitson.

'Oh yes, he will,' answered Eli. 'He 's got the king's measure, you may be sure. Oliver won't hurt him, at least not yet, not till he gits at the secret of the clubs that spit fire. After that I wouldn't say.'

As the canoe left the shore, Na Ulivou turned again, and strode haughtily towards the great temple.

It was nearing noon, and the priests and the men from Levuka were already waiting in front of the *Mbure* the arrival of the hero of the day. As soon as the king reached the temple, the enclosure surrounding it was quickly filled by those whose position gave them the right to be there, all of them seated upon mats which had been spread in anticipation of their arrival, while the *kai si*, or common people, crouched submissively outside, dotting the hill with a multitude of picturesque groups. The sun was shining in a clear sky, and the whole scene was one of such brilliant light and colour that it was difficult to realise the grisly deed which had marked its commencement.

'It's a pretty sight, that I will say,' observed Whitson. 'Look at those girls with flutes and drums. You can scarcely see them for flowers.'

'And not one of them seems to give a thought to the poor murdered man,' sighed Guy.

'They're used to sights like that, I 'magine,' said Eli. 'They don't strike 'em ez they do you an' me. Look at them girls. They're playin' the flutes with their noses. Waal, ef that don't beat all!—Hello! thar's Captin Larkin shovin' off. I s'pose Oliver thinks to impress him with the sight o' what's goin' on.'

'He seems to be bringing the entire ship's company,' said Anthony, rising to his feet to get a better view. 'I wonder he did not leave some aboard to guard the brig.'

'Why should he?' asked Eli. 'The brig won't run away, and Larkin is 'cute enough to know that Oliver won't play any tricks so long ez he lacks the secret he's dying to know.—Sit down, Anthony. Standin' up is too risky.'

'Oh, they can't see me,' answered Anthony without changing his position.

A great banging of wooden drums, big and little, announced the landing of visitors from the brig, and the convicts, drawn up in an irregular column, began to march towards the temple, followed by Faatu, whose eyes still wandered distressfully in the direction of the grove.

'There's that brute Larkin,' said Anthony, as with his arm thrown round the stem of a dead banana tree, he craned forward to look. 'Wouldn't I enjoy a pot-shot at him !'

Crack ! The treacherous stem gave way under his weight, and with a sharp cry of dismay he stumbled into the open. He was back again in an instant, but the wild scream of surprise and terror that rose from below told that he had been seen.

'You've done it now, Anthony,' exclaimed Eli, rising to his feet and grasping his musket. 'I thought you would. Why couldn't you be content to lie down like the rest o' us ? '

Anthony looked so dreadfully distressed that tender-hearted Guy was sorry for him.

'Never mind, old fellow,' he whispered. 'You didn't mean it, and we must do the best we can. Perhaps Faatu was right when he said that they would not dare to follow us in here.'

'It ain't that,' said Eli, overhearing the re-mark; 'but that Larkin won't be put off by any sech superstitious nonsense. See, thar's a score o' them speedin' to tell him. Boys, we've got

to fight and may be to die. Hands round before
we start in.'

'It was my fault. I have killed you,' cried
Anthony passionately as he clasped Eli's hand. 'Oh
I will go down and offer myself as a hostage for the
rest of you!'

'None o' that,' said Eli, laying a strong detaining
grasp on the young man's shoulder as he made an
effort to rush from the grove. 'Thar ain't no sense
in that. It wouldn't do us any good, an' you're more
use to us here. Quit foolin', Anthony,' he added,
with more sternness than he felt, as the lad wrung
his hands in grief.

Anthony ceased to struggle. 'I can die first,' he
muttered, 'and I will.'

Meantime the messengers had reached Larkin, and,
through Faatu, communicated to him the strange
news that after all the prisoners had not left the
island. Not even Na Ulivou's haughty spirit could
face the prospect of an advance into that haunted
spot, but he was quite willing that his white allies
should make the attempt, if they were so inclined.

Evidently they were, for when Larkin understood
the purport of the message, he laughed aloud, and
shaking his musket aloft, urged on his men and
began to march upon the grove, the more confidently
that he had been informed that the muskets of the
refugees were safe in the keeping of the gods in the
temple.

'Steady, boys,' said Eli, 'let 'em come well within
range, an' then fire one by one. Each man to load
before another fires. I'll take Larkin. Once git
rid o' him, an' our chances are doubled.'

Na Ulivou stood in front of the great *Mbure*, staring at the grove, and around him sat the privileged classes, and the priests and the guests from Levuka, their faces turned in the same direction. On the hillside still crouched and knelt the common people, expecting they knew not what from the vengeance of the outraged spirit, and every man's eyes were fastened on the haunted spot. Below, swinging upwards from the beach, tramped the convicts, laughing and shouting, their muskets ready primed in their hands. Above, the little knot of defenders, shoulder to shoulder, and with white, set faces waiting for the end.

Then suddenly a scream, wild and weird, rang out, and the chief priest, standing on a platform in front of the *Mbure*, beat his hands upon his breast, and, foaming at the mouth, shrieked incomprehensible words.

And from the kneeling multitude arose the echo of that yell of terror, and every man cast himself upon his face, even the great king, Na Ulivou himself, not daring to look upon the wrath of the gods.

For suddenly a strange, terrible, unlooked - for thing had happened. The shining sun grew red as blood, then black, the stars twinkled in the heavens when it was but high noon, and darkness covered the face of the land.*

And as the cries and groans of fear filled the murky air, a hollow voice to the right of the grove cried '*Come!*'

---

* Some traditions fix the date of this eclipse some years earlier; but all agree that it occurred at the ceremony of conferring the title of *Vu-ni-Vulu*, a privilege vested in the men of Levuka.

CHAPTER XII.

HRICE did that sepulchral monosyllable fall upon the ears of the astounded group in the grove before they grasped its meaning. Small wonder, coming as it did through the noise of shrieking men and wailing women, the sharp resonance of clattering drums, and the mad ravings of the priest, prophesying that the era of blood had begun. Small wonder that the ghostly voice coming out of the gloom should seem to them almost like a summons from another world. But at the third repetition Eli came to his senses, and, seizing Jerry by the hand, sped to the end of the grove remote from the temple.

'It's Faatu!' he cried joyously under his breath. 'I didn't think the heathen would have had so much spunk in him. Come on, boys. Catch hold of Jerry's other hand, Anthony! I've got his gun. Now then, race all. We'll knock up agin the nigger somewhar.'

Down the long hill they sped, colliding with bush and brake and stone, but never heeding, and presently they became aware of a solitary figure, fleeing through

the dusk with feet winged by terror, and him they
followed, seeing no other living thing, till turning,
doubling, and turning once again, they dashed through
a fringe of trees that completely concealed a tiny cove,
and there in the dark they halted.

'Whar is he?' panted Eli. 'He seemed to come
in hyar.—Faatu, whar have you gotten to?'

There was a smothered sound, half awe, half
joy, and the next moment some one fell prostrate
before Eli and began to clasp his feet.

'Hyar he is,' cried Eli. 'Git up, you or'nery fool.
Thar's no time to lose. Whar's the canoe?'

'Here it is,' called Anthony, who had been groping
about the beach. 'Here, at this end of the cove.'

'Git up, ye critter,' cried Eli, stooping over the
grovelling Faatu and shaking him violently. 'What's
come to you? You can go through all this by-an'-by
ef you've a mind to. Up with you an' show us how
to manage this yer craft.—By time! Why won't the
silly nigger get up?'

'He is completely overcome with terror I fancy,'
said Guy, bending over Faatu and gently patting his
shoulder. 'I'm sure I don't wonder at it. I can't
think how he summoned up courage to come for us at
all.—Faatu! Faatu!'

'*Malohi hootooa, iki tamatea Faatu!*' (Potent god,
don't kill me) mumbled Faatu, relapsing into his
native Tongan.

'Git him up fer any sake,' groaned Eli despairingly,
as he vainly strove to free his legs. 'It won't take
Larkin long to figger out what has happened, an'
then he'll try the grove an' find us gone. The sooner
we're out o' this the better.'

'Get up, Faatu. We won't hurt you,' implored
Guy, catching at the sense of the words which the
Tongan muttered miserably over and over again.
'Faatu! Don't you know us? We are your friends.
Come, Faatu, get into the canoe. Na Ulivou will be
here presently.'

But Na Ulivou's name had just then no terrors for
Faatu.

'You gods,' he gasped. 'You big gods. You
make um night when sun shine. Oh, big gods, no
kill Faatu.'

'Get up,' persisted Guy. 'We are not gods, but
men like yourself. We won't hurt you. Help us,
Faatu. Dear, good Faatu, help us.'

Thus adjured, poor Faatu took heart of grace,
loosed his hold of Eli, and stumbling to his feet,
staggered in the direction of the canoe, on board
of which were already Anthony, Whitson, and Jerry.

'That's better,' said Eli, as they waded through
the shallows, and joined their comrades. 'Now then,
you brown sinner, show us what to do, or I'll lay I'll
eat you myself, body, bones, skin, and hair an' all.'

In spite of the predicament they were in, Guy
burst out laughing, as Faatu, with a cry of terror,
seized a pole, and thrusting it first upon one side and
then upon the other, rapidly propelled the canoe out
of the dense shadows of the cove into the clearer
darkness outside.

'What a shame to frighten him so,' said Guy.
'He doesn't know any better.—What next, Faatu?'

Faatu took up the long sculls, and adjusting them
in their places, motioned to Anthony to take one,
while he manipulated the other.

'Git out a bit,' he answered unsteadily. 'Wind come by-'n-by.'

Grasping the oar in his strong hands, Anthony stood up and imitated Faatu's movements as exactly as he could. He was not very successful at first, but in a few moments he improved, and presently they were well under way.

'It's a good thing thar's all that howlin' an' screechin' goin' on,' said Eli, 'else there'd be a mighty good chance o' some one hearin' the click click o' them big oars in the rowlocks. Whar are you goin' to take us, Faatu?'

'To the great river,' answered the Tongan. 'Me got friends t'ere.'

'Umph!' grunted Eli, 'I'm as wise as ever. Let's run up the sail ez soon ez you can. Ef we can git out o' sight before old Sol shows his nose agen, so much the better.—Waal, Jerry, lad, an' how do *you* feel? I han't had time to ask you till now.'

'I'm all right,' answered Jerry stoutly. 'I was horribly frightened at first, though. I thought it was the end of the world. It's an eclipse, isn't it? I've never seen one before.'

'Jest that,' replied Eli. 'No more did I—leastways not to sech an extent ez this. I guess we may call this a total eclipse.'

'I guess you may,' Guy laughed softly, 'and without any fear of contradiction. Look, oh, Jerry, look, what a beautiful sight!'

The eclipse was at its height, and around the sun and the moon appeared a luminous corona, at the base of which, projecting beyond the dark edge of the moon, gleamed blood-red points and prominences.

As they looked, certain of these prominences surged this way and that, flickering and dancing in all manner of fantastic shapes, while others, curling upwards like lambent tongues of flame, shot with incredible velocity high into the murky sky.*

'I don't wonder,' said Jerry, as the yells and screams on the island broke forth with redoubled intensity. 'I don't wonder. It's splendid, but it's enough to frighten anybody into fits who doesn't know what it means. Poor old Faatu! just listen to him.'

For the Tongan, scarcely able to retain his hold upon the oar, uttered hollow and most moving groans.

'Cheer up, Faatu!' said Guy, patting him on the back. 'You will have the sun out again by-and-by. Hullo!'

He sprang to the oar, and caught it just in time, for the unfortunate Faatu dropped heavily to the deck, fainting from excess of emotion.

'He's got it pretty badly,' said Eli, scooping up some water and dashing it in the Tongan's face. 'Jest ez I hoped he'd show us how to hoist the sail, too. No matter; he'll come round presently. Can you manage the oar, Guy? Take it from him, Whitson.'

'Yes, you take it,' acquiesced Guy, relinquishing the oar to the mate. 'I'll look after Faatu. Oh dear! what's that? That's not part of the eclipse, is it?'

---

* Incandescent hydrogen gas. These flames are a part of the phenomena of a total eclipse of the sun, and often shoot up tens of thousands of miles.

From the island came a succession of bright, rapid flashes, followed by sharp crackling sounds.

'Hev you lost your wits, too, boyee ?' chuckled Eli. 'Don't you know the sound o' musket-firin' when you hear it ?'

'Everything seems so strange and altered just now,' said Guy, busy with Faatu, who showed signs of returning animation. 'What does it mean ?'

'It means that Bill Larkin has got over his fright, that is, ef he was frightened, an' is firin' into the grove,' answered Eli. 'He, he! killed us all at the first fire. No, by time, he ain't sure. Thar's another volley. Done fer us that time, William. Ho! ho! ho!'

'He 'll be rather surprised when he goes in to pick up the bodies,' giggled Jerry. 'He must have thought us precious fools to wait there all this time. Ah! what 's that ?'

For a dark shadow loomed up just in front of them.

'Oh dear! oh dear!' sighed Guy again. 'Haven't we had scares enough for one day. What is it ?'

'It 's the brig,' cried Eli joyously. 'Bullee! I didn't know we were goin' in her direction.—Stop, Whitson.—Pull hard, Anthony. So,' as the nose of the canoe swung round. 'Steady, belay a bit. I 'm goin' on board.'

'What for ?' asked Whitson. 'Hadn't we better get on as fast as possible ?'

'You fergit all our things went down with the boat,' replied Eli, as the canoe grated against the side of the brig. 'Thar's two or three things aboard hyar ez 'll be useful wharever we go an' whatever we

do.' He swung himself on board. 'You come along
with me, Anthony.—Stay by the craft, Whitson.—
Guy, keep your eye on that Tongan. First thing
he 'll try an' do when he comes round 'll be to jump
overboard. Come on, Anthony.'

Anthony leaped on board after him, and together
they made their way below.

Scarcely had they disappeared when Faatu came to
himself. For a moment he sat up and stared into
the surrounding gloom, and then, before Guy could
anticipate the action or move a muscle to prevent it,
flung himself overboard with a shrill cry. Whitson,
however, was too quick for him, and by great good
luck managed to seize him by the foot before he disappeared under water, and amidst the suppressed
shouts of laughter of all three, the unhappy Tongan
was hauled back on to the deck of the canoe.

'Faatu, you foolish fellow,' said Guy, as soon as
he had recovered breath, 'what are you about? Do
you want to be eaten by the sharks?'

Faatu made some incoherent reply, and then suddenly began to cry, the low-voiced, helpless, whimper-
ing of a little child. It was pathetic to hear him,
great strong man as he was, and the laughter of the
three comrades died away into sympathetic murmurs.

'Poor old fellow,' said Jerry, putting his arm
round Faatu's dripping neck. 'Were you frightened
then? Cheer up, Faatu. It is all right; there is
nothing to be afraid of. I 'll take care of you.'

Faatu buried his wet nose in Jerry's jacket, and
snivelled miserably. 'Faatu frightened,' he sobbed,
while Jerry stroked his cheek, and soothed him as if
he were a baby.

'There, there, Faatu,' said Guy, adding his minis-
trations to those of Jerry, while Whitson, turning his
quid in his cheek, spat vehemently right and left,
feeling more than half inclined to cry himself.

'Faatu,' went on Guy soothingly, 'try and get it
out of your head that we are in danger. This darkness will soon pass away. God—our God, that is—
will not let it hurt a good man like you. Do you
believe me?'

'Yis,' sighed Faatu, fondling Guy's hand. 'Me
lofe you.'

'If you love us,' pursued Guy, 'you will help us.
We can't do without you, Faatu. Surely you won't
leave us now.'

'No-o-o,' answered Faatu plaintively.

'Then show us how to hoist the sail, like a good
fellow, so that we may be ready when the others
come back,' said Guy, and slowly and listlessly Faatu
rose and set about the task.

While they were securing the fore and back stays,
Guy looked up and caught the gleam of a light
through the port-holes. In an instant it disappeared. He looked up again, and it was there once
more.

'What a time they are,' he thought, 'and how
foolish of them to show a light. It might be seen
from the shore.'

The same thought struck Whitson, and he expressed
his dissatisfaction in strong language.

'Never mind,' said Guy; 'they can't be long now,
and we are all ready for a start when they do
come.'

'I can't imagine what Banks wanted to go aboard

K

for at all,' grumbled Whitson. 'What's to be gained
by it?'

'Eli generally has a good reason for whatever he
does,' said Jerry, taking up the cudgels for his friend.

'Hush! listen!' cried Guy.

From the direction of the island came the sound
of splashing blades and the swift, irregular rattle of
oars in the rowlocks. Almost at the same moment a
faint crackling was heard within the brig; from the
port-hole above Guy's head curled a thin stream of
smoke, and then a lurid, leaping tongue of flame.

'Oh!' gasped the boy, and seized a rope that
hung from the brig.

But before he could swing himself aboard, there
was a hurried trampling upon deck, a rush to the
side, and Eli, closely followed by Anthony, looked
over.

'Take these,' Eli jerked out, lowering a couple of
canvas bags. 'In with you, Anthony, quick.' And
almost together they dropped on to the deck of the
canoe.

'Shove off,' cried Eli hoarsely. 'Shove off, and
don't lose a moment. The brig's afire, and thar's a
store of powder we knew nothin' about in the hold.'

Whitson shoved strongly off, and Faatu, whose
nerves were all right when he had anything to deal
with that he understood, sprang astern and fixed the
steer oar. The canoe hung back for a moment, and
then, wind and tide both catching her, she lay down
to it, and skimmed like a swallow over the water.

'Did you set fire to her?' asked Jerry.

'Not knowingly,' said Eli, 'but I dessay a spark
from my flint got dropped among them oil casks.

Thar she burns,' as the flames burst through the hatchway, and raced hungrily up the masts. 'She won't be long now.—Hello, William, hev you put off to see the fun ?' For a howl of rage and disappointment rang out above the confusion of sounds that still poured from the island.

'We heard him coming just as you rejoined us,' explained Guy. 'Well, well, Eli, I always did hope to go back in the brig, but you have burned our boats.'

'I 've burned theirs anyway,' said Eli, ' an' I wish they were in it. Whoosh ! thar she blows.'

A lurid stream of light poured high into the air, illuminating everything far and near, and for one brief second revealing the occupants of the canoe and the boat to one another; then through the fiery column swept a vivid, blinding flash, followed instantly by a dull roar. For a moment or two the air streamed sparks and blazing fragments, then all grew dark once more.

At the sound of that awful roar the mournful wailings on the island were blent in one universal scream of terror, but above it all, pealing clear across the water, came the loud, stern shout of Larkin:

'I will hunt you down for this if I follow you to the ends of the earth.'

CHAPTER XIII.

THE JUDGMENT OF MBONAVINDONGO.

THROUGH the darkling waters the canoe rushed southwards, and from the villages on the coast of Viti Levu came the sound of many lamentations, as the afflicted savages called upon their gods for deliverance from the great horror that overshadowed the land. And their gods were deaf to their cries. The canoe, which was a middle-sized one of the build called *thamakau*, the clipper of the South Seas, behaved splendidly, the more when it is remembered how ignorant of the management of such a craft were all on board save one.

But there is nothing like danger for sharpening the wits, and while Faatu looked after the steer oar, Eli, acting under his directions, kept his hand on the sheet in case a change of tack became necessary. The light wind held, however, and as the shadow began to steal off the face of the sun, and the murky twilight to brighten, they entered the Kamba mouth of the Rewa River, the Wai Levu, or great water of Fiji.

'Kamba,' said Faatu, indicating a wooded point,

whence, as from everywhere else, came sounds of wailing. 'Ndoku,' as in the increasing light another village peeped out from amidst its groves of bananas; and then they were fairly in the river. Silently Faatu beckoned Anthony to take his place at the steer oar, and moving forward took the sheet from Eli's hand, lowered the sail, and began to unstep the mast.

'Goin' to try scullin' fer a change, air ye?' asked Eli cheerily.

''St!' ejaculated Faatu, laying a brown finger on his lips. Ignorant whether some new danger might not lie in their path, Eli held his peace; but nothing appeared to justify Faatu's warning, and presently, as they were hugging the bank, Jerry raised his hand and carelessly caught at the overhanging bough of a mangrove. Instantly Faatu leaned over and rapped his wrist so sharply that the boy uttered a low cry of pain.

'What did you'—— he began hotly; but again Faatu made a sign commanding absolute silence.

'See hyar,' said Eli, in a low voice, looking round from his post at the starboard scull; 'let us know what to expect. I don't see anythin'; I don't hear anythin'. What is it?'

Faatu made no reply until the canoe had shot past the mouth of a small creek, then pointing vaguely into the mangroves behind them, he said in a low, awed whisper: 'In t'ere god; angry if um talk.'

'Is that all?' exclaimed Eli, in a tone of relief; while Jerry railed lightly at the Tongan.

'God in t'ere,' persisted Faatu. 'Fery big god; glad got by.'

'God is everywhere, Faatu,' said Guy, seeing an opportunity.

'Oh no,' answered Faatu simply; 'god t'ere— and t'ere,' he pointed ahead, 'and plenty place. Not eferywhere; by-'n-by no gods for long way.'

'Let him alone, Guy,' advised Anthony; 'you will only confuse the poor soul. Have at him some other time.'

'God,' began Faatu again, when immediately in front of them, almost in their very ears, they heard the awful banging of the *lali,* or great wooden drum, but beaten with terrific force, and louder than they had ever heard it before.

Eli ceased sculling, and quietly took his musket from the spear rack at the back of the deck-house.

'Be ready, boys,' he said.

Faatu's face was grave, but his expression was one of awe rather than apprehension, as, sinking his body reverently to the deck, he intoned the *tama.*

The beating of the drum increased in speed and force until the noise became appalling. Not a village, not a human habitation was in sight, not a human being could be seen; and suddenly it struck every one that there was nothing to account for the sound, which apparently proceeded from the open and clearly visible centre of a ring of mangroves just ahead of the canoe.

'Waal, that's queer,' muttered Eli; 'it sounds like a drum. I b'lieve it is a drum. Yet wan solitary drummer couldn't make that astonishin' row, you'd think.'

'I defy him to,' said Jerry. 'It must be a ghost, or one of Faatu's gods.'

It would take a very substantial ghost to raise such a din as that,' said Anthony, as the canoe glided past the circle of mangroves.

And the sound ceased as they went by.

'God,' exclaimed Faatu, catching Jerry's remark. 'Mburerua. Him fery big god. Him haf big *lali*—oo! fery big.' He held up eight fingers. 'Take so many men to beat um. When Mburerua beat big *lali*, t'en mans eferywhere begin to fight.' He waved his hand comprehensively around. 'Fiji mans not beat *lali*,' he went on; 'Mburerua beat um. See! no mans t'ere.'

'Rubbish!' grunted Anthony. 'We can't see them; but they must be there.'

''Tis a trick of the priests to impress the people, I expect,' suggested Whitson.

'Then it's very well performed,' said Guy.

'Ain't it?' chimed in Eli. 'Kinder gives you the creeps.'

Rubbish! A trick! It may have been. But at Mbau and Viwa, at Rewa and Nakelo, at Navuso, and at far away-Namosi, listening thousands heard that day the beating of Mburerua's great drum, and fell with their faces upon the ground, while the priests sitting in front of the *Mbures* became inspired, and shrieked prophecies of bloody wars and battles, when the air should be darkened with clouds of spears, flying swiftly, and the rattle of club against club should drown the noise of the groans of the wounded and dying, and blood should flow from the land until the rivers ran red between their banks.

'Mburetu,' said Faatu, pointing to a village on their left, and adding cheerfully, 'No more gods till by-'n-by.'

'Faith! I'm not sorry to hear that,' declared Jerry emphatically; 'for what between their silence and their noise, they're most disturbin' crachurs.'

'You're right,' agreed Eli; 'I never could abide harnts myself.'

Some little distance farther and they reached the canal of Kele Musu, which shortens the passage to Rewa by twenty miles, and is a wonderful piece of engineering for natives whose only spades were wooden stakes, and whose sole means of removing the excavated earth was to scoop it up with their hands and carry it away in baskets. Into this they were about to turn when Eli abruptly asked Faatu where he intended to take them to, and on being informed 'to Rewa,' called on Anthony, and sculling strongly, shot past the mouth of the canal, and drove the canoe into the midst of a dense clump of mangroves, where he dropped his oar and made fast.

'Why for you do t'at?' demanded Faatu. 'Rewa not come so quick t'at way.'

'May be not,' returned Eli. 'We ain't in sech a hurry ez all that, an' ef we never git thar at all it won't matter much. Fact is, I'd sooner go anywhar else than Rewa. After what Larkin said, I don't think it's safe.'

The three boys held their peace, waiting for further explanation, but Whitson said, somewhat impatiently:

'Why not, Banks? Rewa seems to me to be the safest place we can go to. The Tongan has friends there, and, besides, how on earth is Larkin or anybody else to know which way we have gone, or where?'

'A good man, but pow'ful slow,' was Eli's inward comment, while aloud he proceeded to explain his reasons for avoiding Rewa.   If Larkin's threat of following them were to be taken seriously, and in their position they could not afford to take it otherwise, Rewa was sure to be the first place which he would be likely to visit.   For two reasons: the first that he and the Mbauans would certainly remember that it was from Rewa Faatu had come with his message, and what more likely than that he should return to his friends ?   The second, that Larkin, remembering Faatu's remark that there were other Tongans at, or in the direction of, Rewa, who would go there in the hope of picking up an interpreter among them.

'Of course there is a chance that Na Ulivou, furious at the loss of the brig and its precious contents, may have turned upon Larkin and swept him from the face of the earth,' said Anthony, as Eli brought his argument to a close.

'Not likely,' returned the latter; 'remember, Oliver don't know the secret of the muskets, so he can't tell ez thar was anythin' aboard the brig ez would be useful in that line, an' fer the rest, Larkin an' them with him hev a good supply o' ammunition, quite enough to keep Oliver in order fer a time. You mustn't fergit thar's a couple o' dozen o' the varmints.'

'The want of an interpreter will be his chief inducement, I should think,' remarked Guy.   'If he can supply that, and live quietly and comfortably where he is, why should he trouble to go on a wild-goose chase ?   He must know that, given he doesn't light on us at Rewa, he has no chance of finding us. Why, we might have put out to sea for all he could tell.'

'An' we will, too,' nodded Eli; 'I'd sooner trust the salt water than any one on these islands, black or white. Ef we were provisioned fer sech a trip, I'd say start right now.'

Here Faatu, who had been following the conversation most attentively, broke in, saying:

'Tree Tonga mans at Rewa spik *papalangi* talk. Leetle, all same me. Lakini want um. He go Rewa. We not go Rewa. Hey?'

'Quite right, Faatu,' said Guy, smiling at him. 'Where are we to go then?'

'Go over sea,' answered Faatu. 'Faatu lofe sea plenty, big, much, fery.'

'Good gracious! what a string of adjectives,' laughed Jerry. 'Keep some for next time, Faatu.'

Faatu grinned responsively.

'Faatu talk *papalangi* good, hey, Jelly?' he said.

'Here, don't you call names,' cried Jerry, in mock wrath. 'Try it again. Jerry, my boy, Jerry—not Jelly, stupid.'

'Jelly, my boy, Jelly—not Jelly, stupid,' repeated Faatu, with much gravity, as though he were saying a lesson.

'Let him alone, Jerry,' laughed Guy. 'You can educate him later on.—Is there no place where we can get some pigs and yams?' he went on to Faatu. 'Plenty—enough to take over sea?'

Faatu shook his head and spread the palms of his hands upwards.

'No hab whale's toof,' he sighed despondently.

'What, whales' teeth,' echoed Eli. 'Oh, but I

reckon we have, though—plenty. I got some when we were aboard. I jedged they might come in handy. See hyar.'

He thrust his hand into one of the canvas sacks, and brought out several of the precious teeth, which, at that date, were of more value in Fiji than their weight in gold.

A grin of delight overspread Faatu's handsome face.

'That is splendid,' he exclaimed; 'now we can go anywhere and do anything.' Only, of course, he did not express himself quite so correctly.

'Hurrah!' cried Jerry softly. 'Then, Faatu, as we've had nothing to eat since very early breakfast, I vote you pilot us into port without delay. I'm so hungry I don't know what to do.'

Faatu pulled some yams and coco-nuts from beneath a mat within the deck-house.

'You want eat, Jelly, my boy, Jelly—not Jelly, stupid,' he said, mastering the whole of Jerry's, to him, extraordinary name, by a tremendous effort of memory.

'Oh, shut your head, Jerry,' guffawed Eli, as the boy began an indignant protest. 'Or fill yourself up with them yams while we talk sense. Thar's some biscuit in that other bag.——See hyar, Faatu, whar are we to go?'

'Me t'ink,' began Faatu, and stopped, holding up his hand. 'Canoe coming,' he whispered softly, and stepping aft, softly parted the mangrove boughs and peered down the river.

Eli joined him, while the rest stared at one another, for, listen as they would, they could hear nothing. Presently, however, they became aware of a monotonous rhythmical beat, faint at first, but growing momentarily louder. It was the sound of sculls rocking from side to side in their sockets. Five minutes passed, and then round a bend in the river swept a great canoe with the black and white pennon of the Vu-ni-Valu streaming from her masthead. On she came, heading straight for the spot where they lay concealed, until it seemed as if she were about to run them down. Then with a sweep of the sculls her nose was turned, she shot into the canal, and disappeared from sight. For some little time no one ventured to speak; but at last Eli said, with a mild air of triumph: 'What did I tell you?'

'You were right as usual,' answered Anthony. 'Larkin has lost no time in organising the pursuit. But there were no white men aboard that I could see.'

'The *Mata* was there, though,' said Whitson. 'They're on the hunt for us; that's certain.'

'*Mata* take whale's toof to Tui Rewa,' explained Faatu, seizing a pole and thrusting the canoe away from the bank. 'Him say p'raps gif us back. Him fery angry we not t'ere.'

'I'm sorry fer his feelings,' said Eli drily, as he took his stand at the scull. 'Come on, Anthony. Time's up.'

For an hour or more they sculled steadily on; then, as they left the monotonous green of the mangroves behind them, Whitson and Guy relieved their comrades at the oars and they entered a reach of the river bordered by low, flat shores and grassy meadows. It was verging towards evening, and the sun was shining again in a clear sky. The eclipse was over, but the impression remained, and as they swept by village after village with its collection of low, thatched houses, not a living being was to be seen; for the priests had told the people that the gods were angry, and it was *tambu* for man or woman to eat food, or drink water, or to step outside their dwellings till the morning dawned. If now and then from some house peeped out a scared face, it was instantly withdrawn, its trembling owner firmly convinced that it had been his to look upon a portent of still deeper meaning, which should serve him for discourse when next he met his friends and neighbours; for had not his eyes beheld the shadowy canoe of Ndengei as it rushed by with its freight of gods and pale ghosts to the gloomy caverns of Na Vatu?

And so on and on they went until the sun sank and the songs of the birds died away in feeble twitterings as the sharp and sudden darkness of the tropics covered the land and the fireflies lit their tiny lanterns. Here and there from one bank or the other came the grunt of a wakeful pig, or the shrill call of a bird startled out of its sleep, and then Faatu, seizing a piece of biscuit, or yam, or, coco-nut, would hurl it ashore as a *soro* (propitation) to the *Luve ni Wai*, the Children of the Waters, those wild and fearful 'little' gods who might, unless promptly appeased, work them much mischief. On and on, while some slept exhausted, and the arms of those who tugged at the labouring oars ached for pain and weariness. On and on against heavy tide and swift current, now bumping against a snag, now poling clear of a shallow, till at last Faatu, who with

tireless eyes had kept watch in the bows, called a
halt, and with sighs of relief, Anthony and Whitson,
who had been alternately sculling and poling for the
last hour, dropped wearily to the deck.

'Don't wake Eli,' said Anthony; 'he is quite
worn out. I am fresh enough except about the
arms. I'll keep watch for an hour and then call
you.'

'No; lie down both of you,' said the voice of
Guy at his elbow. 'I've had a most refreshing
sleep. Faatu and I will keep watch together.'

Too tired to argue the point, Anthony and Whitson
fell heavily asleep, and Guy and Faatu, not choosing
to wake them, kept watch all through the long
silent hours. At last a light breeze rustled the
foliage, a faint whiteness glimmered through the
darkness, here a bird twittered and there a parrot
shrieked; there was a humming of mosquitoes, a
wreathing mist rose from the river, the air chilled
suddenly, and all the signs foretold the approach of
dawn.

As Guy laid a hand upon his shoulder Eli sat up
suddenly.

'Why—whar'—— he began, and then as recollection flashed upon him, 'Oh, Guy, boyee, this is too
bad. You've let me sleep the night through.'

'You needed it, old fellow,' answered Guy. 'I
would not have roused you even now but for that
noise. Listen!'

From far away down the river came once again
the measured sound of rocking sculls.

'Suthin comin',' said Eli. 'Wake, Anthony! Up
with you, Whitson! We must get on.'

The sleepers started up, yawning and rubbing their eyes as Faatu unmoored the canoe and rapidly poled away from the bank.

'What is it?' inquired Anthony, springing to his place.

'Can't say,' answered Eli. 'We know it can't be friends, an' we can't be sure it ain't enemies. Forward!'

On again with tireless energy through reach after reach of river, each more beautiful than the last; between banks whence the rich foliage stooped to drink of the rushing water; past green pasture lands, whereon as yet no flocks nor herds grazed, nor would for many a year; past points and curves and spits where the graceful *niu sawas* * spread their delicate leaves to the morning air, heavy with the scent of violets, robbed from the white blossoms of the ivi.† Past it all, careless of the beauties which at another time would have delighted their eyes; for their ears were ever strained to catch the sound of those rocking sculls, warning of certain danger and possible death.

Onward still with a change at the oars; past the rough hills on the right and the lower banks on the left, till at last they swept round a wooded point, to where the river narrowed abruptly, and a small waterfall poured its slender silver stream over the black face of a perpendicular rock, beneath which some boys and very young men were disporting themselves and bathing their faces assiduously.

'*Wai ni Kumi*' (Water of the Beard), said Faatu

* A beautiful palm—*Kentia exorrhiza.*
† Tahitian Chestnut—*Inocarpus edulis.*

with a grin. 'Me know um. Mans t'ink um make um beard if um wash um face t'ere.'

But, however keen the desire of the boys to obtain the mark of manhood on their faces, it yielded to fear as their astonished eyes fell upon the extraordinary beings in the canoe, and with yells of terror they sped up the bank, and fled inland.

'Now we're in for it,' said Eli, as in obedience to Faatu's directions, the sculls were finally laid aside and the canoe poled through the shallowing waters. 'Thar's a village hyarabouts I jedge, an' them lads is goin' to give warnin' of our comin'. Faatu and Guy, you do the polin'.—Jerry, lie down.—Anthony and Whitson, look to your primin'.'

'Don't shoot unless it is absolutely necessary,' implored Guy. 'Perhaps they will let us pass. What place are we coming to, Faatu?'

'Naitasiri,' was the answer. 'T'ere,' as they rounded a wooded point and entered a broader reach of the stream; 'T'ere um am.'

'Yes; and there they are,' added Anthony. 'What a crowd of them. Thank heaven, they have yet to hear the sound of a musket.'

It was indeed a fearful sight that met their eyes. The curving bank on their right was black with savages, all of them armed with club and spear, and yelling wildly—ferociously, as it seemed. But Faatu, with a genial grin upon his face, poled steadily on and betrayed no alarm.

'I guess it's all right,' said Eli, observing this. 'Look at the Tongan.—Shall we fire, Faatu?'

'Not, not,' was the hasty reply. 'Peace! See, womans and chillums wif um. T'at mean Fiji mans

Half-measures wouldn't work there.

Fiji.   PAGE 178.

not angry—not fight. Oo'i! Oo'i!' he shouted,
following the hail with a torrent of Fijian, the music
of which was spoiled by his harsh Tongan pronuncia-
tion. A tall, handsome chief stepped half way down
the grassy bank to answer him.

'Whence come you, Tongan?' he demanded; 'and
who are these with you in the canoe? Are they
men or gods? They do not look like men, for they
have painted their faces white. Yesterday the gods
were angry and put out the sun. The priests saw
visions, and told us you would come. You are welcome, if you come in peace.'

This was of course intelligible to no one but Faatu,
whose quick intelligence leapt to an idea.

'I am a Tongan, as you can see and hear,' he
replied; 'but those with me are "little" gods from
over the sea. They did me a kindness and I wish
to recompense them, for though they are "little" yet
they are very powerful. The men of Mbau would
have eaten them, and they were angry and turned
their backs upon Mbau. But first of all they
darkened the sun.'

'Did they?' said the chief, much interested. 'That
is strange, for the priest told us it was Ndengei.'

'Perhaps Ndengei darkened it here,' answered
Faatu diplomatically; 'but they darkened it at Mbau,
or, if they did not, they asked their God to do it
for them. I heard them. Oh, they are very wise
and very powerful, and when they are angry, they
make their long clubs talk with tongues of fire and
men fall dead.'

The chief looked incredulous. 'I will believe that
when I see it,' he said. 'See, there is one whose

L

brains have turned to soup. He is of no use to any-
one. Speak to him with a club.'

He pointed to an abject creature, who, seated
astride a branch, moped and moaned and swung his
long arms to and fro.

Faatu nodded, and laying hold of a musket, levelled
it at the unfortunate and fired.

Just in time Anthony knocked up the barrel, and
the charge expended itself harmlessly among the
branches. But the shock was too much for the
wretched idiot, who lost his hold of the bough, and
fell with a shrill yelp of terror into the river. In a
moment he was out again and speeding up the bank,
followed or preceded by the entire crowd, howling
lustily as they fled.

'Come back!' shouted Faatu. 'Why for do
t'at?' he said angrily to Anthony. 'Now um not
belief can do.'

'Bah! you savage,' returned Anthony, shaking his
fist in Faatu's face.

'Let him alone,' ordered Eli. 'That canoe is
creepin' up, an' unless that shot frightens the rowers,
she'll be here in no time. Call 'em back, Faatu.'

Faatu shouted reassuring words, and presently the
chief stopped, turned, and retraced his steps, followed
slowly by some eight or ten others.

'Well now, you see,' said Faatu blandly.

'It is not true what you said,' replied the chief in
trembling accents. 'The madman is yet alive.'

'Quite so,' admitted Faatu, who was of the stuff
that ambassadors are made of; 'but that is because
I am a fool. If one of them had made it speak, you
would have seen. Now they are angry and will not.

Let them come ashore and promise to treat them well, and they will, perhaps, teach you the trick of it.'

A loud shout of ' Here they come !' from Jerry cut short the parley; and the pursuing canoe came proudly round the point and bore down upon them.

'Now you will hear them talk in earnest,' said Faatu to the chief; 'and men will be killed, for they are angry.'

'Hail them, Faatu,' said Eli. 'Warn them that they must come no nearer.'

The expression of the Naitasirian chief was one of smug satisfaction, as he listened to Faatu's address, for he did not greatly love the men of Mbau, who had recently digested some of his best warriors, and he was quite content to secure a cheap and perfectly safe revenge.

That discretion is the better part of valour was as well, if not better, known in Fiji as elsewhere, so the men at once stopped poling, and brought the canoe to a standstill. A chief then stood up and engaged in an animated conversation with him of Naitasiri, which, as may well be imagined, lost not a little of its dignity and eloquence in the translation which Faatu furnished to his white friends. Said the Mbauan chief :

'Hail, great Stinking Mangrove !' which was the malodorous English of Tui Naitasiri's name, Mbonavin- dongo. 'Hail, O Mbonavindongo ! Na Ulivou sends love and this whale's tooth in earnest of it. The little bird which carries the news told the Root of War that the wicked white men who brought much trouble to Mbau would flee to the waters of the Great River. One canoe is gone to Rewa, another waits at

Kamba, a third is hastening to Suva, and a fourth to
Navua. I am come to you, and—why,' he broke off
with a start of admirably feigned surprise, 'there are
the very men before my eyes. Truly my good fortune
is wonderful. Give them over to me, Mbonavindongo,
for their lives are forfeit to the gods.'

With a dexterous sweep of his arm he sent the
whale's tooth whirling through the air with so good
an aim that it fell at the feet of Mbonavindongo, who
stooped, touched it, and then, changing his mind, let
it lie. At the same time he acknowledged with a
courteous bow the Mbauan's profuse apologies for the
unceremonious method of the presentation.

Then up rose Eli with two whales' teeth in his
left hand and his musket in his right.

'O Mbonavindongo, the man from Mbau is a liar,'
he cried, speaking very slowly, so that Faatu might
interpret every word. 'We are not bad men. The
Mbauans would have slain us, but our great God
made a thick darkness cover the sun and we came
away.'

Mbonavindongo nodded. This chimed in with
Faatu's version.

'Moreover,' went on Eli, 'for every tooth that the
Mbauans will give, we will give two. See, here they
are.' He plunged waist-deep into the water, waded
to the bank, and crouching at the feet of Mbonavindongo, presented his offering.

The boldness of the act pleased Mbonavindongo,
who accepted the gift with a smile. Instantly a great
clapping of hands arose from the people, many of
whom had stolen back to the bank, and Faatu cried
joyously. 'Him lofe you now. When um take

whales' toof um not can hurt. When Fjii mans take
whales' toof um do what um say.'

With a touch of his foot Mbonavindongo spurned
the whale's tooth from Mbau into the river, privately
resolving to recover it after the departure of the
visitors. This was a most outrageous insult, for of
course etiquette required that the tooth, if not accepted, should be returned. But Mbonavindongo's
mind was made up.

'Tell that to Na Ulivou,' he cried. 'I will give
up my guests to no one—least of all to him. Who
is this Na Ulivou that he thinks he has only to ask
and to have? These are not wicked men, even if
they be not gods. Perhaps they are "little" gods. I
do not know. But they have a God of their own
that is stronger than the Mbauan god, and I will not
give them up.'

'Bah!' returned the Mbauan. 'Mbonavindongo's
father was probably a fool. These are wicked men
who have stolen the clubs that talk and kill from the
good men left behind at Mbau. There are twenty-
five of them, and their clubs speak much louder and
can kill men. These people can only kill birds.'
This was a pretty little fiction which Na Ulivou had
impressed upon the crew of each canoe in order to
give them courage if they came to close quarters with
the fugitives. 'We heard the club talking as we
came up,' went on the chief. 'Was any one
killed?'

'No,' answered Mbonavindongo with a troubled
look.

'There, then, is the proof that they are impostors,'
said the Mbauan, very much relieved in his own mind,

if the truth must be told. 'Well, Mbonavindongo, since you will not give them up we will take them, and then, perhaps, Na Ulivou will forgive you for spurning his gift. Yet I do not know that he will. Forward, my brothers. Those clubs speak but do not kill.'

'Don't they?' muttered Eli as Faatu translated this to him, while the Mbauans poled swiftly forwards and the men of Naitasiri, believing they had been tricked, swept threateningly down the bank. 'Don't they? I'll give 'em one more chance. Tell 'em to go back.'

'Bah!' laughed the Mbauan chief derisively. 'You are but empty boasters.' He hurled his club with so good an aim that had not Eli fallen flat on the deck of the canoe, to which he had returned, his brains would assuredly have been dashed out. Like lightning the Virginian sprang up, and taking quick aim, shot the Mbauan through the heart.

'It had to be done, boys,' he said regretfully as the chief fell with a splash into the river. 'It was his life or ours. Half measures wouldn't work there.'

This prompt illustration of the killing powers of Eli's club produced the desired effect. The advance upon both sides was checked, and the Mbauans, after hauling the dead chief back into the canoe, poled swiftly down stream.

'Ié!' yelled Mbonavindongo after them. 'The Mbauans are liars. Tell Na Ulivou I am greater than he. By-and-by I will come to Mbau and root it up and throw it into the sea, and Na Ulivou and his cowards will I cook and eat. Ié!'

Foaming with rage, a Mbauan chief rose in the

canoe and shook his spears at Mbonavindongo.
'Mbonavindongo,' he screamed, 'do you, filth of
Naitasiri, dare to threaten? Before you can stir a
step on the way to Mbau, Na Ulivou will be here,
and there shall not be so much left of Naitasiri or
its people, or its pig of a chief, as shall fill a cooking
pot. Beware of Na Ulivou! Beware!'

'Pooh!' cried Mbonavindongo defiantly as the canoe
rounded the spit, '*Sa ndui thangi ni tomba*' (every
man is a wind in his own bay). 'Let him come and
we shall see.'—He stretched out his hands with a
friendly gesture to Jerry. 'Little god with the red
head,' he said, 'come and dwell in my house, and I
will give you everything you can desire.'

'Look at that now,' said Jerry proudly, when the
grinning Faatu had translated this. ''Tis I am the
boy to get you out of a scrape, so I am. Faatu, say
I'm obliged.'

'What is the name of the little redhead? inquired
the chief.

'Jelly-my-boy-Jelly-not-Jelly-stupid,' replied Faatu
promptly.

'What!' exclaimed the bewildered Mbonavindongo,
and Faatu, amid the uproarious laughter of the
whites, slowly repeated the perplexing syllables.

Mbonavindongo struggled within for a few moments,
and then with an expansive grin stretched out his
hand once more, exclaiming benevolently, '*Sa loloma,*
Jelly-my-boy-Jelly-not-Jelly-stupid!' and amid ac-
clamations and hilarious greetings, the refugees
stepped ashore, ascended the grassy bank, and passed
through the scented groves of blossoming shaddock
trees in the direction of the town.

CHAPTER XIV.

THE BITER BIT.

THE delight of Mbonavindongo knew no bounds when he found that the curious and apparently all - powerful white men really meant to accept his invitation and stay at Naitasiri. He threw aside his royal dignity and behaved with the abandonment of a child who has suddenly acquired a new and unlooked-for toy. His merriment was infectious, for the feelings of the Fijians lie very near the surface, and the noise soon became uproarious, the women and children, reassured by the turn of events, peeping from the door-ways and swelling the din with shrill cries. Nor were the white men less affected. The strain under which they had laboured for so long gave way, and they joined in the laughter as they walked along, smiling pleasantly at the dusky warriors who surrounded them, and waving their hands good-naturedly to the girls, many of whom had sped home when the new arrivals landed, and hastily arraying themselves in their best garb, and twining garlands of vines and scarlet blossoms coquettishly about their graceful

figures, now stood about in groups, giggling, and
ogling their swains in the crowd.

All of a sudden, Jerry, whose red head seemed to
be the centre of attraction, drew a deep breath,
swelled out his chest, and without any preliminary
warning, burst out with 'See the conquering hero
comes!'

At the first sound of his beautiful voice the noisy
laughter ceased, and men looked at one another,
nodding their heads with delight and whispering, 'It
is sweet. It is better than a bird.'   But when the
martial strain ceased, sharp and sudden, upon the last
full note, a ringing cheer from the whites and a roar
of applause from the Fijians rent the air, mingled
with cries of '*Nambu! Nambu!* (Reward!)   A gift
for the little god with the red head!'

Na Mbonavindongo turned quickly.   Even at this
exalted moment the claims of Fijian etiquette must
not be entirely forgotten, and as he turned, the shouting ceased and the crowd made deep and reverent
obeisance.

Na Mbonavindongo's good-humoured face fell.   It
was evident that he was deeply disappointed.   A
gift! the people had shouted, and a gift he was prepared to give to this wonderful singer whom he
wished to make his own.   Certainly a gift; and
what could be more appropriate than a nice *mbakolo?*
Had but one man been animated by proper feeling
and remained erect, Na Mbonavindongo would have
been delighted to give him a tap on the head with his
club—only one; it would have been quite enough—
but he had not turned quickly enough, and there was
no excuse for converting anybody into a dish for

breakfast. It was very trying. Stay! There was
the madman, who was of no use to any one; he
would do very well. The chief shouted an order, and
immediately the wretched man, who had been hover-
ing on the outskirts of the crowd, was dragged forward, raving and shrieking. A sane man would have
calmly accepted the inevitable; this miserable creature had so little sense that he actually preferred to
live when the chief had determined that it was better
for him to die.

The smile returned to Na Mbonavindongo's face;
but before he could raise his club to administer the
coup de grâce to his unfortunate subject, Eli, who
suspected mischief, said something rapidly to Faatu,
who as rapidly translated it to the chief.

'What!' cried Mbonavindongo in astonishment.
'They do not wish to eat *mbakolo*! Oh! there must
be some mistake. Ask them again. It is for the
little one with the red head. It is a gift for his
song.'

'Then tell him I'll never open my mouth again
unless he lets that poor man go,' said Jerry emphatically, when he understood, and seeing that he was in
earnest, the chief reluctantly signed to the guards to
release their prisoner.

'Well, what does he want?' he inquired rather
sullenly. 'I wish to give him a gift.'

'Breakfast,' returned Jerry promptly to the solemn
Faatu, who in his heart of hearts thought that his
white friends were making a very unnecessary fuss
about one miserable man. 'Let him give us breakfast; but not that.'

'Tell him that our God would be angry with us

if we ate the poor man; then he will understand,'
suggested Guy.

'Well, well,' grumbled Mbonavindongo, turning to
give orders for breakfast to be prepared, 'let him sing
again, and I will think of something else.'

'It strikes me I'm like little Tom Tucker; only
'tis breakfast, not supper, I'm singing for,' said Jerry
with a grin, and without more ado struck up 'The
Fine Old English Gentleman,' substituting for the
last line, 'Like a fine ould Fiji Tu-u-i, all of the
olden time,' his friends swelling the chorus, to the
huge delight of the enchanted listeners.

'Like a fine old Fiji Tu-u-i!' sang Anthony, and
sat suddenly down upon the ground, roaring with
laughter. 'Oh, if you could but see yourself!' he
shouted. 'Jelly, my boy, Jelly, &c., you're a blessing
in disguise; you've quite won their hearts.'

'*Vinaka! Vinaka!*' said Mbonavindongo, nodding
his head and smiling, his good - humour being
quite restored. 'Now eat, and afterwards we will
talk.'

'He's a sensible chap,' remarked Jerry a quarter
of an hour later, as with a sigh of satisfaction he dis-
posed of the last fragment of *vakalolo*, a dish to
which he had become particularly attached. 'I like
him better than Na Ulivou.'

'Look to your primin' all the same,' said Eli grimly.
'Oliver was civil enough at first, remember, and
Boney thar may turn round on us when it suits
him.'

'No,' put in Faatu. 'Him take whales' toof.
Him not fool you. Fiji mans take toof, him do like
him say.'

'But what if Na Ulivou offers more ?' asked Guy.

'Waal, he may,' admitted Eli thoughtfully; 'but I guess thar's no sense in meetin' trouble half way. Faatu says we're all right just now, and he knows the beggars.'

'Yis,' said Faatu. 'Sleep, eat, walk, talk; Naitasiri mans not hurt you.'

'Then I vote for sleep,' proposed Anthony. 'We've had nothing but snatches for so long.'

'Waal, we did pretty well last night, thanks to Guy,' said Eli. 'However, I'm agreeable for an hour or two.—Faatu, you look pretty fresh; you set thar an' call us ef anythin' out o' the way comes to pass.'

He cast himself down just where he was, pillowing his face upon his arms. The others followed his example, and soon all were apparently fast asleep.

An hour passed, then another; and suddenly, as a wild, unearthly yell rang through the village, Eli bounded to his feet.

'By time, we're done! The trouble's come,' he cried.

The others sprang up and stood by him, shoulder to shoulder. One glance, only one, served to show them the desperate nature of their position. Faatu was gone. Jerry was gone. The muskets were gone! And round the corner of the *Mbure ni sa* rushed two or three hundred savages, who, brandishing spears and clubs, and shouting discordantly, bore furiously down upon them. Not a sound did the four whites utter, not a word did they say. Once only their eyes met in mute farewell, and then they drew together and with grim, determined faces waited for the end. The savages, their bodies blackened with charcoal of

the *kumu*-tree,* their faces fantastically painted, swept
along with horrid cries, keeping slightly in rear of
their leader, whose appearance would, under circumstances less grave, have provoked a hearty fit of
laughter. He was very small and stout, and but for
the scanty strip of *masi* round his middle and the white
turban which covered his head, absolutely naked. In
ludicrous contrast with his blackened body, his nose
had been painted a shining red, and while in the
vigour of his shouts and yells he outdid the lustiest
of his followers, he attempted to brandish an enormous
club, which was not only too heavy, but many sizes
too long for him.

Suddenly the little man put on a tremendous spurt
and dashed well in advance of the crowd. For a
moment he halted as if to regain his breath, and then
with a terrific screech essayed to swing his club above
his head. But the effort was too much for him, and
as he rushed forward the heavy weapon fell to the
ground, dragging the small warrior with it. The
shock of the fall loosened the light folds of his turban,
and as the wind caught and blew the gauzy *tapa* far
away, there over the hideous painted face which
grinned up at the waiting victims, bristled a stiff crop
of flaming red hair. Shrieking with laughter, the
Fijians halted, pointing their fingers at the white men
and screaming unintelligible words, while their redoubtable leader, turning over upon his back, kicked
his sturdy legs in the air and fairly howled with joy.
For a moment the four comrades stared in bewilderment at this extraordinary scene, and then as
Anthony's deep bass guffaw rolled out, Eli sprang

* *Acacia Richei.*

upon the pigmy chief, and grasping him under the arms, swung him clean off the ground.

'You outrajus imp, you; so it's this way you go back on your friends,' he cried hilariously, as he hugged the quivering black body to his breast to the great detriment of the only shirt he possessed. 'By time! You'll never know what a scare you gave us. But I fergive you; I fergive you, seein' it's you.'

'Oh! let me go,' gasped Jerry. 'I want to laugh.' He writhed out of Eli's arms and flung himself down upon the ground once more, screaming, panting, sputtering.

'Oh dear! oh dear!' he got out at last. 'If only you could have seen your solemn faces! I'd have had to laugh in another minute even if I hadn't tumbled down. Oh! oh! he! he! he!' His laughter died away into a faint, exhausted giggling.

'Well, you have had your fun,' said Anthony good-humouredly, for sharp as had been their fright, Jerry's appearance was enough to disarm anybody. 'But I tell you what it is, youngster, if you'd come within reach of my fist before I knew who you were, there wouldn't have been much left of you.'

'Moreover,' said Guy, 'if we had had our muskets, the consequences might have been serious to you and to a good many more. I really think, Jerry, that'——

'Oh, don't blow him up,' interrupted Whitson, laughing at the absurd expression of penitence which Jerry immediately assumed. 'He certainly scared us badly; but it was only a joke, and the poor boy hasn't had any fun for a long time. How did you manage this transformation, youngster?'

But before Jerry could answer, Faatu, accompanied by Mbonavindongo, whose fat sides were shaking with laughter, stepped out of an adjoining house with the muskets in his arms.

'You brown sinner,' said Eli, noting the grin on the Tongan's face, you know more of this than you choose to own up to, I bet.'

'He! he!' giggled Jerry. 'It was Faatu painted me. I wasn't asleep, and when I saw all these fellows dressing up for something, I asked him what it was, and he told me it was a dance and he! he! he! I said let's frighten them, and so he said yes, and we took away the muskets and he! he! he! I was painted, and the other fellows laughed so loud I thought you would wake, and then Faatu told them what to do, and they said yes, and we charged down upon you. He! he! he!'

'Well, all's well that ends well,' said Anthony, when Jerry had brought his lucid narrative to a close. 'There's no harm done. In fact, I think you have rather improved our position, for they seem to have taken a greater fancy to you than ever.'

Meanwhile Mbonavindongo, divining that the incident had not terminated unpleasantly for his young favourite, made a sign to the painted warriors, who immediately sprang up from the ground where they had crouched on his appearance in the open, and arranging themselves in two long lines, began a fantastic dance, or sham fight, spears *versus* clubs. The scene was very effective, for the dancers were not novices, and as they swept hither and thither executing the most intricate and complicated evolutions with faultless precision, their swart, glistening

bodies swaying in graceful curves, loud shouts of
applause broke from the white spectators, while Jerry,
temporarily naturalised, yelled his approval in choicest
Fijian, being privately prompted thereto by the delighted Faatu.

At last the spearmen made a furious forward rush,
in response to which the heroes of the clubs fell flat
upon their backs, and lay still without the least
appearance of animation.   Then, as if horror-struck
at the result of their own daring, the spearmen shifted
from their left hands to their right the broad palm-
leaf fans they carried, and began with every appearance of solicitude to fan their defunct adversaries
back to life.   So successful were their efforts that in
a few moments the prostrate warriors sprang to their
feet with loud yells, and the mimic combat began
once more.

'By time! That's a good idee!' ejaculated Eli.

'Isn't it?' said Jerry.   'It's like a scene out of a
play.'   He glanced up as he spoke, and to his surprise
found that the Virginian, so far from looking at the
dance, was staring solemnly up into the sky.   'What's
a good idea?' asked the boy.   Then observing the
thoughtful frown that puckered Eli's brow, he
nestled up to him, whispering, 'You are not angry
with me, Eli, are you?'

'Angry with you, bub!' echoed Eli, coming down
to earth again.   'I should say not.   Why that idee
——— Thar,' he broke off, 'the dance is over; you run
away and play, or bathe in the river, or do what you
like fer a spell.   Me an' the boys must have a chat
with Boney.   Hello! what's the matter now?   My
land! the pooty little dears is dressed fer the ball.'

From a grove of palm-trees in which they had been waiting, issued a procession of one hundred and twenty young girls, walking in single file, and each bearing a basket of ndalo. Their costumes consisted of a girdle of hibiscus fibres, black, red, white, or yellow, according to the taste and fancy of the wearer ; while their heads and shoulders were coquettishly garlanded with the scarlet blossoms of the same plant. None of them were beautiful according to the European standard of beauty, but all were splendidly moulded, and moved with the easy gait and free unhampered grace of the savage in his native wilds. If not exactly handsome, there was a healthy look about them all which was very attractive.

As soon as the procession started, a number of young men darted forward and spread a quantity of leaves on the ground in front of the white men. Then as each girl came to a halt, they relieved her of the basket she carried, and emptied the contents upon the improvised mat, which was soon covered with a goodly heap of vegetables. Five young men now advanced with as many roast pigs, which they laid upon the heap of taro and retired. Then Mbonavindongo, with a good deal of ceremony, presented the whole to his guests, and begged that they would do him the favour to accept of what he was pleased to term a very small mark of his love and esteem.

'Bedad ! I wonder what he 'd consider a large mark,' laughed Jerry, smacking his lips as he regarded the sucking pig which formed the top of the pile. 'I declare I think it must be dinner-time.'

'Not it,' said Guy. 'Be off, you imp of gluttony, and do what you like with yourself for the next

M

couple of hours. We want to have a chat with his highness here.'

'What about ?' asked Jerry instantly.

'About providing for your insatiable appetite for one thing,' jeered Guy. 'I expect the taxes will be raised if you stop here very long.'

'Faith ! I don't want to stop any longer than can be helped,' retorted Jerry. 'But what am I to do without Faatu ?—Here, I know. Guy, lend me your note-book and pencil.—Now, Faatu,' as Guy produced the required articles, ' how do you say " what is that ?" in Fijian ?'

'A thava ongo,' answered Faatu, with one of his genial grins.

'Thanks,' said Jerry, making a note of the words. 'A thava ongo,' he read out aloud to the unbounded amazement of the great Mbonavindongo. Seeing this, Jerry, always ripe for mischief, wrote 'Mbonavindongo,' and holding the book where the chief could see it, gravely pronounced the word.

'Ah,' said Mbonavindongo, after a few moments of profound meditation, 'it is kalou ! Could I do it ?'

'Not yet,' Jerry informed him through Faatu, who having witnessed just such a performance at his own home in Tonga, was intensely delighted and amused.

'Come here,' said the mystified Mbonavindongo, beckoning Jerry to one side. 'Perhaps the others would be good enough to turn their backs ? Thanks,' he added politely. 'Now, little Red-head, put down him and I will see.' He indicated a huge person of about twenty stone in weight, who was standing somewhat apart, regarding vacancy with an equally vacant stare.

'What's his name then?' inquired Jerry when Faatu had communicated the wish of the chief.

'Na Ngari Kau' (the big fat man), replied Faatu.

'Faith! he's well named,' smiled Jerry, writing down the name in a large clear hand, and passing the book to Mbonavindongo, who took it gingerly between his fingers as though he expected it to bite.

'Ha,' he ejaculated after he had turned and twisted the book about for some time, regarding the writing from every point of view. 'Jelly-my-boy'——

'That 'll do!' cried Jerry. 'What is it you want? No need to waste your breath over the rest of it.'

'Let him, too, turn his back,' commanded Mbonavindongo, which Jerry obediently did.

Eli, Anthony, Guy, and Whitson were then brought, each in turn, to see what Jerry had written, and as one after the other they pronounced the name of the big fat man, the astonishment of the onlookers was prodigious, and loud shouts of '*Kalou!*' went up everywhere.

'But how is it done?' inquired the mystified chief.

'It is not like anything or anybody. It has no eyes; it has neither head nor legs nor arms; yet they recognise it to be Na Ngari Kau. I do not understand it at all.'

'Give me the book, Jerry,' said Guy, and holding it so that no one should see what he was about, he sketched rapidly for a few moments and sent the book back to Mbonavindongo once more.

A shout of amazement broke from the chief. 'This is more wonderful than ever!' he cried. 'This is Na Ngari Kau! It is the man himself.—Come here, Ratu Ngari Kau, and see yourself.' But the fat man was dreaming of the pigs so unfortunately bestowed on these disturbing foreigners, and it required a vigorous poke in the back to bring him down to earth again. As he sank upon his ample hams, Na Mbonavindongo laughingly thrust the book under his eyes. 'See, Ratu, it is you,' he said.

'Ugh!' snorted Ngari Kau. 'The *papalangi* is a liar. I am a man; that is a pig;' and with many a resounding grunt of disapproval he crawled heavily off into his *vale* (house). Na Mbonavindongo, who was not particularly slender himself, roared with joy. 'Now Mbonavindongo,' he said, returning the book to Guy.

But Eli interposed. 'Faatu,' he said, 'ask his highness to put off this game for an hour or so. By-and-by Guy will make pictures of the whole tribe if he likes. Just now we want to talk to him. Say that I have two more whales' teeth for him as well as other presents. By time! It's ez well I got that bag o' tricks before the brig blowed up.'

Na Mbonavindongo's face fell when Faatu began his intimation; but it cleared again at the mention of whales' teeth, and with a courteous gesture he invited the white men to step into his *vale.*

'Here is the book, Jerry,' said Guy, handing it to him. 'Don't be too hard on the pencil. Mind now, by the time we meet again we shall expect you to talk Fijian at least as well as Faatu talks English.'

'*Sa lakki mothe!*' (Farewell!) cried Mbonavindongo, waving his hand, to which Jerry, prompted by Faatu, replied airily, '*Roa-roa!*' (Au revoir!) And with a delighted laugh, the chief disappeared into his house.

Left to himself, Jerry wandered here and there throughout the village, note-book in hand, asking of everyone he met ' *A thava ongo?* ' pointing to the object the name of which he desired to know, and jotting down the answers. At first the Fijians fought rather shy of him, but encouraged by his affable manners, and the fact that his skin was no longer of that unnatural white tint, they took heart of grace, and presently he had quite a following as he passed out of the town and took his way to the river, intending to wash away his acquired hue.

Now it so happens that if a Fijian sees anything in the possession of another which he particularly desires to have, he has no hesitation in asking for it, nor is it considered good manners to refuse the request. This of course Jerry could not be expected to know; so, when a somewhat surly-looking man stepped forward and made signs that he would like to have the wonderful note-book, the boy, thinking he merely desired to look at it, immediately handed it over. But when the fellow with a grin of delight began to retreat towards the village with his prize, Jerry, divining how matters stood, made after him in hot haste.

'Here, stop!' he cried. 'I thought you only wanted to look at it. Give it back.'

'Noungouloa will keep it,' grumbled the savage. 'It was a gift.'

'Will you, though?' said Jerry, catching at the sense of the words. 'We'll see about that.' And making a rapid dive, he snatched away the book and bounded back among the men, who scattered at his approach, fearing the anger of the little *papalangi*, of whose power they had seen ample evidence.

Noungouloa stood for a moment, fingering his club

wrathfully, but the fear of the chief was before his eyes, and turning on his heel he strode back to the village, muttering darkly to himself.

'Now I 've offended him, I suppose,' said Jerry. 'Well, I can't help it. Hullo, you fellows! Where are you off to ? Come back, I say.'

But one by one the men slunk away after their comrade, thinking that if the stranger was really angry it was best to be out of his reach.

'They 're a rum lot,' mused Jerry, looking after them. 'All smiles one minute and frowns the next. Heigho ! I suppose I 'd better follow them. Oh what lovely flowers ! I must get a bunch for Guy.'

He had cast his eyes upwards and caught sight of the rich purple blossoms that adorned the *kavika* tree * by which he was standing, and without more ado swung himself up among the branches. Here he plucked a great bunch of the glowing flowers, and casting them to the ground, prepared to descend. Some eight feet from the ground a stout bough jutted out horizontally, and, boy-like, he threw himself upon it, and, hanging by his hands, prepared to drop upon the soft turf beneath. A guttural grunt just below made him pause, and after a swift downward glance he crooked his leg over the bough, swung up on to it once more, and ran like a squirrel up the tall trunk.

Immediately beneath the bough, their spears uplifted, ready to impale him had he dropped, were four savage-looking Fijians, and with a thrill of dismay he thought he recognised among them the malevolent countenance of Noungouloa.

* *Eugenia Malaccensis*, the Malay Apple.

CHAPTER XV.

NOUNGOULOA'S TREACHERY.

'*HUI mpu ku mdow nou tothar!*' growled the tallest of the savages, swinging his long arms and jabbing up in the direction of Jerry with his spear.

'*Hevaj unco roca tim!*' foamed another, clawing vigorously at the tree trunk, and making as though he would climb up.

'*Lemmeg eta tu!*' vociferated the third.

'*Putiminapi!*' howled the fourth.

'*Fate nimu panba kim!*' chorused the entire company, circling round the tree and grimacing up at the boy.

Frightened though he undoubtedly was, Jerry's wits did not entirely desert him, and while he straddled on a bough and glared down at the besiegers, he determined to temporise.

'I'm all right so far,' he thought; 'but if they take it into their heads to throw their spears at me, I'm a gone coon, as Eli would say. Curious! I must have learned a good deal of Fijian in the last couple of hours, for some of their words sound quite familiar. Perhaps I can make them understand.

If I can only keep them quiet for a bit, Eli and the boys are sure to come this way.'

He took out his note-book and rapidly ran his finger down the column of words.

'Hi, Noungouloa!' he shouted. '*Sa loloma!* You mustn't touch me, you know. I'm *tambu.* I'll tell Mbonavindongo—I wish I may get the chance— *Sa lakki mothe!* Good-bye, old chap! Yah! you grinning black baste, if only I had a couple of coco- nuts, I'd let a little sense into your ugly head. Good Noungouloa, *mole saka, mole.* Only go away and I'll *mole* you till I'm black in the face—Faith! I'm that already. Noungouloa!—Oh murder! none of these words will do. Eli! Anthony! Mbonavin- dongo-o! Coo-ee!' he yelled at the top of his voice. 'Help!'

'Hello, boyee! What's got you now?' came the immediate answer, to Jerry's intense relief.

'Oh Eli'——— he began, and stopped, staring down at the group, for though the grinning face of Noun- gouloa still looked up at him, yet from between the parted lips came the reassuring voice of Eli.

Like a flash the truth dawned upon Jerry, and while the four conspirators doubled and twisted, and held their shaking sides, he slid down the tree, and rushing at the tall Virginian, pommelled him vigorously.

'You mane spalpeens!' he cried, 'to think that you would play me such a trick. Och! but I'll be even with you yet, so I will.'

'How do you like it yourself?' gasped Anthony, wiping his eyes. 'Oh dear! a monkey on a pole was nothing to you.'

'You are paid out for the fright you gave us, Master Jerry,' said Guy; 'only I don't think you got half enough. Didn't you suspect us?'

'Not for a moment,' giggled Jerry. 'You acted too well. To be sure, I thought I recognised some of the words, but I couldn't find them in my book. Where did you pick up all that Fiji talk?'

'I said, "Ah, you imp, you come down out o' thar," ' chuckled Eli.

'And I, "Heave a junk of rock at him." '

'And I, "Let me get at you." '

'And I, "Put him in a pie." '

The four went off again into shouts of laughter, in which Jerry joined heartily. 'But your hair?' he said at last; 'that's what disguised you so well. Wherever did you get those astonishing wigs from?' For each was decorated with a most fantastic head of hair after the most approved Fiji fashion.

'Ah, thereby hangs a tale,' answered Anthony.

'Let's have it then,' cried Jerry; 'but first of all let me take a plunge into the river and wash this filthy black off. I should advise you all to do the same.'

'Would you really?' jeered Eli. 'You ain't so smart ez I took you to be, Jerry, ef you 'magine we went to all this trouble jest for the purpose o' frightenin' you. Though I 'low you deserve to be nat'ally tore in two, sech an outrajus imp ez you are.'

'Fudge!' cried Jerry, all excitement. 'What did you dress up for, if not for a joke?'

'I should call it undressing,' put in Guy. 'But there is no joke, Jerry; we are perfectly serious.'

'You look it,' returned Jerry. 'Well, perhaps you will condescend to explain.'

'Cert'nly, once you give us a chance,' drawled
Eli. 'You see, boyee, when you came tearin' down
on top o' us at the head o' your gang of heathens, you
kind o' knocked the stuffin' out o' me fer a spell; but
pretty soon I began to see thar was sense in it, an'
I laid alongside that idee and made fast.'

'What idea?' inquired Jerry. Then with a flash
of recollection—'Oh! the idea that struck you while
the dance was going on.'

Eli nodded. 'Jest that. You gimme that idee
yourself, boyee, an' before all's done I jedge we'll one
an' all be 'bleeged to you for 't. You see, it's only a
matter o' days—may be hours—till Bill Larkin starts
out to hunt us down, an' to look fer a crowd o' white
men in these parts ain't jest the same ez searchin' fer
a needle in a truss o' hay; wharez, niggers ain't so
onusual that he's goin' to ketch the first one he sees
and scrub him down to look fer a white skin onder-
neath. 'Sides, when we start out on tour on our own
account, niggers ez we seem to be'll hev a better
chance o' escapin' rumpuses with niggers ez really is.'

'Oh, then you don't intend to stay here?' queried
Jerry.

'Waal, I 'low we hadn't thought o' it,' said Eli
drily; 'that is, onless you're so took up with your Fiji
friends you don't want to git home to your pa an' ma.'

To the surprise of all, light-hearted Jerry burst
into a sudden passion of tears.

'Oh! oh! oh!' he sobbed stormily. 'How can
you say such a thing? I've tried not to worry you,
because I thought you would think that I was a baby,
and in the way if anything had to be done; but the
nights I've lain awake on board the brig and cried

my eyes out—I couldn't help it, and I don't care what you think,' he finished defiantly, dashing the tears from his eyes, and producing a broad bar of white down the middle of his vermilion nose in the process.

'What should we think, dear lad?' said Guy affectionately. 'We know that you feel the separation just as keenly as the rest of us; and Eli was saying as we came along just now to look for you how bravely and manfully you bore your troubles.'

'That's so,' affirmed Eli; 'an' I 'low, boyee, I'd sooner have cut out my silly tongue than let it wag to hurt you.'

'You're the best man in the crowd by a long way,' declared slow-witted Whitson with such a solemn and distressed countenance that Jerry burst out laughing through his tears.

'It's a fact,' said Anthony. 'Why, even Eli admits that it is to you that he owes the idea that may be the saving of us all. Cheer up, Jerry boy; nobody thinks the less of you for being the merry grig you are. I am sure I do not know what we should have done without you. Go and take a look at your face in the river,' he broke off with his rollicking laugh. 'If that doesn't cure your doleful dumps, nothing will.'

'Go on with the yarn,' said Jerry, looking quite unnecessarily ashamed of himself. 'I'm all right now.'

'I'll finish it,' said Guy. 'Meantime, we can stroll back to the village and begin upon your sucking pig. There's a panacea for you! You see,' he went on as they started, 'we have had a long chat with Mbona-

vindongo and his chief men, in which we have discovered that we are on an island.'

'You didn't suppose it to be the continent of
Europe, did you ?' interposed Jerry cheekily.

'Not exactly,' was the smiling reply; 'but we had
no idea how large or how small it was. I don't think
we should have any idea now, for these stay-at-home
Fijians could give us no help in that matter; but
Faatu has fortunately coasted all round it with the
more adventurous Tongans, and from what he says
we judge it to be about ninety miles across. Naitasiri,
where we are now, is only some twelve miles from the
east coast, as the crow flies, though, of course, by
river the journey is much longer; so that leaves us
something over seventy miles.'

'You don't mean to say we are to walk across the
island !' cried Jerry.

'Waal, we han't struck any kerridges so far,'
observed Eli; 'but thar 's no sayin' what we mayn't
run agin before we 're through. You see, boyee, this
is the way we 've settled it with Boney, who, ef he
don't know everythin', yit ain't by any means a fool.
The men of Mbau are numerous and brave, standin'
head an' shoulders above the rest o' the Fijians fer
sense, even accordin' to Boney. What 's more, they 've
got at their backs a comp'ny o' white men ez is
blacker inside 'n what the Fiji men are outside, an' ez
won't stick at nothin'. Ye heard yourself what the
feller in the canoe said. The east is guarded, the
south is guarded, likely they can watch the north, ez
they hev friends thar; only the west remains. That
is to say, straight ahead.'

'But how are we to find the way ?' inquired Jerry.

'Eli put a small compass into one of his wonderful bags,' Guy told him. 'You ought to see what a quantity of things he has brought—whales' teeth, axes, knives, coloured handkerchiefs——'

'Yes,' interrupted Eli; 'an' we've told Boney he shall have the whole kit, savin' what may be wanted on the journey, ef he'll only git us thar.'

'What! Is he coming, too?' cried Jerry excitedly.

'He can't bear to part with his red-headed god,' chuckled Eli. 'It seems that up in the mountains we'll have to cross thar's some mighty wild folk, an' Boney 'lows we'll do better ef we go in strength. So he's going to escort us to the other side with a comp'ny of fifty men. He 'lowed he'd bring more after we'd rammed it into him that we warn't gods at all, but only mortals like himself, an' a heap wuss off at that; but I told him enough was ez good ez a feast. He seemed powerful disapp'inted we warn't gods—pertic'ler you. It's you, boyee, that's made him so kind; fer he's took sech a fancy to your voice that he 'lows he jest nat'ally loves you.'

'Well, I never!' exclaimed Jerry. 'This is a yarn and no mistake. But what are we to do when we get there?'

'Faatu says we can get a canoe there in which we may be able to sail home,' explained Anthony. 'Allowing for exaggeration, one need not be afraid of a thousand miles or so in a well-built one.'

'We'll chance it at all events,' put in Whitson.

'But what about Larkin when he comes here and finds us gone?' asked Jerry shrewdly.

'That's all right,' said Eli. 'Boney has got a bit o' bluff ready fer him. Don't you pester. Sail in an' enjoy yourself to-day, an' be ready for a start airly to-morrer. Ye 'll need to give your coat a touch up hyar an' thar, an' you must go to the barber's an' get a wig like ours.'

'The barber's!' echoed Jerry.

'Yes,' said Anthony; 'hairdressers and wigmakers flourish here, I can tell you. All the chiefs have their own personal attendants, who are *tambu* to every one else, it appears; but there are two or three very clever fellows who practise on their own account, and one of them provided us, as you see. He has one in reserve for you that, but for the colour of it, is the image of those worn by barristers.'

'Wonderful!' said Jerry. 'I say, though, aren't they very hot?'

'Rather; but what would you? One must suffer in a good cause. By the way, you are not the only red-head in the village, though you bear the palm for brilliance of colour, and yours is natural, while theirs'——

'Is warranted to wash, like my new coat,' supplied Jerry. 'Hi, Faatu,' as the Tongan appeared, his face beaming with smiles, 'how do we look?'

'Fus' rate, I guess,' returned the brown man, who was making rapid progress under Eli. 'Fiji mans t'ink you Fiji mans.'

'You couldn't say more,' laughed Jerry. 'Why, there 's my friend Noungouloa. What is he doing? He looks very sulky.'

The others glanced across to where Noungouloa, squatting upon his hams, was busily planting a row of small sticks in the ground alongside his house.

Every now and then he paused in his occupation to cast a malevolent glance at Jerry.

'Him fery angry,' explained Faatu. 'Him put um stick t'ere make um 'member him angry.'

'Is that it?' said Jerry carelessly. 'Then I must look out for squalls.' He told his companions how he had offended the Fijian.

'It's a pity,' observed Eli. 'However, it don't amount to much, for we'll be out o' this to-morrer mornin', and I'll take good care he ain't o' the comp'ny. Come, boys, this is the house they've allotted us, and I've hoisted the old flag in front o' it to show it's *tambu*. We don't want them niggers pokin' their noses in every ten seconds.'

'Was that in the bag, too?' asked Jerry, looking up at the union-jack which, hoisted above the stars-and-stripes, flung its fold proudly to the breeze.

'Ay,' answered Eli. 'It riz a small sensation when I run 'em up. The niggers war awful took with 'em. I don't know ez I oughtn't to hev put the stars an' stripes on top, considerin' the lickin' we gave old mother England,' he added quizzically.

'You'd better not try it. We're four to one, remember,' said Anthony, and amid merry laughter, ignorant of the vengeful look which Noungouloa sent after them, they entered the *Mbure*, where Jerry found his barrister's wig awaiting him.

The afternoon and evening passed uneventfully, and ere the sun had well set, they flung down their tired limbs upon the heaps of soft mats provided for them, thankful for the prospect of a long and quiet night's repose.

At sunrise a loud shout roused them, and hurrying

to the door of the *Mbure,* they perceived the *Mata*
standing in front of the king's house, crying at the
top of his voice, '*Yangona! Yangona!*'

Instantly numerous heads were popped out of the
sleeping *Mbures,* and hundreds of voices joined in
the answering shout: '*Mama! Mama!*' (Chew it!)
And presently a number of chiefs and gentlemen
were seen hurrying towards the royal residence.

'Um going to drink *kava,*' said Faatu, employing
the term in use in Tonga. 'By-'n-by we go.'

Sure enough, a good-looking young woman, one of
the king's numerous wives, approached just then, and
after a graceful obeisance, presented his majesty's
compliments, and expressed his hope that they would
join him in a bowl of grog before the labours of the
day began.

'Waal, my dear, it's early yet fer that sort o'
comfort,' answered Eli with a grin; 'but, waal, seein'
it's you, I don't mind. Come on, boys, we may ez
well see all thar is to be seen in this sing'lar
country.'

Mbonavindongo greeted them graciously, and they
seated themselves on mats in the midst of the assembled company, all of whom were provided with
cups of polished coco-nut. The new-comers were
furnished with similar articles at the king's command,
and then the ceremony began.

A great wooden bowl was brought in with a rope
of coco-nut fibre attached to it, the free end of which
was thrown towards the king to indicate his sove-
reignty, and, further, to warn any one who entered of
his presence, and the necessity for obeisance, otherwise the intruder, carelessly maintaining an erect

attitude, would have been promptly clubbed. The *yangona* root, scraped and cut into small pieces, was then distributed to a number of young men, each of whom, popping his piece into his mouth, chewed it vigorously, frequently rinsing his mouth with fresh water, and, finally, after some time, producing a lump of finely masticated white fibre, which he deposited in the bowl.

'Sir,' said the herald at this stage, 'permit me to inform you with the deepest respect that the *yangona* is collected.'

'*Loba !*' (wring it) replied the king, and the *Mata* having repeated the order to the man who was to prepare the draught, water was poured into the bowl, and the whole strained with much ceremony through a large piece of hibiscus fibre. As the straining proceeded the *Mata* prayed aloud, thanking the gods for past favours, and beseeching their protection and goodwill throughout the day and for all time to come, the assembly intoning a reverent '*Ei mana ndina !*' Amen.

All being now ready, the cup-bearer knelt and presented a cupful of the yellowish fluid to the king, the herald at the same time offering another short prayer or grace. Mbonavindongo received the cup, and having poured out a few drops as libation to the gods, lifted it to his lips, and drained it to the dregs. Instantly all the company clapped their hands rhythmically and burst into a chant, the last note of which, high and prolonged, was taken up and echoed by the waiting people outside, till it rolled through the village from one end to the other.

He would have been a disloyal man and a bold

N

who refused to shout when Mbonavindongo, the king,
emptied his morning cup. Yet one man was silent.
Noungouloa, squatting on his hams and intently considering his row of sticks, scowled balefully and held
his peace.

Blowing the moisture from his lips with a hissing
sound, Na Mbonavindongo inclined his head towards
his guests, and proposed the toast, or sentiment, which
always accompanied ceremonious *yangona* drinking.
'*Me loma vinaka na kalou!*' (May the gods be
gracious), he said, 'waft you on your way rejoicing,
and let us never be enemies,' which piece of politeness the blackened whites acknowledged with a respectful, '*Mole, Turanga!*' (Thanks, my lord !)

Na Mbonavindongo glanced deprecatingly at the
powerful chiefs who surrounded him, as much as to
say, 'Excuse me if I pass you by this once,' and
then indicated that the cup should be offered first
to Jerry, one of the highest honours in his power
to bestow.

With the cup in his hand, the cup-bearer halted in
front of the boy, and looked inquiringly at the *Mata*,
who, poor man, kept mumbling something under his
breath, while his face expressed the deepest perplexity. Finally he whispered something to Faatu,
withdrew, returned and whispered again and yet
again, and then, raising his head proudly as one who
has mastered a difficult lesson, proclaimed in stentorian tones, 'Jelly-my-boy-Jelly-not-Jelly-stupid, drink
next after the king.'

It was etiquette to name the person so highly
honoured, and the *Mata* had forgotten Jerry's name.
Small blame to him !

Out of consideration for Jerry's youth, a very small quantity of *yangona* had been placed in the cup, but it was an honour the poor boy could well have dispensed with, and with a very wry face he swallowed the nauseous mixture, which has been accurately described as resembling nothing so much as soapsuds, jalap, and magnesia.

But Jerry was a little gentleman, and not to be outdone in politeness. He blew away the moisture from his lips as the king had done, and said respectfully, '*Sa loloma, Tui Naitasiri,*' at which Mbonavindongo was hard put to it to preserve his dignity and a straight face.

The others then drank in turn, each according to his rank, and immediately afterwards the meeting broke up, the herald proclaiming in a loud voice, 'The bowl is empty.'

As they issued from the *Mbure*, Anthony pointed out a company of men who were walking towards the river, bearing among them three or four baskets, covered with banana leaves, from one of which protruded something that looked uncommonly like a human foot. This being referred to Faatu for explanation, the Tongan coolly replied : 'Ho yis, t'at de man wif soup in his head.'

'The madman !' cried Anthony in horror.

'Yis,' answered Faatu ; 't'ey bake him in night. Him cooked now. Mbonavindongo send him to Na Ulivou, and say him white man. T'en Na Ulivou not come here for you. Him t'ink you am ate.'

So this was Mbonavindongo's game of bluff. It was some seconds before they grasped the full horror of it, and then Eli said in a voice full of emotion :

'Boys, that poor man has died for us, although he never knew it. If I'd had an idee, but thar I hadn't. Who could have had? His blood be on their heads ez shed it, not on ours ez would have stopped the bloody murder ef we could.'

'God send us safe out of this island,' muttered Whitson, 'for, friends or foes, they're all devils alike.'

Two hours later they marched out of Naitasiri, Mbonavindongo and his fifty warriors leading the way, and a yelling crowd accompanying them to the outskirts of the village. There was no fear that the secret of the movement would be betrayed. Loyalty to his feudal chief was a prominent Fijian characteristic, and there were no traitors in Naitasiri.

Were there not? There was indeed one. But no one saw Noungouloa, as with a gratified, backward glance at his row of sticks, he plunged into the bush with his face set in the direction of Mbau.

CHAPTER XVI.

JERRY'S FOLLY.

'THUS far into the bowels of the land have we marched on without impediment,' quoted Jerry, a few days later, as he issued forth from the *Mbure ni sa* of beautiful Namosi, and swaggered up and down in the warm morning sunshine, the small naked boys and girls scattering on every side and gazing with awe and amazement, not at his face, which they could understand, for art had rendered that not unlike their own, but at his boots, which were to them incomprehensible. How the five strangers who had come among them could manage to get along without toes the boys of Namosi were puzzled to explain, and, quick to ascribe to witchcraft whatever lay outside the range of their experience, they were careful to give the new arrivals a wide berth.

Jerry certainly looked comical enough with his shining, naked body, his enormous wig and his seaboots, from each of which the frayed and ragged top of a blue worsted stocking protruded. In common with his companions, he had not felt the loss of his clothes, for the black paint with which he was coated had prevented the sun from blistering his skin; but he soon recognised that he could not do without his boots; so, though exceedingly anxious to act entirely *vaka viti*, had followed the example of the others and drawn them on, to his unspeakable relief, if the truth must be told, though he would have died rather than admit it.

At every town along the route the fugitives had been cordially welcomed, for Mbonavindongo had been careful enough to send a herald in advance, bearing a whale's tooth—or more, according to his state and dignity—for the chief, and craving permission to pass through his town and territory. The journey had been taken in a very leisurely fashion, for your Fijian loves not to hurry himself at any time; and whenever Eli, by no means certain that the wily Larkin would not manage to get wind of their departure, had urged fat, good-natured Mbonavindongo to break camp and push forward, the chief merely smiled and replied '*Malua*,' that word ever on the lips of the ease-loving men of Viti, and as pregnant in its meaning and effects as the Spanish *Mañana*.

As they entered the superb and wondrously lovely pass that leads to Namosi, they were met by the king Na Nga Ndamu (the Red Duck), who was an old friend of Mbonavindongo's, and anxious to do him honour. The Red Duck's keen eyes had at once picked out the five strangers upon whose legs grew such an extraordinary skin; but though burning with curiosity, he had politely repressed the questions which sprang to his lips, and after much sniffing at cheeks and pressing of hands, had turned again and led the way to the town, where a great feast had been pre-

pared. This was followed by a *tuku-tuku*, or speechi-
fying, wherein Mbonavindongo related to Nga Ndamu
all that had happened since last they met, and Red
Duck returned the compliment. When told that the
five visitors from a far country wore white skins
beneath their coating of black, he smiled incredulously;
while at the story of the clubs that talked he laughed
outright, apologising for his rudeness, but declaring
that he was too old a soldier to be taken in by the
travellers' tales which his friend Mbonavindongo was
good enough to invent for his amusement. Somewhat
annoyed, the chief of Naitasiri had urged Eli to give
a demonstration, but the Virginian had begged to be
excused, realising as he did that every round of ammunition was of value, in consequence of which, Nga
Ndamu, delighted to have got the best of the argument, strove more than ever to show his hospitality
and expressed the deepest regret that the shortness
of the notice he had received had rendered it impossible for him to provide a baked man or two for
supper. To his great relief Eli informed him that
the eating of human flesh was their greatest and
most peculiar *tambu*, and that the omission was,
therefore, a fortunate one. Then there had been
more speeches, lavish protestations of lasting goodwill, and after a parting cup of *yangona* they had
been allowed to retire to the *Mbure ni sa* and sleep
in peace.

As Jerry stood there, yawning and stretching, one
of the boys, taking heart of grace, came timidly up
to him, and making a profound reverence, exclaimed
'*Sia ndra, na Turanga!*' 'Good-morning, my lord.'
'I believe you, my boy,' returned Jerry. 'What

do you propose to do with yourself this fine day ?
I 'll be very happy to join you in anything you please
to suggest, that is, after breakfast, and always pro-
vided that my very good friend and captain, Eli
P. Banks, has not arranged to start immediately.
Now what are your plans ? '

The young Fijian opened his eyes very widely at
this address, of which he understood not a word.
Then lightly touching his breast, he uttered the one
word, 'Mbeka !'

Jerry fetched a deep breath. 'Mbeka,' he repeated,
'Mbeka—now what does that mean ? I wish I had
Guy's note-book. Mbeka—Oh ! I suppose it 's your
name. *Sia ndra*, Mbeka ?'

The boy grinned delightedly, and dashing his
short spear among the eaves of the *Mbure*, disturbed
a bat, which flew away in a headlong, irresponsible
fashion, very much disgusted and bewildered at being
turned out into the sunlight.

'Mbeka !' cried the boy, pointing after the little
animal. 'Mbeka leka !' And he touched his breast
again.

'*Leka* means little, I know that,' said Jerry with
satisfaction, 'and *Mbeka* must be a bat. Mbeka leka,
Little Bat. That is your name, I imagine. Hi !
You Mbeka Leka ?' He pointed to the boy.

'*Eo, saka* (yes, sir), Mbeka Leka,' replied the delighted boy.

'Oh, is it ?' returned Jerry. 'Well, we 've been a
long time getting at it, and if our conversation is to
proceed at this rate, I 'm afraid—however,' touching
his breast, 'I am Jerry.'

'Jelly !' echoed the young savage confidently.

'No, not Jelly,' began Jerry and stopped, moved by a reminiscence. 'Very well, have it your own way. Jelly be it.'

'Jellybeet,' repeated the boy.

'Oh, I say, this is getting to be too much of a good thing,' exclaimed Jerry. 'I shall have as many names presently as a centipede has legs. Hi, Mbeka, *a thava ongo?*' For as he mentioned the centipede, one of those wriggling creatures escaped from under a stone which he had turned over with his foot.

'*Thikinovu,*' replied Mbeka, jumping out of the way; but Jerry set his heel upon the venomous thing and squashed it.

'Ié! Ié!' cried Mbeka, and poured out a torrent of Fijian.

'Not at all,' said Jerry loftily, catching at the sense of the words. 'I'm not hurt. Look how tough this is.' He tapped his boot. 'Feel.' He caught hold of Mbeka's hand and pressed the brown fingers against the leather.

'Ié! Ié!' said Mbeka again, and stretched out his own foot, working the toes up and down energetically.

'I believe he thinks I haven't got any toes,' said Jerry with a grin, and, seating himself upon a stump, he rapidly drew off both boot and stocking, holding out a piebald leg and foot for the inspection of the amazed Mbeka, who with staring eyes and mouth agape, pointed to the other leg.

'Take the other one off? Certainly,' said Jerry, suiting the action to the word, and with the boots in one hand and the stockings in the other, rose from his seat.

'*Thikinovu! Tamata thikinovu!*' (A man centipede!) shrieked Mbeka, and fled into the midst of
the group of children who had assembled on the *rara*,
or village green, to watch the performance.

'A man centipede I am now,' said Jerry. 'I
wonder what they will call me next?' He resumed
his stockings and boots, and advancing towards the
group, made signs to them not to be afraid. 'Hi!
Mbeka, come and talk to me again,' he called.
'I'm not going to eat you,' he went on as the boy
approached diffidently. 'Oh, by the way, do you like
mbakolo, Mbeka?'

The Little Bat's countenance underwent a change.
He had understood but one word, but that was
enough, and he folded his hands over his stomach,
smacked his lips, and nodded emphatically.

'Faugh! You filthy little beast!' cried Jerry in
great disgust. 'Get away! I won't have anything
more to say to you.'

The Bat recoiled before the angry face and up-
raised arm, and then, rushing to the conclusion that
the word *mbakolo* contains a direct and pointed
allusion to his own impending fate, stood transfixed
with horror, emitting loud howls of dismay, while
tears of anguish poured out of his eyes and rolled
over his cheeks.

'There, there,' said Jerry contritely, as he patted
the weeping boy on the shoulder. 'Don't cry,
Mbeka. It was my fault. I oughtn't to have asked.
Of course you don't know any better. Come now,
let us make friends. See, I want a coco-nut. Will
you get me one?—*Niu ndina*,'* he repeated, pointing

* The true coco-nut; *Cocos nucifera.*

to a clump of the graceful trees, which grew at one
end of the *rara*.

Anxious to propitiate the offended stranger, Mbeka
dashed away his tears, and springing to a coco-nut
tree, literally walked up it, his hands clasping and
his feet lightly touching the trunk, while his lithe
body was curved outwards, far from it. In an in-
credibly short time he was seated amid the feathery
crown, tapping the nuts with his finger and listening
acutely, to judge, by the sound produced, of the
various stages of ripeness which the fruit had reached.
Presently he cast three or four to the ground, and
rapidly descending, stuck a stout stick obliquely into
the earth, with which he deftly stripped off the husks.
Next, taking one nut in his hand he hammered away
at another until he had produced a small round hole,
performing the operation so neatly that not a drop
of the milk was spilt. Then with a graceful bow he
handed the nut to Jerry, who eagerly quaffed the
delicious fluid it contained.

'That's a great deal better than *mbakolo*,' he
muttered. '*Mole* Mbeka, *mole*. Hullo! Eli, is that
you? When are we going to start?'

'Right after breakfast,' answered the Virginian,
approaching and accepting the nut which Mbeka
politely offered him. 'I've got Boney stirred up to
an early move at last. I thought we'd never git
past that eternal *malua* of his; but he seems to have
fergotten it this mornin', fer a mercy.'

'He eats man,' said Jerry, pointing to Mbeka.
'Poor little beast, it's no use blaming him; he doesn't
know any better.'

'No; and he gits plenty encouragement,' answered

Eli, indicating some rows of stones neatly set into the *rara*. 'See them stones? Every one of them stands for a man cooked and eaten. Pleasant, ain't it? The big ones are for chiefs, the small ones for common men.'

'Ugh!' Jerry shuddered. 'I wish we were out of this country, Eli.'

'Same hyar, boyee; and we will be soon, please God, ef we kin only keep Boney up to the mark. Come away to breakfast.'

'Can you spare me a knife?' asked Jerry. 'I'd like to give one to Mbeka here.'

'You'll find one in one o' the bags,' replied Eli. 'But don't be too free with your presents, for we've a bit o' distance to cover yet, and Boney grudges everythin' we give away. I can see that.'

Jerry darted into the *Mbure*, and presently returned with a jack-knife, which he handed to Mbeka, who received it with unbounded delight, and immediately pranced off to show his comrades his new acquisition.

Two hours later the Little Bat attempted to join himself to the company as they marched away; but being sternly repulsed, and threatened with the club if he followed, sat him down upon a boulder and wept.

That night as they camped in the forest, Jerry was startled to find himself clasped in a soft embrace, while a warm, palpitating body nestled against his own. Only for a moment, and then the intruder, whoever he was, slipped away. So quickly did it all happen that Jerry, scarcely half awake, laid himself down to sleep again under the impression that he had dreamed a particularly vivid dream.

Towards noon next day they crossed the river Singatoka, repulsed without much trouble the attack of a small body of *Kai Tholos*, or Hillmen, and afterwards conciliated the chief by a present of two whales' teeth and an axe, with both of which articles he was unacquainted. From him they learned with some difficulty—for the dialect here differed considerably from that of the eastern tribes—that a large body of men had been observed that morning some miles to the north, moving in a westerly direction. Who they might be he was unable to imagine; but probably they were men of Ndrau, bent upon a marauding expedition. But as a matter of fact he had not been close enough to see.

Anxious to set the question at rest if possible, Eli persuaded Mbonavindongo to despatch half-a-dozen scouts to the top of a high hill in the vicinity, whence a good view of the surrounding country could be obtained. The main body was to proceed on its way, leaving the scouts to follow and overtake it that night or early next morning. In case of any alarming discovery a strong runner was instantly to be sent off with news.

The scouting expedition offered such a prospect of variety from the monotony of the daily marches that Jerry at once begged permission to accompany it; but this was peremptorily refused, for, as Eli pointed out, he could not possibly be allowed to go alone with the Naitasirians, while to divide the small force of whites would be highly injudicious, since no one could say when some serious danger might not arise which would tax their powers of resistance to the uttermost.

Now Jerry, though headstrong and self-willed, was

as a rule obedient and easily controlled, but every one
has his moods, good and bad, and on that day the
boy was feeling fretful and generally out of sorts; so
instead of responding readily to Eli's advice, he shook
off Guy's detaining hand, laid kindly upon his
shoulder, and marched sulkily to the rear of the
column.

Guy was for following him, but Eli restrained him.
'Let him be,' said the Virginian. 'He's got the
tantrums jest now, same ez we all git now an' agen.
It's only his high sperrits. He'll come round agen
before long.'

'Yes, leave him alone,' advised Anthony. 'He's
in the blues and won't listen to anything you say.
I think his supper last night must have disagreed
with him, for he told me of some extraordinary
nightmare which seized him somewhere in the small
hours of this morning.'

'He's downhearted and perhaps homesick,' said
Guy. 'Poor little chap, I would like to try and cheer
him up. However, just as you think best.'

So Master Jerry was suffered to 'gang his ain gait.'

With a gloomy brow, and halting first on one foot
and then on the other, the boy watched the scouts as
they filed away in the direction of the mountain.
His brain was filled with mutinous thoughts, and his
bosom swelled with a sense of the injustice with
which he had been treated.

'Such a shame!' he muttered. 'They are grown
up and can do what they like. Just because I am a
boy they think I am not fit to be trusted. As if it
mattered. Those fellows will be back in no time, and
there's no saying what fun they mayn't have while

they're away. We haven't seen a wild beast since
we came into the country, barring pigs and flying
foxes ; but I shouldn't wonder if there were plenty
on that range. It's just the place for them. I might
get a shot.'

He hung back still farther, fingering his musket
lovingly. He had forgotten, or did not choose to
remember, Eli's strict injunction that not a shot was
to be wasted upon duck or game of any sort. The
tail of the column, composed entirely of Fijians, was
just disappearing round a bend in the ravine through
which they were marching, and the men, chattering
and laughing, paid no attention whatever to the discontented laggard. Jerry cast one swift glance after
them, and then acting upon the impulse of the moment,
darted rapidly into the thick bush and sped upon the
trail of the scouts.

'Do you Tongans eat men, Faatu ?' inquired
Whitson as they marched along through the rough
boulder-strewn valley.

'No,' answered Faatu. 'Yis ; sometimes when um
little.'

'What do you mean by that, you brown horror ?'
said Anthony. 'Babies ?'

'No,' replied Faatu with a grin. 'Little mans
want be big mana. He eat um.'

'I suppose he means that some do it occasionally
out of bravado,' said Guy, adding, 'did you talk much
to the missionaries, Faatu ?'

'Misinaries all killed,' answered the Tongan.

'Killed !' echoed Guy. 'I thought that. Then
how did you pick up your English ?'

'*Papalangis* in Tonga,' explained Faatu. '*Papa-*

langis say kill misinaries. So Tongans kill um. T'en Tongans kill *papalangis.* T'en more *papalangis* come in brig. Lif wif Tooboo Finow. Fight wif big guns.'

'Like this,' said Whitson, holding up his musket.

'No; oh no. Big! Efer so big! Go boom!' *

'Can he mean cannon?' said Anthony. 'No, that would be impossible. How many Englishmen were there in Tonga, Faatu?'

'T'at many,' answered Faatu, holding up ten fingers. 'Me learn *papalangi* talk from um.'

'And very creditably you've done it, too,' said Guy, turning his head to emit a shout of 'Jerry!'

'Sulky little beggar! Leave him alone; he'll come to his senses by-and-by,' laughed Anthony.

'Come over hyar, Faatu. I want to talk to Boney,' called Eli. 'Thar's a place up thar, just ahead, whar we might ez well camp fer the night. It'd be good in case o' surprises.'

'You are not on the lookout for surprises, are you?' asked Anthony.

'Waal, I don't know. I han't been comfortable in my mind sence we struck news o' that marchin' column. It may mean nothin'; it may mean anythin'. Anyhow, I 'low we might be worse off than up thar, ef thar's business to be done.'

The place he indicated was a remarkable looking fortress, situated upon a projecting spur of the cliffs which overhung the river. It was in reality a fighting-place to which the inhabitants of a town in the vicinity were wont to retire before the attacks of their fierce and powerful enemies of Ndrau. But just now it was deserted, for a few weeks previous the

* Faatu probably referred to the period of Mariner's captivity.

men of Ndrau had swept down the valley upon the
unsuspecting villagers, and massacred them all before
they could reach their airy fort. Mbonavindongo and
his party were of course ignorant of this; but after
some consultation it was judged safe from the appearance of the place to occupy it for the night at least.
A narrow path wound upwards from the ravine to
the spur, which latter was divided midway between
the cliff and the fort by a deep, wide ditch, spanned
by a couple of slender logs. On the farther side of
the ditch a strong palisade of upright posts, with
wicker-work between, ran across the whole breadth
of the neck, entrance being effected through a gate
so low that one could only crawl through it, and so
narrow that but one person could enter at a time.
Beyond the palisade was an open space some forty
yards wide, and at the very extremity of the spur
towered a colossal rock, eighty feet high at least, in
which was cut a single series of steps leading to the
broad, flat top, where grew a huge old banyan tree,
whose vast roots, flung downwards over the face of
the rock, formed a natural balustrade to the steps.
Under the banyan tree was a small house or temple,
and a second stout palisade ran across the side of the
plateau facing the cliff. The outer face needed no
such protection, for one looked over the edge sheer
two hundred feet down into the river.

'Waal, this is a nice place for a picnic,' said Eli
critically as they reached the open space under the
rocky citadel. 'These yer fellows know a thing or
two about fortification, that I will say. I reckon we
can camp hyar. That is, unless anybody wants to
climb up to the house. I don't.'

o

'It's the sort of thing that would please
Jerry,' said Anthony with a laugh. 'Come along
Jerry, boy; here's a bit of genuine excitement for
you.'

'Yes, come along an' shin up, boyee,' called Eli.
'Smart now, thar ain't no sense in gittin' riled.
You've kept it up long enough. 'Tain't like you to
sulk all afternoon.'

'Jerry, you ought to be ashamed of yourself, and
I hope you are,' hailed Guy, scanning the black faces,
as one by one the escort crawled through the gate
of the palisade.

But as the last man entered, and there was no sign
of Jerry, the four comrades exchanged glances of
alarm, and the question burst simultaneously from
their lips, 'Where can he be ?'

'I thought he was with the rear guard,' said Guy
helplessly. 'Oh, I wish I had gone back.'

'So he was, too,' said Anthony. 'I looked back
just as we were rounding a curve and saw him.'

'I was behind you,' put in Whitson, 'and I saw
him, too. He was gradually falling farther and
farther to the rear.'

'Then you may depend upon it the little rascal
has bolted after the scouts,' cried Anthony. 'I'll
punch his jolly young head when he comes back for
scaring us like this.'

'I b'lieve you've struck it,' said Eli. 'He meant to
have his way and he has had it. Don't take on, Guy.
He'll come to no harm. He'll be back along with
the scouts. Hyar, let's arsk some o' them ez was in
the rear.'

But no amount of questioning elicited anything

further than that Jerry had been last seen shortly
after the altercation. Those in front supposed him
to be still in the rear, while those in the rear imagined
that he had gone forward again. In a word, no one
knew anything about him.

The conclusion, however, was so obvious that after
the first shock they felt no alarm, but only a natural
anxiety for the safe return of the truant with the
scouts. Guy, indeed, wished to take a party and
scour the valley, but this was overruled, the general
consensus of opinion being that the boy was with the
scouts and safe, for the road by which they had come,
though difficult, had not been dangerous, and it was
impossible that he could have come to any harm in
pursuing it without attracting the notice of some one
in the company, and equally impossible that, as Guy
forlornly suggested, he had been snatched away unobserved, for, thanks to the recent foray of the men
of Ndrau, they had not encountered a human being
since they parted from the *Kai Tholos* in the early
afternoon.

In anticipation of the return of the scouts, a huge
fire was built in the courtyard to give them warning
of the whereabouts of their friends, and while the
light-hearted Fijians, tired after their fatiguing march
and the substantial supper which had followed it,
snored peacefully, the four whites and Faatu kept
anxious watch, listening to the sounds that floated up
the valley on the wings of the night wind.

At last, towards midnight, as Eli was charging his
pipe for the sixth time, the long-drawn shout of the
tama arose from far below.

'Thar they are,' cried Eli, springing to his feet.

'Hail 'em, Faatu, an' warn em to be careful o' the
boy comin' up the path, unless they elect to stay
whar they are till dawn.'

Faatu shouted his message at the pitch of his voice,
and almost immediately the answer came faintly up
to them, 'What boy ?'

'Jelly-my-boy-Jelly-not-Jelly-stupid,' yelled Faatu,
frantic with excitement. 'Is he not with you ?'

'No,' came the startling reply. 'We have not
seen him since before we left the main body.'

In the flaring light of the great fire the five stared
into each other's eyes as this fateful news reached
them. Then Guy with a short, dry sob, sprang
towards the gateway.

'Stop, boy,' said Eli, holding him back. 'They
are comin' up. Let's hear what they've got to say.'

'Oh! what can they say ?' cried Guy, struggling
to free himself. 'He is lost! he is lost! And it is
my fault. I should have taken care of him. Let
me go and look for him.'

'An' git lost yourself,' said Eli sadly. 'No, that
mustn't be. It's my fault, if it's any one's, for
speakin' so quick to him. But nothing can be done
now ; ef we're to do any good, we must wait for the
mornin'.'

CHAPTER XVII.

THE CONSEQUENCES OF THE SAME.

JERRY'S first idea when he left the main body had been to join himself at once to the scouts, whose footfalls he could still hear not far away; but after a moment's reflection he altered his plans, and determined instead to follow them at a distance, until they had gone far enough to render it impossible for them to return and hand him over to the authorities; for he was a stubborn little rascal; and now that he had once broken bounds, he meant to pursue the adventure to the end. Certainly, now and again he felt a pang as he thought of the distress and alarm which his absence would cause when discovered, but he took what comfort he could out of the fact that his friends would be sure to conclude that he had accompanied the scouts.

'Besides,' he finished, shoving his conscience into a corner, 'Eli didn't positively say I wasn't to go; but only that it would be a good deal better if I stayed where I was.' By which sort of casuistry older and wiser people than Jerry have more than once come to bitter grief.

For a time all went well, and, keeping closely

under cover, Jerry followed the guiding sounds until about half-way up the wooded hill, when he thought that he might show himself without fear of disastrous consequences. But he had reckoned without making allowance for savage customs, for, just as he was preparing to make a forward rush, the sound of footsteps ceased suddenly, and he paused, momentarily at a loss what to do. The fact was that the scouts, fancying that they heard suspicious noises ahead of them, had sunk silently to earth amongst the ferns. Still apprehensive of some trap, they presently decided upon a change of direction, and, gliding away without a sound, continued their ascent of the mountain at a point about a quarter of a mile to the left. The summit gained, they discovered nothing for their pains, and after remaining on watch for a couple of hours, descended to the valley and hurried to overtake the main body.

It did not take very long for Jerry to arrive at a partially correct solution of the mystery. 'They have been alarmed and have stopped to reconnoitre,' he said to himself. 'If they move on again presently I'll call out. If not, I'll go cautiously forward and join them.'

He waited for ten minutes or so, by which time, though of course he did not suspect it, his friends the scouts were far away upon another line, and then, deciding that the best thing he could do would be to go on, advanced stealthily in what he supposed to be the direction whence the sounds had come. He knew by his sensations that he was always ascending, but having nothing else to guide him, bore too far to the right, putting as he went on an ever-increasing dis-

tance between himself and those of whom he was in
search. In five minutes he stopped again, looking
bewilderedly about him. The trees grew so close
together and the foliage was so dense that he could
see but a very short distance in any direction; perpetual twilight reigned in the forest belt he had
entered, and the deep and unbroken silence began to
affect his nerves.

'I must have passed them by,' he thought. 'I 'll
go back.' He did, always unconsciously trending to
the right, and five minutes took him farther down
the hill than he had been when he made his first
halt and still not a sign of the scouts. A cry rose to
his lips, but he choked it back, remembering in time
that there were others to be considered besides himself, and that any indication of his presence might
not only warn a lurking enemy of his whereabouts,
but also bring disaster upon his friends.

'I 've brought it on myself,' he mused forlornly,
'and I must get out of it the best way I can. Let
me see. I can't go down, for I should never be able
to find my way after the main body. I must go up
as quickly as possible. The scouts are sure to wait
for some time at the summit, and once there I can't
miss them.'

He made a wry face at the unpleasantness of his
position, and putting his best foot forward, trudged
steadily up the mountain once more. But again that
fatal tendency to bear to the right assailed him, and
all unconsciously he worked his way eastwards, then
for a short distance northwards, and finally, by the
time his face was set once more in the right direction,
westwards, he had gone half-way round the mountain

and was still at some distance from the top. Still he
pushed on, refusing to think of the consequences to
himself if he should fail to discover the scouts, and,
fortunately for his feelings, ignorant that already
some two hours had elapsed since their departure,
until at last, shortly before sunset, footsore and weary,
hungry and thirsty, he stood upon the summit.

For a moment he forgot his troubles in the mag-
nificence of the prospect that lay outstretched upon
every hand.   Below him, to the east, rolled mile upon
mile of tropical forest, bread-fruit, wild nutmeg,
chestnut, and banyan, *ivi* and *kavika*, blending the
rich tints of their foliage and their varied forms of
leaf and bough in splendid confusion, while here and
there through openings in the maze the eye wandered through long vistas of giant stems innumerable,
or stayed suddenly, caught by the delicate tracery of
vines and pendulous ferns and airy mosses that hung
like fairy screens between the great pillars of the
mighty aisles.   Dotting the landscape, the bright
green waving fronds of tree fern and the clumps of
broad-leaved bananas, or, it might be, a cultivated
patch of yams or *ndalo*, showed where a village
nestled among the trees, while far, far away in the
immense distance the ‘beautiful isles of the sea,’
Ovalau, Moturiki, Ngau, Mbenga, and many others, lay
dreamily upon the placid bosom of the ocean.   Westwards how different! The plateau upon which Jerry
stood was almost as a dividing line between the wet
and dry regions of Fiji, and towards the setting sun
the country, though not without a quiet beauty of
its own, seemed dull and uninteresting by comparison.
Open plains and valleys, low, rolling hills, bare, or

covered thickly with the sombre *noko-noko*, all trended
away to the high coast-range, which shut out the
view of the sea, the goal towards which the fugitives
laboured.

'Now where can they be, I wonder?' thought Jerry,
as after a short breathing space he turned irresolutely
this way and that, hesitating in which direction to
prosecute his search. 'I think I might venture
to call out now. Hullo! Why, there they are.
Hurrah!'

His eye, roving restlessly here and there, had caught
the gleam of white loin-cloths and turbans among the
trees, and without stopping to think, he ran towards
the spot, shouting as he went the names of the scouts.

'Raivalita! Mothelutu! Malata!' he called. 'Eke!
Eke! Here! Here!'

The next moment he dashed in among a group of
stalwart natives, painted for war, and pulled up short
with a gasp of dismay. For there, lounging against
the trees, or lolling upon the ground, were half-a-dozen
of his sworn foes, the convicts.

Proceeding upon the principle that it is best to act
first and ask questions afterwards, one of the warriors
advanced towards Jerry with uplifted club, but Hunt,
the boatswain, waved him back, and, stepping in front
of the boy, inquired roughly:

'What brings you here?'

Fear froze Jerry into silence, which was as well,
for at Hunt's next question: 'Where did yer get
that gun and them boots?' he saw in a flash that he
had not been recognised, and leapt to the conclusion
that if he could but properly act the savage he
appeared to be, he might yet escape. So, looking

straight at his interrogator he shook his head vigorously as a sign that he did not understand.

'Seems to me,' said Hunt, 'seeing he's got a gun
and is wearing them boots, as them whites must
have fallen in with his tribe and got massacred.
And a good thing too, I says.' He made signs to one
of the Fijians, who at once poured out a flow of talk
upon Jerry, of which, needless to say, he understood
not one word.

But necessity makes a quick wit, and lessons were
not usually thrown away upon Gerald Blake. He
remembered the difficulty the men of Naitasiri had
experienced in conversing with the *Kai Tholos*, owing
to difference of dialect, and the thought flashed across
him that he would pass himself off as a Hillman,
understanding nothing of this stranger's tongue. So
once again he shook his head, ejaculating Ndrau!
and following up the name of the town with a string
of meaningless syllables. The Fijian looked puzzled
in his turn, and after several vain efforts fell back,
muttering *Kai Tholo*, and making signs to Hunt that
conversation was impossible.

The boatswain, therefore, took up the ball once
more. 'See 'ere,' he said, tapping first his musket
and then his boots, 'where did you get 'em?'

Jerry appeared to consider for a moment, and then
nodding his head vigorously, pointed to the valley
below.

'Got 'em there, did you?' said Hunt. 'And what
became of the owner, I'd like to know. Hi! Did
you kill him and eat him?' He made a pretended
onslaught upon Dobbs and then pointed to his own
open mouth.

Sick with disgust, Jerry yet nodded furiously, laying his hand upon his stomach, and twisting his mouth into a horrid grin.

'So that's the way of it,' went on Hunt, grinning responsively. 'Now I wonder which of 'em it was, or if it was all of 'em. Ah! 'ere comes the capting. He'll be glad to 'ear this bit o' news.' Jerry felt his face pale under his coating of paint; but it was not so much at the sight of Larkin as at that of the man who followed in his steps, for in that sulky, lowering countenance he recognised the traitor, Noungouloa.

'It's all up now,' thought Jerry. 'So that ruffian has betrayed us. It's a pity we didn't find him out before we left Naitasiri.'

Wild with apprehension though he was, he yet managed to preserve a calm exterior, as Hunt, addressing Larkin, informed the latter of what had passed, and gave his opinion that the fugitives had come to a bad end.

'Humph! That's your idea, is it?' said Larkin, eyeing Jerry keenly. 'It seems to me that '——

What he would have said further must remain unknown, for at that moment Noungouloa made a sudden rush at Jerry, clutched the fuzzy wig and tore it from the boy's head, and, dancing and gibbering like a maniac, waved his trophy in the air.

There was a universal shout of surprise, and for an instant every one stared open-mouthed at the singular picture presented by the boy, with his red head, his black body, his blue stockings, and his long boots. Then Larkin, recoiling against a tree, laughed until the tears ran down his cheeks.

All the wrath in Jerry rushed to the surface.

Was he to stand there and make sport for this murderer, this brute who had been the cause of all their troubles? A mist swam before his eyes and cleared; his brain reeled and grew steady; his gun leaped to his shoulder; for one instant the dark muzzle covered Larkin's heart and then the hammer fell.

Alas! there was no report. In his climb up the mountain the powder had been shaken out and the pan was empty.

With a bitter cry, Jerry flung down the weapon, and with clenched fists and flashing eyes, faced Larkin, who, sobered by the narrowness of his escape, advanced upon him.

'You little devil!' hissed the convict, striking the boy a blow on the mouth that brought the blood spurting from his lips, and sent him heavily to the ground. 'What! You'd murder me, would you? We'll see. You vermin, I won't waste words over you. Pick him up, Hunt, and bring him along. No use waiting here; the sun will set in a few moments.'

Hunt raised Jerry in his arms, and, followed by the mixed crowd, strode after Larkin, who led the way along the crest of the hill to where a huge fire blazed and crackled, near which several large freshly-dug pits yawned widely.

A great number of Fijians, perhaps a couple of hundred, were concentrated at this spot, and the forest was apparently full of them, for Jerry could hear them laughing and talking afar off. But it was not upon them that the boy concentrated his horror-stricken gaze, but upon twenty dead bodies, which, ready dressed for the oven, lay beside the pits.

'You see, you little whelp. That's what's in store for you by-and-by,' said Larkin, noting the piteous glance which Jerry cast at the bodies. 'Meantime, Hunt, lash him to a tree.'

Larkin was very much changed in the brief interval which had elapsed since Jerry had last seen him. The veneer of refinement and suavity had disappeared, and only the coarse, crime-stained convict remained.

'Cut a stout switch, Hunt,' he resumed, when Jerry had been made fast with some tarry cords the boatswain drew from his jacket pocket. 'Now, young Blake, I'm going to punish you for your murderous attack upon me. Later on we will talk of something else. But I will give you one chance. Tell me how you come to be here alone, and where your comrades are, and I will let you go.'

'I don't believe you,' answered Jerry in a muffled voice. 'You are too wicked a man. But I got lost, and the others are far away from here by this time.' His voice shook with a slight sob. He was only a boy, and he was very frightened. Moreover, the ghastly sight immediately under his eyes made him feel sick.

'I should have thought they would have taken better care of you,' sneered Larkin. 'Where are they? In what direction, I mean.'

Jerry twisted his head round and stared into Larkin's eyes.

'You may flog me into strips if you choose; but I won't tell you,' he said tremulously.

'Won't you?' jeered Larkin. 'We'll see. Why, you are funking now. Lay into him Hunt. Imagine you are dealing with young Hawkins, and let that nerve your arm.'

The taunt stung Jerry, and with his under-lip fast between his teeth, he vowed he would die before he made a sign.

Hunt raised his muscular arm. Swish! the pliant rod curved round the shrinking back and chest, and the quivering body shrank closer to the tree. But not a sound.

'How do you like it?' scoffed Larkin. 'Will you speak?'

'No,' muttered the boy.

Hunt raised his arm again. There was a sound like the twanging of a fiddle-string, a faint whistling noise in the air, something flashed past Jerry's bewildered sight; he heard a deep groan, a shout of mingled wrath and amazement, and, turning his head once more, beheld the boatswain dead upon the ground with the shaft of an arrow protruding from the socket of his left eye.

CHAPTER XVIII.

THE DOINGS OF MBEKA.

FOR the time being Jerry was forgotten, for white men and black, expecting an organised attack from what quarter they knew not, sprang hurriedly to arms. But when minute after minute passed, and still there was no sign of an assault, nor did any sound break the deep silence of the forest, a wrathful shout arose from five hundred throats, and, shaking their spears and clubs aloft, the Fijians poured into the bush to hunt for the ambushed assassin.

Larkin stood gazing meditatively down upon the dead body of Hunt, and for a long time he neither moved nor spoke. His white friends, ten in number, grouped themselves at a little distance behind him, conversing in low tones, and now and again glancing and pointing at Jerry, who, with his head still twisted round, watched the singular scene, as much as and more at a loss than any one there to comprehend its meaning. For he did not know that there had been a conflict that morning, and the bodies that lay by the pits were those of the *Kai Tholos* who had been slaughtered. Larkin, however, and the convicts

with him, had leapt to the conclusion that the death
of Hunt had been due to some wandering member
of the tribe, who had followed them up and, seeing an
opportunity for revenge, had promptly seized it.

'It must be so, lads,' said Larkin, rousing himself
at last from his reverie. 'Poor Ted Hunt has met his
death at the hands of one of the fellows with whom
we were engaged to-day. Well, he's a good man
gone. One consolation, if the Mbauans lay hold of
the shooter, there won't be much left of him by
to-morrow morning, even if they wait to cook him,
which I very much doubt. Hullo! what is this now?'

Apparently the Mbauans had failed to catch the
man, for as Larkin spoke, the remaining convicts filed
into the firelight, a melancholy procession, bearing
among them the dead body of Skipper Adams, shot,
as Hunt had been, through the eye.

Larkin swore a fierce and terrible oath; the fiercer
and more terrible that he so seldom condescended to
that sort of talk. 'What is this? what is this?' he
cried. 'How—when did this happen?'

'Not five minutes ago,' answered one of the convicts. 'We heard the rumpus down here, and
wondered what it meant. Then a while later we
heard some one tramping by, stealthy like, and Tom he
sticks his head through a bush and "Who's that?"
says he. The sun were just going out of sight, it
were, as he says it. "Who's that?" he says, thinking,
no doubt, poor chap, as it were a Mbauan, when
whang! comes an arrer and takes him in the eye.
He never said a word, he were that surprised, but fell
right down upon his face, and when we picked him
up he were dead. We'd have charged into the bush,

but just then the Mbauans came sweeping by, so
what was the good ?'

'Well, well, so poor Tom is gone,' said Larkin, in a
melancholy voice. 'I could have better spared a
better man. But really this is getting beyond a joke.
—If I thought your friends had a hand in this!' he
vociferated, wheeling round and glaring at Jerry.

'They hadn't,' said Jerry. 'It is not their style,
and besides they are far away, as I told you.'

'Yes, and you'll tell me a good deal more before
I'm done with you, or I'll know the reason why,'
raged Larkin. 'I hold you and the miserable pack
of curs you call your friends responsible for the death
of these two men. If it had not been for you, we
should not have been here.'

'And if it had not been for you, we should not
have been here,' retorted Jerry, unable to resist the
temptation, though he clearly recognised that speech
would be dangerous.

Larkin, however, had again fallen into a brown
study, and did not notice the remark, if he heard it.
'I tell you what it is, lads,' he said at last; 'we must
draw off to-night to that fortress among the rocks up
yonder. This may be only the first indication of a
serious attack. I wish it had been some of those
wretched blacks who had been killed, instead of two
of my best men.'

One after another the Mbauans returned from their
unsuccessful hunt. Their blood was up, and they
glared angrily at Jerry, shaking their clubs and
muttering wrathfully, '*Mbakolo! Mbakolo!*'

The boy was horribly frightened, though he kept
his feelings well under control; but his lips moved

P

tremulously, and his eye wandered from the great fire into the thick darkness of the forest as though searching for aid which never came. He tried not to think of it, but he had little doubt as to the fate in store for him, and the thought paralysed him. He had a faint hope that if he could only get hold of Na Ulivou, the Mbauan king might be induced to intercede in his favour; but unfortunately for the proving of this theory the *Vu-ni-Valu* was not present, having remained behind with a second column to punish the men of Naitasiri for their audacity in opposing his commands, for to such he considered his request equivalent, and for causing the death of one of his favourite chiefs. Mbitakau, the *Mata*, was, subject to Larkin's orders, the head of the pursuing column of five hundred chosen men, and the convict captain had sworn that if he came up with the runaways, he would bring their bodies back, so that Na Ulivou might learn by actual experiment whether they were, or were not, better than those of his black countrymen. So, even had the Root of War been present, Jerry's chances of making a favourable impression upon him would have been slender indeed—except, of course, in a gastronomic sense.

After some conversation with Mbitakau by means of a Tongan interpreter, whom he had obtained from Rewa, Larkin turned again to Jerry.

'I do not believe that you are the sort of boy who can be flogged into obedience, or I should myself proceed with your whipping,' he said coldly, as he untied the cords which bound the boy to the tree; 'at the same time, you must not think that you are to get off scot-free, so I am going to teach you a

lesson. If it makes the impression upon you that
I believe it will, you will be submissive enough by
morning. If not—well, you will have seen what is in
store for you, and can take your choice. One thing
I will say to you: sooner or later, with or without
your aid, I will come up with your friends; for I
swear that I will not rest while one of them walks
the earth.'

Jerry made no reply, and the convict turning him
round bound him again with his back against the
tree, so that he was unable to escape a full view
of the great fire, the stark, prone bodies, and the
yawning pits.

'Now,' resumed Larkin, 'we are going to leave
you; for I confess that I have not much stomach for
the sight you are going to see. We shall not be far
away, only four hundred yards or so, in a natural
fortress, where we may resist an attack if one should
happen to be made; for I cannot afford to lose any
more men at present. Palavali,' he said to the Tongan
interpreter, 'tell Mbitakau that when he has finished
his performance here, he had better join us among the
rocks.'

'Larkin, you are never going to leave me alone
here among these fiends!' panted poor Jerry, with a
shuddering sense of what was before him.

'Indeed I am,' answered the convict; 'for the present
at least. Later on I shall send some one to look after
you, in case you wriggle out of your bonds, though'
—examining the fastenings to which he had added
some strong vines—' I don't think that is very likely.
Come on, mates.'

He drew the switch which he held in his hand

sharply across Jerry's naked chest, and with a mocking laugh made off, followed by the convicts and the
bulk of the savages. Mbitakau, along with some half
dozen chiefs and as many warriors, remained behind,
nor was the unfortunate Jerry left very long in un-
certainty as to their intentions.

A quantity of fuel which had been provided
beforehand was thrown into each pit, a layer of large
stones being placed upon each heap. The wood was
then kindled, and soon columns of smoke and
quivering tongues of flame were rolling and leaping
from the vast hollows. A further number of large
stones, placed just within the original fire, very
quickly became red hot.

So far, the *Mata* and his gentlemen friends had sat
quietly by, watching the preparations; but now they
began to exhibit signs of impatience, and addressed
several excited remarks to one of the warriors who
was directing operations. The man nodded, disappeared for a moment into a grove of trees, and
returned, bearing a basket of green withes, from
which, to Jerry's unspeakable horror, he produced a
heart and liver. Squatting down, he adjusted these
upon the stones in the fire, and then diving once more
into his basket, brought out a further supply of the
dreadful food, which he placed to roast beside the
first.

Sick, almost fainting with disgust and terror, Jerry
closed his eyes and kept them tightly shut; but after
a time an irresistible fascination forced him to open
them again. The *tafa tamata*, or butcher, had deftly
divided the tit-bits with a bamboo knife and a piece
of sharp shell, and was handing them, nicely served

upon green leaves, to the expectant *Mata* and his friends. The boy shut his eyes again, but the champing of jaws and smacking of lips told him all too truly what was going forward. Presently he roused himself to look again. The fire in the pits was burned out, and the stones were red hot. Lifting the bodies carefully by the head and heels, the butcher and his assistants laid them upon the glowing stones, some of which were placed within the abdomens of the victims. A thick coat of leaves was then laid over the bodies, and upon this again earth was shovelled to the depth of three or four inches and then smoothed. All was now finished, and when the steam should penetrate this double covering, the *mbakolo* would be cooked and ready to be divided among the warriors.

The *Mata* rose, and, after taking a drink from a bamboo tube, which was handed to him by an attendant, approached Jerry. Laying hold of the boy's arm, he pressed his greasy fingers into the soft and yielding flesh, prodded the well-covered ribs, and turning to a chief at his side, remarked with a leer, ' *Roa roa !* ' (to-morrow).

A strong shudder shook Jerry from head to foot, the pupils of his eyes dilated with fear and horror, and with a faint sigh his head fell forward upon his breast, and a merciful unconsciousness shielded him from the terrors of a hideous imagination.

When he came to himself the fire had been replenished, and as memory slowly returned to him he saw, to his relief, that he was not alone. Under such circumstances any company was better than none, and it was with almost a sense of comfort that

he recognised the ugly face of Noungouloa scowling
up at him.   At a little distance from the squatting
Fijian lay, with mouth wide, and peacefully snoring,
Luke Rogers, one of the convicts, who, after examining Jerry's bonds to see that they were all secure, had
turned over the duties of the watch to his dusky
companion.

'Rogers,' said Jerry faintly, remembering how on
one occasion the man had protested against the
behaviour of Larkin ; 'Rogers, I never did you any
harm.   Won't you help me ?'

The low, despairing tones failed to break in upon
the convict's slumbers, but Noungouloa arose, and
flourishing his club over Jerry's head, made signs to
him to be silent, while with a fiendish grin he pointed
to the great pits.   Then he squatted down once more,
holding his club across his knees, and every now and
again casting malevolent glances at the miserable boy.

Jerry watched him wearily, making no further
attempt to arouse Rogers, and presently found himself wondering blankly what the time was, and
wishing that the dawn were come, that his troubles
might be brought to an end, for he had made up his
mind that death alone could bring him relief, and
anything was better than this agony of suspense.

Suddenly his eye, wandering listlessly to and fro,
was attracted by a slight stir among the bushes
beyond the fire.   The night was very still, scarcely a
breath of wind stirring.   What could it be then that
so softly parted the drooping boughs ?   The question
did not interest him greatly, and his eyes were
closing again, when all at once he was startled into
thrilling, throbbing wakefulness.

Out from among the gently-moving branches emerged a lithe, black figure, creeping stealthily on hands and knees towards the squatting Noungouloa, who, all unconscious, and with nodding head, now dozed lightly.

A wild flame of hope shot up in Jerry's breast. Could this be Eli or one of his friends come to his rescue, or was it only one of the cannibals, stolen back from the camp to observe the progress of the cooking ? He did not dare to think, but with starting eyes and breath hard held, watched the crawling figure as nearer and nearer it drew to the all too careless Noungouloa. Now but six feet separated the two, now but three, now but one. The crouching figure rose to its knees, something gleaming in its right hand, while the fingers of the left hovered for a moment over Noungouloa's head. There was an instant's pause, a sudden forward snatch at the mop of hair, a quick bending backwards of the ugly head, a strong sweep of the figure's right arm, and with his head half-severed from his body, the traitor of Naitasiri rolled sideways without a groan to the ground.

Instantly the figure sprang up, and with one wet hand pressed over Jerry's lips, stifling the cry of horror that threatened to burst from them, slashed rapidly with the knife grasped in the other at the bonds which bound him to the tree.

In a moment the boy was free, and as the fire flared upwards and lit the face of his benefactor, he recognised him.

'Mbeka !' he breathed softly. 'You !'

The Little Bat made a swift sign of silence and pointed to the woods.

Jerry needed no stronger hint, but instantly dropping to the ground, began to crawl away. A gruff exclamation arrested the movement, and looking round he saw to his horror that Rogers was sitting up and staring at the tree. The boy's heart sank, but instantly throbbed hopefully again, for the quick-witted Bat, warned by the restlessness of the white man, had reared himself against the trunk, and now stood, silently counterfeiting the late prisoner.

Rogers blinked heavily at him once or twice, yawned, muttered something, and then, casting himself down once more, fell almost instantly asleep.

For a few minutes silence reigned, and then the Bat, stooping swiftly, possessed himself of Noun-gouloa's heavy club, and swinging it aloft, let it fall.

Jerry buried his face in the ground, and dug his fingers into his ears, so that he should not hear the dull, sickening crash, and when he looked round once more Mbeka was busy about the body of Rogers, his shoulders working, and his right arm moving backwards and forwards with a quick sawing movement.

'Whatever is he doing, and why doesn't he come?' thought Jerry fretfully, as Mbeka transferred his attentions to Noungouloa. 'Oh! oh! oh! how frightful!'

It was all he could do to repress a scream, for as the Bat rose at last to his feet and advanced towards him, Jerry saw that he carried in his left hand two ghastly human heads.

'*Vinaka! vinaka!*' chuckled the Bat gleefully, swinging the heads to and fro as he passed Jerry, who, chilled by the horror of the thing, rose and staggered after him.

Half-a-mile from the scene of the tragedy Mbeka came to a halt under a large tree, among the roots of which Jerry could distinguish by the light of the moon a bow and arrows, a couple of spears, and a small heap of yams, upon one of which he greedily pounced, for he was desperately hungry. Mbeka watched him appreciatively for some minutes, and then with a guttural exclamation, passed Roger's musket to Jerry, seized his own more primitive weapons, and sped away down the mountain. Questions were needless, for as Jerry tore after him, a wild yell in the direction of the camp told him that his flight had been discovered, and that the pursuit was begun.

CHAPTER XIX.

A REMARKABLE DISAPPEARANCE.

THOUGH they recognised the force of Eli's argument, that it would be hopeless to look for Jerry during the night, yet never had hours seemed so long to Anthony and Guy as those which dragged on between midnight and morning. As the first shaft of light shot up into the eastern sky they sprang to their feet, and before Eli and the twelve warriors whom he had selected to accompany them had stirred a step, were half-way down the rocky pass which led to the valley.

'Keep a sharp lookout, Whitson,' said Eli to the mate, who was to remain in charge of the reserve. 'Not ez I 'magine you're likely to be bothered; but you never know. It might be ez well ef while we're away you sent some one up to the top o' the rock to explore. Good-bye! We'll be back at once ef we find the little chap; ef not, some o' us'll return towards evenin' an' let you know what's doin'.'

For himself he meant never to come back until he had found his little friend, while if he did not find him—well, still he meant never to come back.

Wherever Jerry was gone he meant to follow him, were it over the edge of the world.

'We'll march to the spot whar he was last seen, unless we pick him up on the way,' he said when he came up with the cousins, 'and then we can ascend the mountain, for I guess he follered the scouts, though they never saw him. He's no fool, ain't Jerry, and once he found out he was lost, he'd not go monkeyin' round, but sit right down an' wait till we came to look for him.'

'I dare say he would,' said Anthony gloomily; 'but in this abode of cannibals there are worse things than being lost.'

'Don't, Anthony, don't,' implored Guy piteously. 'Don't let us start with such dreadful ideas. God knows it is hard enough as it is. I—shall we not shout as we go along, Eli? There is no saying where he may not be.'

'Ay, shout away,' answered Eli, and set the example with a ringing coo-ee.

Strangely enough sounded the wild Australian cry in the ears of the Fijian escort, but though its penetrating syllables must have travelled an immense distance in that clear air, yet there came no answer.

'Never mind,' said Eli encouragingly. 'We couldn't expect to run up agin him not a hundred yards from home. Try again, Guy.'

'Coo-ee! coo-ee!' halloaed Guy, and the Fijians, delighted with the musical sound, took up the shout until the valley resounded with the shrill call.

Still no response; and as they turned a curve Eli paused to wave a farewell to Whitson, who was watching them from the fort, a quarter of a mile

away. Another moment and it was hidden from
sight, and for another quarter of a mile the valley
stretched almost in a straight line in front of them,
though here and there the view was partially obscured
by huge boulders and outjutting or fallen trees.

'Coo-ee! coo-ee!' shouted Anthony in his sonorous tones.

'Coo-ee! coo-ee!' came back instantly in a shrill
treble, and then, 'Help! help!'

'By time, it's him!' roared Eli. 'Whar are ye,
boyee? Good land! Thar he is, an' they're after
him!'

Round the next curve of the valley, flying on the
wings of the wind, came Jerry, his musket tightly
grasped in his right hand, and his red hair streaming
behind him in curious contrast to his sooty skin.
Twenty paces in his rear raced another small figure,
evidently a son of the soil, for in one hand he bore
two human heads, while with the other he shook aloft
his spears, yelling in true Fijian fashion. Behind
him, again, four tall savages, armed with ponderous
clubs, which they swung as lightly as though they
had been batons, charged furiously forwards.

'Ye blood-thirsty little rip!' screeched Eli at the
diminutive Fijian. 'I'll stop your rush.—Back,
Anthony!—Back, Guy!' For they had sprung forward. 'Keep together, an' look to your primin'.
There's maybe more behind. Jerry's all right.
He's ahead, an' he knows how to run.—Dodge to
right or left, Jerry,' he roared, 'an' let me git a cl'ar
shot at the little devil behind you.—By time! lads,
we're in for it. Look at 'em.—Dodge, Jerry,
dodge!'

But Jerry held straight on, wasting no breath in words, and covering with his body the small native in his rear, while round the bend, terrific sight, poured what seemed to be a never-ending column of warriors, each as he came into the straight emitting a howl of joy at the sight of the prey in front. Suddenly Jerry's little follower stopped, swung round, fitted an arrow to his bow, drew back the string to his ear, and sent the gaudily-feathered shaft deep into the heart of the foremost savage, who with his hands flung up above his head, toppled heavily to the ground. An instant later both boys disappeared from view behind a boulder, there was a sharp crack as Jerry's musket rang out, another savage fell, and once more the two small heroes came into sight.

'By time, the little chap's a friend!' cried Eli. 'Forward, boys, and pick 'em up. We'll easy stop the other fellows' rush.'

Like hounds slipped from the leash, the cousins bounded forward to meet the boys. In a few strides they were together, and Anthony, swinging Jerry up in his arms, turned and rushed madly back again, while Guy, catching hold of the black boy's hand, tore after them.'

'To one side!' yelled Eli, and, as they obeyed, his musket cracked and a third pursuer fell wounded to the ground.

'They're Mbauans!' panted Jerry, for there was, as may be supposed, no time for congratulations. 'Five hundred of them if there's one, and Larkin and his convicts behind. That's Mbeka with me. Don't hurt him.'

'Set the boy down, Anthony,' cried Eli.—'Catch

him up, some of you,' he vociferated at the Fijians,
who were engaged in yelling defiance at the foe.
'Quit screamin', you 'tarnal ijits, an' hoist up Jerry
an' the Baker, an' leg it for the fort. God be thanked
it ain't fur away!'

He caught up Jerry and simply flung him into
the arms of the nearest native, who, considerably
astonished, suddenly grasped what was required of
him, and made off up the valley as fast as his legs
would carry him, while another performed a like
good office for the Baker, as Eli called him.

As the men of Naitasiri started, Anthony and Guy
emptied their muskets at the advancing crowd, which
gave suddenly back, as a wave that breaks upon a
rock.

'That's the ticket!' shouted Eli. 'Away with you
now. Load as you run an' turn when you hear me fire.'

He finished loading his piece as coolly as if he had
been out duck-shooting, and, as the savages, em-
boldened at the sight of his solitary figure, swept
forward again, once more stopped their advance and
bolted after his comrades. He had reloaded by the
time he reached them, and swinging round they fired
a rattling volley and took to their heels.

But the men of Mbau had had enough for the
present, and while those in the rear, who had not yet
rounded the curve, cried 'forward,' those in front,
who were getting all the peppering, cried 'back,' and
so the dusky column rolled and twisted and bent
upon itself till the wave of commotion reached the
extreme rear, where Larkin, wild with wrath at
the unexpected check, struggled furiously to force a
passage to the front.

The confusion gave the whites the time they required, and before the pursuing column had been again set in motion, they had gained the top of the path, dashed across the bridge, pulled the logs after them, crowded through the gate of the stockade and fallen all together upon Jerry, who had sprung to meet them, laughing, crying, kissing, and hugging by turns. Faatu and Mbonavindongo, too, were not behind-hand in their congratulations, while the members of the escort, particularly those who had been instrumental in bringing Jerry out of the fight, sang and danced, and capered with glee, making the courtyard ring with their laughter. Only a deep, ominous growl from far below seemed to threaten that this scene of delight and good humour should be rudely changed. But no one paid any attention to it until Whitson, who had mounted upon a platform and was looking over the stockade, called out suddenly, 'Here they come! Crowds of them!'

'By time! I forgot all about 'em,' cried Eli joyously. 'Waal, let 'em come an' welcome.'

'If they have a fancy for a walk up here it is about all they will get for their pains,' laughed Guy.

'Excepting a few ounces of lead by way of early breakfast,' put in Anthony.

'Ah! Larkin ain't the man to be set back without one try for us,' said Eli. 'Jerry, my dear, we'll have to hear the rest o' your story by-an'-by, please God.'

'There's not much more to tell,' returned Jerry, who had been gabbling away at a great rate. 'We got clean away, thanks to Mbeka. Wasn't it fortunate I gave him that knife you were so mean

about, Eli ? I expect they had given us up and were
simply marching west in the hope of coming up with
somebody or something, when suddenly we, who were
resting under a rock, caught sight of their vanguard,
and then the race began.'

'Waal, waal,' said Eli, 'we've got to quit foolin'
an' tend to business.—Faatu, take them boys an' see
ez they git suthin to eat. I 'low they must be
hungry.'

'Hungry!' echoed Jerry. 'Starving you mean.
I've had nothing but a stomachful of yam since I
saw you; while as to Mbeka I don't know what he
had, but I do know that it was all I could do to
prevent him eating me. Hey, Mbeka!'

Mbeka grinned responsively. He had stood apart
all this time holding on to his grisly burden, and
waiting like a faithful dog for some notice to be
bestowed upon him.

'Put those things down, Mbeka,' said Guy, indicating the heads; but the boy leaping lightly to one
side, sprang up and stuck the heads on top of the
palisades by Whitson, who with a snort of disgust sent
them spinning into the ravine.

Mbeka looked angry for a moment, then disappointed, and finally with a philosophical laugh went
off to join Jerry at breakfast.

'They have halted below there,' announced
Whitson from his post of observation.

'Quite so,' observed Anthony ironically. 'Larkin
is not such a fool as to try that path while our
muskets command it. Besides, even if he reached
the spur, he could not cross the gap, as he can very
well see from below.'

'It ain't that we've to think of so much,' said Eli. 'Thar's only one way down ez well ez up, an' ef Larkin chooses to camp below thar, he needn't take the trouble to come up, fer we must go down or starve.'

'That is true,' said Whitson; 'but Larkin does not know it.'

'He has got sense enough to know that we must live from hand to mouth as we march,' said Guy. 'I wonder if food could possibly be stored in that house up there, Eli.'

'A good idea,' answered the Virginian. 'Did you send some one up thar, mate?'

'No; there wasn't time,' replied Whitson. 'You were back so soon.'

'I'll go,' said Guy, moving towards the steps; but Eli pulled him back.

'No, no,' he objected. 'Let one o' the niggers go. Hi, Faatu, ask Boney to send some one to see what's in yonder house.'

A tall fellow instantly sprang at the steps, and clinging to the roots of the banyan, worked his way rapidly up the face of the rock. Scarcely, however, had his head risen above the level of the palisades than there was a sharp crack, a cloud of dust started from the rock, and the Fijian dropped swiftly to the ground, bleeding profusely from a graze along the scalp.

'Kalou! Kalou!' exclaimed his comrades, crowding round the fallen warrior, who, much more frightened than hurt, lay upon his face and kicked his heels in the air.

'Rubbish!' said Eli. ''Tain't nuthin' when you're

Q

used to it. First blood to them,' he added grimly.
'But whar did the bullet come from. It's jest ez
well you'd quit your post at the palisades, mate; fer
I guess that feller was after you.'

'He must be somewhere on the path then,' said
Guy; 'for the shot could not possibly have come from
below.'

Anthony drew his knife from his boot and rapidly
cut a loophole in the palisade. 'Who is game to go
up and draw the fellow's fire while I watch him?'
he said.

'Nobody,' answered Eli promptly. 'Thar ain't an
individooal hyar ez hasn't got more sense. But this
yer's an old dodge. You kin try it.' He drew his
wig from his head. 'Ready?'

'Wait a moment,' said Anthony enlarging the loophole slightly and settling himself at it. 'Now.'

Eli set the wig upon the point of a long spear and
slowly pushed it up the face of the rock. As soon as
it reached a certain level, two reports rang out almost
simultaneously, the wig was flattened against the
gray stone, and Anthony with a nod of satisfaction
pulled back the smoking barrel of his musket through
the loophole.

'Did you git him?' demanded Eli excitedly. 'By
time, he is a good shot.'

'Was, you mean,' said Anthony. 'He won't shoot
any more.'

'Bullee!' chuckled Eli. 'Countin' Tirrel an'
Jenkin, that's six Master Bill has lost one way or
another. Ef we kin git rid o' them mean whites, I
do believe our blackies an' theirs would make terms
easy 'nuff.—Good land! Guy, what are you doin'?'

For Guy, with his musket slung at his back, was
running lightly up the steps, aided by the gnarled
roots of the banyan.

'Come down!' shouted his friends in chorus, while
a roar of wrath arose from the valley and several
ineffectual shots were fired, but with a triumphant
laugh he swung himself on to the flat top, darted
through the palisade, and disappeared. In a moment
he was back again, shouting and waving his hands.

'There is food enough and to spare to feed us for
a fortnight,' he cried. 'Come up! come up. They
may force the stockade, but they can't get up here,
and they know it. That's why they're so anxious
to stop us. Yams, taro, bread-fruit, coco-nuts—everything but meat.'

'Up after him!' vociferated Eli. 'I guess we can
be vegetarians fer a bit. Barrin' the pigs, it's been
our luck ever since we came to the country. Faatu,
tell Boney to send his heathen up first. We'll stand
hyar, and drap the first varmint that shows his nose
to climb the path.'

He sprang upon the platform accompanied by
Whitson, while Anthony, rapidly cutting another
loophole, beckoned to Faatu to take his stand at it.

A roar of rage swelled from below as the men
of Naitasiri with wonderful celerity scaled the steep
rock and ensconced themselves upon the palisaded
top, for the Mbauans, used to this style of warfare,
knew very well not only the advantages of the position, but also the probability that a supply of provisions was stored in the house.

'Come on,' yelled Eli derisively, as he noted the
stir in the valley. 'Thar's breakfast waiting fer the

first ez shows himself on the path. Yah! Why don't
you come?—No volleying, boys, or they'll git us
before we can load. Fire one at a time.—Now then,
Jerry, up you go with the Baker.—You next, Whitson,
—don't stay to argufy. Up with you.' For the mate
demurred at leaving him. 'Up an' fire from the
top ef you can.—Faatu, you next.—By time! Thar
they come. Fire into the thick o' them, Anthony,
an' run.'

Enraged at what was going forward, Larkin had
made a passionate appeal to Mbitakau, so, acting under
the latter's orders, a phalanx of the stoutest of the
men of Mbau rushed the path, carrying in the midst
of them three of the convicts, whom they shielded
with their bodies from the bullets of the defenders
until a vantage ground had been reached whence an
effective reply could be made.

Anthony delivered his fire, with what result could
not be seen, though from the yell that arose it was
evident that the bullet had found its billet. Then,
instead of obeying Eli's order, he pulled in his piece
and coolly commenced to reload.

'Away!' ordered Eli. 'They're all up but you an'
me.'

'I know,' returned Anthony, taking his stand at
the loophole again. 'Up with you! I'll cover your
retreat.'

'What are you sayin'?' vociferated Eli. 'Can't
you see ez the pizen critters is under cover from
Whitson's fire? They'll riddle you ez you climb ef
I'm not here to stop 'em.'

'And they'll riddle you as you climb if I am not
here to stop them,' retorted Anthony. 'You are the

brains of this expedition. I can better be spared than you, if it comes to that. Up with you. I stay here till you are safe.'

'Blame you, thar's no time to argufy,' muttered Eli, as, discharging his musket, he leaped from the platform and ran hastily to the foot of the steps. With the activity of a practised sailor he swung himself up, but just as his head came into the line of fire, loosed his hold and dropped with a shrill laugh to the ground, while three bullets flattened themselves against the rock and fell harmlessly beside him.

'Are you hit?' cried Anthony, springing to his side. 'They were too quick for me.'

'Hit! Not much, I ain't,' chuckled Eli, already half way up the rock again. 'The fools fired together, I knowed they would. Up behind me before they can load agen. Old man Eli's been too much for 'em jest this once ez I reckoned he would be.'

So chuckling and complimenting himself, he reached the top of the rock and, followed headlong by the delighted Anthony, dived through the opening in the palisade to the accompaniment of a chorus of yells from the baffled convicts.

'How does that strike you?' he remarked, looking about him with a complacent grin. 'Ah! you may hoot an' yell, below thar. Who cares a Continental? Every charge o' powder you let off's one down to us, for it's one less to you.—Waal, Guy, boyee, whar's them yams? I guess we can afford to take a spell.'

'Guy is not here!' cried Jerry shrilly.

'What!' exclaimed Anthony. 'He ran back into the stockade as the Fijians began to climb up.'

'Him not here,' declared Faatu. 'Me look efery-where.'

'God help us! He can't have fallen over the cliff,' gasped Eli, springing to the edge of the rock, while Anthony dashed into the house, crying: 'Guy, old fellow, are you in here?'

The interior of the *Mbure* was almost dark, the only light it contained being admitted through the low door-way; but Anthony, glancing hither and thither, could just make out that it was, as his cousin had told them, a storehouse of provisions.

'Guy!' he called again. 'Are you here? Are you hurt?'

There was no answer, and with a sense of dismay at his heart, he groped his way to the far end of the *Mbure*.

'Guy!' he began once more. 'G——'

Then the ground seemed to give way beneath him, his musket flew from his grasp, and with a ringing cry he fell down, down, down through space.

CHAPTER XX.

GONE AWAY.

BEWILDERED as Anthony was by the swift rush of air past his face, yet the instinct of self-preservation caused him to throw out his hands and clutch wildly, in the hope that he might grasp something which would arrest his descent. Instantly his fingers encountered some yielding felted substance, and his feet at the same moment striking upon an inclined floor, he jerked himself backwards against what he felt to be a sloping wall, and slid comfortably to the bottom of the huge funnel, for such it was, into which he had fallen, till his progress was arrested by a pile of soft mats, considerately placed so as to break his fall. But before he had time to realise this astonishing termination to his adventure, a pair of strong arms was flung about him, and struggling to his feet, he closed with his antagonist.

'Let me go,' he panted. 'Let me go, or I'll brain you.'

'Oh, it's you!' said a well-known voice, as the detaining arms were loosed. 'I didn't know. I wasn't sure. What a relief!'

'Guy!' cried Anthony in an ecstasy of delight.
'Are you there, old fellow? Is it really you?
Hurrah! we were afraid you had gone over the
cliff.'

'Didn't it strike you where I had gone to when
you came tumbling down here after me?' laughed
Guy.

'By George, no!' answered Anthony. 'I was
expecting nothing but the bump, as the Yorkshire-
man said. How did you get here?'

'Much in the same way as you did, I imagine. I
tumbled through the hole. But there's an easy way
up; I was just going to ascend when you came
hurtling down. This is evidently intended as a way
of escape in case of the carrying of the citadel. But
let us go up and relieve Eli's mind. We can explore
the place later on if necessary.'

'Where does the light come from?' asked Anthony,
watching Guy, as the latter prepared to ascend by
crawling on hands and knees up the steep sides of
the funnel.

'From outside. The mouth of this cave opens
some twenty yards to the right, immediately over
the river. But I expect there must be another opening somewhere, for no one would choose to bottle
himself up here while an enemy occupied the top of
the rock. Moreover, there are immense bundles of
bamboo torches stacked all along the walls. I'——

'Below there!' came in stentorian tones from
above?' 'Is that you two chattering down there,
or is it your ghosts?'

'Pretty solid ghosts, Eli,' laughed Guy. 'We were
just coming up.'

'Waal, I should say so. What have ye struck ez
makes you fergit your friends has feelins ? Hyar's the
whole kit o' them given you up fer lost, an' howlin'
an' cryin', while thar you are, discussin' the facts ez
cool ez you please. By time ! I'm glad, though.
Say, how did you manage 'thout breakin' your necks ?
I mighty nigh fell through the pesky hole myself.'

'There is no occasion to fall through,' said Guy.
' Put your feet through, and feel for the sloping wall,
and then let yourself slide, if you want to come down.
I think you had better, for I should say that we
can slip out of the back door somewhere down here
while our friends the enemy are hammering at the
front.'

' I wouldn't wonder but you 're right,' returned Eli.
' Not ez they show much disposition to hammer so
far, fer they 've withdrawn into the valley agen.
But no doubt they will. Hold on till I tell the folk,
an' I 'll be with you in a jiffy. Hi ! what's that ?
Ketch him ! Stop him ! My land ! Phew ! you outrajus imp, you. You 'll make an old man o' me
before my time. Say, is he all right ?'

That, it is scarcely necessary to explain, was Jerry,
who, closely followed by Mbeka, came flying down
the funnel.

' All right,' laughed Guy. ' Now, youngster, what
do you want ?'

' It sounded interesting,' panted Jerry, 'so we
thought we 'd come.'

' I 've told 'em,' halloaed Eli down the shaft, ' an'
they 're all jes' keen to come, but I 've said to hold
on till I git back an' tell 'em it 's worth the journey.
Meantime——ready below ? whoosh ! Hyar I am.

My land ! it's all lined with cloth or suthin'.   Never knew such easy travellin'.'

'You went into it with your eyes open,' said Anthony ; 'a very different matter from tumbling down it as I did.'

'I reckon. But you can bet your boots it ain't thar fer nothin'. What's that you said about torches ? Let's have a light, an' take a squint around. I've fetched my tinder-box.'

He struck a shower of sparks, to the profound amazement of Mbeka, who shrank against Jerry, murmuring 'Kalou.'

'Never see anythin' like that in all your born days, did you, Baker ?' said Eli, with a quiet grin, as he blew the tinder into a flame and lit the torches Guy handed to him. 'My ! we won't run short o' lights, no, nor o' provender neither. I say, ain't that a pooty sight ?'

The flaring bamboos revealed not only an immense quantity of other torches, but also, in a pocket of the cave, a large number of baked pigs, piled one on top of the other.

'Fresh, too,' said Eli, sniffing gingerly at the carcases. 'I opine the owners of this yer fort had got it provisioned fer a siege, an' were cut off before they could get up,' which had indeed been the case.

'Well, aren't you going to explore, you greedy old thing ?' said Jerry, as Eli continued to poke his finger into the sides of the pigs.

'I'm makin' sure ez they reely are pigs,' answered Eli. 'You can't be too careful in this sing'ler country. However, I reckon them pigs is pigs, so we'll sample 'em by-an'-by. Lead on, Guy.'

'Where to ?' very naturally demanded Guy.

'Waal, I didn't know. I thought maybe you'd explored the place already.'

'Oh no; I went as far as the mouth of the cave, but there's no means of descending there; it's a sheer precipice to the river.'

'Waal, lead on in the other direction, but go cautious, fer you don't know what may be in front. You may run agin the owners likely ez not.'

They followed the trend of the vast cavern for perhaps fifty yards, and then Guy pulled up with an exclamation.

'There's another shaft here,' said he. 'Shall we go down ?'

'Let's have a look,' said Eli, thrusting in his torch. 'Why, yes, it's only a few feet deep. Not more 'n five, I should say.'

So it proved, and presently they stood in another cavern, the roof of which was so low that they were forced to stoop, nor was there any exit towards the river. A hundred feet farther, and they stood upon the brink of a third hole.

'I'm off,' said Guy, sliding in. 'Ah! Oh!' The cry came faintly up to them.

'Are you all right ?' Anthony called down anxiously.

'Yes; but it's the longest yet, and my torch is out. No matter; I can see daylight. Come on.'

One after the other they slid to the bottom of the shaft, and moving towards the light, found Guy standing at the mouth of the cave on a ledge of rock not three feet above the level of the river, which here formed a deep pool.

'This appears to be the end of all things,' observed
Anthony. 'There's the river, and there is a sheer
face of rock opposite. I suppose the idea is to swim
or wade farther up the stream, and so reach land
on this side or that.'

'Ain't thar nothin' at the other end, I wonder?'
said Eli; 'I'll go an' see.' He kindled a fresh torch
and went off. 'No,' he said, when he rejoined them,
'thar's nothin' but a blank wall thar. See now,
this is curious; jest above thar the river is runnin'
pooty strong; then comes this yer pool, which I
reckon must be deep, 'cause it's quite still; then,
below the pool agen the rush begins once more.
Curious, I—Hi! look at the Baker. What's got
into him?'

But a momentary consideration of the soles of the
Baker's feet was all that was possible under the
circumstances, for he had plunged head first into the
pool, and almost instantly disappeared from sight.
As he had no clothes on, the first supposition was
that the temptation of a nice cool bath had proved
too much for him, but as second after second passed
and still he did not reappear, the comrades stared at
one another in dismay, for, as the newspapers say, no
reason could be assigned for the rash act.

'Out of the road!' cried Anthony, when it became
evident that if Mbeka remained under water for
another thirty seconds he must be drowned past all
chance of restoration. 'The poor little beggar has
got caught in a snag.'

The last words were lost as, having thrown aside
his wig, he shot past them into the pool.

'He'll fetch him up; don't you fret,' said Eli

encouragingly to Jerry, who looked miserably at the water, for he had grown quite fond of the Little Bat. 'Ef he can be reached, Anthony 'll reach him.'

But this Anthony had apparently failed to do, for the widening circles met the rocks on either side and vanished, the surface of the pool resumed its ordinary quiet aspect, and still no sign of either of them.

With a cry of despair Guy joined his hands above his head, and prepared to take the fatal plunge, but Eli held him firmly back.

'Stop!' he said sternly, though his voice shook. 'Ain't it enough ez we 've lost him 'thout—Oh, thank God! thank God! thar they are!'

'Thank God!' echoed Guy. 'But what can it mean?'

'P'raps you 'll explain, one o' you,' said Eli, his tone changing to one of intense relief. 'It 'll be interestin' to know what sort o' patent bellows the Baker carries inside him that he can stay ten minutes under water, an' come up 'thout so much ez a puff, let alone his comin' up at all.'

Here the Baker burst into voluble Fijian.

'That 's all right; that 's all right,' said Eli, 'an' I b'lieve you mean no harm by it, though it sounds powerful like swearin'. But leave it to Anthony. Anthony, boy, what is it?'

'Why, the fact is,' answered Anthony slowly, and enjoying the other's perplexity, 'the fact is, there 's another series of caves in the opposite cliff, but to get to them you have to dive through this pool.'

Exclamations of astonishment burst from the three listeners.

'My land!' said Eli. 'And the Baker spotted

that. 'Cute little 'possum. That 's why he took the dive.'

'Precisely,' answered Anthony. 'And when I entered the cave, which you may suppose I was very much surprised at doing, there he was sitting on a ledge, swinging his legs, and admiring the beauties of nature through a hole in the top.'

'In the top of what ? his legs ?' demanded Jerry. '*Vinaka*, Mbeka, *Vinaka !*'

'No, stupid, in the roof,' returned Anthony, while the Baker grinned delightedly.

'Waal, I guess we owe the Baker more 'n one good turn,' said Eli. 'Jerry, that knife you gave him bought more 'n it was worth. The little cuss ! who 'd have thought he had so much sense ? While we 're standing hyar debatin' on it, in he goes head first, an' knocks the mystery gallery—west in a second. Baker, my respects t' ye.'

'Well, what are you going to do ?' asked Anthony. 'We don't want to tread water here all day.' '

'Do ! why, we 'll all come over. What else should we do ?'

'Without exploring,' said Guy. 'Isn't that rather rash ?'

'Not it. We know the way in to this yer chain o' caves, an' you bet the Baker has found the beginning of the way out. Ef I 'm wrong, thar won't be no difficulty in gitting back. Ef I 'm right, we 'll save time by going on at once. Any way, I 'm willing to chance it. I 'm going back for Whitson, Boney, an' the rest.'

'I 'll go with you,' said Guy.

'Come away then.—You others stay here till we

git back. We'll not be longer than we kin help.'

The two made their way back to the summit of the rock, and, after informing the company of their astonishing find, set about making preparations for immediate departure. Mbonavindongo, indeed, demurred at first, for, recognising the impregnability of the position, he would dearly have liked to let a little more blood with safety to himself. Eli, however, persuaded him at last by promise of a magnificent present of whales' teeth, and when the astute Mbonavindongo inquired whence they were to be forthcoming, considering the inroads which had been made upon the stock, Eli, assuming an expression of annoyance, asked whether he was still so unconvinced of the power of his white associates as to doubt that the production of a few miserable whales' teeth was a matter which would cost them a second thought, if once they set their minds to it. As a matter of fact, the wily Virginian, on his way back with Guy, had discovered a quantity of whales' teeth stored in a deep recess, and at once made up his mind to apportion as many as could conveniently be carried between himself and his comrades, keeping the Fijians for the present in ignorance of the unexpected acquisition. The discovery pleased him from another point of view, for it showed that they were again approaching the coast, which he judged could not be more than two days' march away at most.

Every one now went to work with a will. The pigs, or a good many of them, were cut up, packed with vegetables in wrappings of native cloth, tied with sinnet, and distributed among the men; the

barrels of the muskets were firmly plugged, and the
locks and supplies of ammunition protected against
the action of the water, and at last everything
was ready. As a final precaution Eli determined to blind the entrance to the caves as far
as possible, and to that end hurriedly lashed a
number of bamboo rods together so as to form a
tray, upon which he piled a quantity of vegetables.
Then setting the tray partially over the mouth of
the hole, he slipped through, steadied himself as with
an upward heave of his hand he adjusted the cover,
and slid rapidly down to join the company, whom he
found waiting for him on the lowest corridor.

Meantime matters had not been standing still upon
the other side. Recognising the hopelessness of an
attack upon the fort from the side of the spur,
Larkin had set his wits to work to discover some
means by which he might dislodge his enemies.
Finding none, he determined upon a cautious recon-
naissance on the side overhanging the river, the
lower half of which was concealed from his view by
an enormous boulder, which had fallen to the opposite bank in such a way as to form a mighty arch,
beneath which the river rushed on its way to the
sea. With some difficulty he scaled this, helped by
the trees which jutted out from the steep cliff at its
side, and after an upward glance to assure himself
that he could not be observed from the fort, cast
himself flat upon it, and, peering cautiously over the
edge, commenced his survey.

A moment served to show him that if the descent
of that sheer face was impossible for the fugitives, so
also was ascent for him, and with a muttered execra-

tion at the ingenuity of nature, he was preparing to withdraw, when his attention was suddenly arrested by a yellow gleam some eighty yards up stream. It was in fact Anthony's head from which, it will be remembered, he had removed the wig, and the contrast was sufficiently striking between the flaxen hair and the now piebald face and body, for the bath of which Anthony was making the most had removed not a little of the black paint.

'By all that's wonderful, it is young Hawkins,' muttered Larkin. 'How in the world does he come to be there? There must be a way down after all; and if a way down, then a way up. No matter; that can come later. Meantime, as a bird in the hand is worth two in the bush'—— He threw forward his musket with a sinister smile.

Already his eye glanced along the barrel, and his finger pressed the trigger, when Anthony suddenly flung his hands up above his head, and sank like a stone.

'Diving, are you, my fine fellow,' said Larkin to himself. 'I'll be ready for you when you reappear.' The next moment the musket dropped unheeded upon the rock, and an expression of unbounded amazement stole over his face.

Out, apparently, from the solid face of the cliff sprang head first a lithe black figure, and disappeared beneath the water. Another, another, then another with a head of fiery red hair. Another and yet another until he had counted fifty-seven. And the astonishing part of it was that not one of them came to the surface again after taking the dive.

'Well,' exclaimed Larkin, sitting bolt upright,

R

'that is the most singular case of *felo de se* I ever saw in all my days, and I 've seen some odd ones at the Settlement.'

He mused for some time, staring at the pool, now grown quiet again. Then a shrill sound between a whistle and a scream escaped his lips, and with gleaming eyes he started to his feet.

'By Jove!' he cried as he scrambled down the boulder. 'Every man of them carried a bundle of some sort at his back.'

CHAPTER XXI

'TWIXT CONVICT AND CANNIBAL.

ONE by one the fugitives, sinking to the bottom of the pool, found the submerged entrance to the cave, and, passing through, rose up to the ledge upon which Mbeka capered, proud of his success as a pioneer. As they moved along, splashing through a thin stream of water, which barely reached their ankles, the light which streamed through a jagged hole in the roof showed them that they were in an enormous vaulted chamber, almost circular, and with, so far as they could see, no outlet except that ragged rent above. Afar off, however, the sound of water musically trickling over different levels of rock could distinctly be heard, showing that, narrow though it might prove to be, there was indeed a way somewhere ahead. The novelty of the situation pleased the light-hearted Fijians, who sang, and jabbered, and shouted, laughing merrily and exchanging broad jests at the expense of the enemy whom they supposed they had outwitted, while the practical Eli, rapidly unrolling the cloth which covered a bundle of bamboo torches, kindled several, and handing them to his comrades, moved in advance to explore the position of affairs.

'This place has been used before,' he remarked to Whitson, pointing to the charred fragment of a torch which lay upon the ledge, 'so I guess thar's a way out. I 'magine we can't go fur wrong ef we foller up this stream, that is, ef the water-way don't narrow to sech an extent ez to stop us. See whar it comes tricklin' over yonder shelf. Thar's a cleft thar. Wonder ef it's wide enough to squeeze through.'

'That is easily settled,' said Anthony, swinging himself up. 'If I don't stick, neither will any one else. Ha! it is a squeeze. No, only just at the entrance. Now I am in a long passage or what appears to be so, and I should say that it led into the open air, for a faint light is streaming in from the opposite end.'

'How long is it?' inquired Eli.

'I can't say. It might be twenty yards, or fifty, or a hundred; the gloom is deceptive.'

'So. Well, take a walk along and find out. Stay, hyar's a torch, and mind you keep a sharp lookout fer holes under foot.'

In a few minutes Anthony was back again.

'Come on,' he cried, 'it is all clear. The passage is about eighty yards long, and leads out into open, hilly country.'

'Any cover?' asked Eli.

'Plenty; many of the hills are covered with forest.'

'Good! Pass the word along the line to close up an' make tracks for the outer world. And, Faatu, ask Boney to git his men to stop that din. It's enough to bring the roof down upon us. Let 'em

keep their hollerin' till they're out o' the wood.—
Ha!' as he emerged into the outer air, 'is this what
you call open country, Anthony? I've a notion you
might call it pretty close.'

'Why, it is open enough for five miles or so,'
argued Anthony; 'then, I admit, comes a barrier of
high hills, which we '——

'Must cross,' interrupted Eli. 'Hyar, let's git the
compass an' take our bearin's. West-south-west is
whar we're lookin'. Waal, I guess that ought to
fetch us to the sea, which, ef we've good-luck, won't
be far from the other side of yonder range.'

'And then hurrah for home!' cried Jerry.

'Right, boyee, an' I wish you were thar,' said Eli,
patting his head. 'We ain't had too much to com-
plain of so fur, though we've had some narrer shaves;
but now we've shaken off that pesky critter, Larkin,
thank the Lord, I jedge we've about seen the worst
of it.—Boney, my respects t' ye.—What is he saying,
Faatu?'

'Him say time for b'ekfus,' expounded Faatu, with
an emphasis which showed that he was quite of
Mbonavindongo's opinion.

'And I agree with him,' cried Jerry; 'the bit of
pig I've got at my back is working through my
shoulders, so anxious is it to get inside.'

'Waal, start in an eat ez you go along,' laughed Eli;
'but we daren't think o' a halt until we reach that
range on the other side o' Anthony's open country.—
Come, Boney, thar's no use lookin' glum. You've
carried a bright face so fur, an' you might as well
keep it up till the end. Thar, that's right, chief;
I knew you wouldn't go back on us now.'

'I 'll sing him a song,' said Jerry; 'that will keep
him in a good-humour;' and, attaching himself to
Mbonavindongo, he tuned up and piped lustily as they
marched along between and over the low rolling
hills that led to the long range.

The sun had passed the zenith before they reached
the foot of the mountains, and, though there were not
a few discontented faces, yet at Eli's earnest request, they did not pause till they had reached the
summit of the first, whence the American hoped to
obtain a view, however distant, of the sea. But he
was doomed to disappointment; for upon the farther
side of a narrow valley rose another hill of equal
height to that upon which they stood, and reluctantly
he called a halt.

It was no light matter to get the Fijians to proceed after their meal; but at last, after a rest of nearly
three hours, the company resumed their march, and
after descending into the valley, began stoutly to
breast the opposite hill.

'It is not unlike Australia hereabouts,' said
Guy, as he tramped through the long grass, and
glanced at the scattered clumps of casuarinas, or
noko nokos, as the Fijians called them, which, with
the acacias and magnolias, dotted the sides of the
hill.

'I 'm sure I wish it was Australia,' sighed Jerry, as
he puffed along, striving to digest his dinner of pork
and yams.   'Oh dear, there 's another of those
terrible hills.'

'I dare say you find pig inside rather heavier than
pig outside,' chaffed Anthony. 'At the same time, a
little reducing won't do you any harm.'

'A little!' groaned Jerry; 'if this sort of heave up and jolt down is to go on much longer, I shall dissolve entirely, so I will.'

'Well, we'll pop your liquid remains into a Fiji bottle if you do, and take every care of them,' promised Guy. 'I tell you what it is, though, Eli, we shall require a new coat of paint at the end of this day's march. Either that or a complete riddance of the old one. I feel in a dreadful mess.'

'An' you look it,' observed Eli suavely. 'However, I jedge we're all in the same boat ez fur ez that goes; so let us hope we'll shake hands with old Daddy Neptune before long. By time! leavin' me out o' the count, he reely ought to do suthin' fer the lot o' you, seein' him an' Mrs Britannia is sech friends.'

'Heigho!' sighed Anthony, as they touched another summit; 'another to go down, another to go up. When will this end?'

'Jest when you least expect it,' said Eli; 'so keep a good heart, boyee, for it ain't in the natur' o' things ez this can last much longer.'

Prophetic words! Painfully, toilsomely, puffing, panting, sighing, groaning, they dragged themselves up the steep grass-grown hill, Mbonavindongo, his *Mata*, and Faatu leading, with Jerry, who, for all his lamentations, still trudged on sturdily, not far behind. With a gasp of relief the Naitasirian chief planted his *titoko*, or alpenstock, upon a broad ledge above him, and wearily heaved himself up. In another instant he stood upon the summit, and his fatigue dropped from him as a garment. Forgetting his royal dignity in his excitement, he cut a caper, exclaiming at the top of his voice, while his broad face beamed with

satisfaction: '*Sara sara! kusa kusa!*'   (Look! look!
Be quick!)

Inspired by the shout, the others hurried after him,
crowding to the top of the hill.

What a sight met their delighted eyes! Immediately below them, from the foot of the hill onwards,
stretched a narrow plain, perhaps half a mile wide,
with one solitary tree-crowned mound rising out of
it, not far from its farthest limit. Innumerable
patches of cultivated land, crowds of men, women, and
children walking hither and thither, working in the
fields or playing at games, and a dense cluster of
queer-looking houses on the left hand, all denoted a
thriving and populous town. But beyond! A great
blaze of splendour! A far-spreading, interminable
golden glory, that rolled, and tossed, and rippled from
beneath the great yellow sun, whose lower border just
touched the distant horizon, past the encircling reef
with its endless shower of rainbow drops to the very
edge of the long strip of dazzling white coral sand
that fringed the plain. And at that gracious sight
a long, loud shout of gladness pealed from every
throat. 'The sea! the sea! the sea!' Jerry cast
himself down upon the ground and sprawled for very
joy.

'Well, by this and by that,' he cried, 'if Xenophon
and his old Greeks that plagued me so much just before
we started for Broken Bay were half as glad to come
upon the sea as I am now, I forgive them all the
worry and botheration they caused me, so I do.'

'It's an inspirin' sight,' said Eli; 'but I'd no idee
we were so close. I'd have said it was another day's
journey off ef you'd asked me.'

'Let us go down,' cried impetuous Anthony. 'Look at the canoes drawn up on the beach—scores of them.'

Guy was silent. He stood somewhat apart with Whitson, whose furrowed weather-beaten face worked strongly, looking with earnest eyes beyond the golden pathway, above the glowing sun, into the great crimson and purple cloud masses piled up in the western sky. His face shone in the light of the departing sun, and though his lips moved, no sound came from them.

Catching sight of his expression, Anthony and Jerry hushed their clamour, and Eli, looking round the group, said solemnly :

'Boys, Guy is right. We 've all been mighty keen about askin' fer what we wanted ; an' now we 've got it, don't let us fergit to be thankful.'

Silence fell upon them all for a few moments, and then Eli, observing a stir among the Fijians, turned and stared curiously at them.

Mbonavindongo, the *Mata*, and another chief walked together towards a little mound some forty paces away, and with a good deal of ceremony set thereon a piece of pork, a yam or two, and a small bit of *yangona* root. Then they rejoined their comrades.

'What is that for, Faatu ? ' inquired Eli sharply.

'Mbonavindongo make um *soro* (offering) to god 'cause him glad him got here. Oh yis, him fery glad,' replied the Tongan, adding on his own account, 'So am me.'

Eli glanced at Anthony, who reddened between his streaks of black. ' By time ! he exclaimed, ' I never thought ez I 'd live to be taught my dooty by a

cannibal chief. Boys, thar ain't no place so dark ez
the Lord ha'n't let a little light shine into it. That's
my belief anyhow.'

'Well, what are we to do?' asked Anthony, after a
pause, during which the sun sank majestically into the
sea. 'It will be dark in a few moments. Are we to
go down to-night or not?'

'Let's hear what Boney has to say,' answered Eli.
'I'm agin it myself, seein' ez we don't know how
we'd be received. But let the chief decide.'

'No,' said Mbonavindongo, when the question had
been submitted to him; 'to-morrow will be soon
enough. They are many and we are few. When the
day dawns, and the king has drunk his *yangona*, then
I will send messengers with a gift, and pray him
to receive us. Were we to come suddenly upon them
in the night, they would certainly slay us, and we
should have to be slain, for, ha! they are many and
we are very few.'

'Right,' agreed Eli. 'I thought so myself; but I
didn't want to disappoint you, Anthony.'

'Oh, I'm content,' said Anthony. 'Here we are,
and there's the sea. A few hours more or less don't
matter. It was a bath I was thinking about. As
soon as the messengers return in the morning I shall
go and have a dip. What a relief it will be to get
this filthy stuff off one's body.'

'It is well,' said Mbonavindongo, when the decision
had been conveyed to him. 'And now, since we are
all very tired, let us build a fire to keep off the
spirits, brew a bowl of *yangona*, and take our sleep
from the bosom of the gods.'

'But hold on,' demurred Eli; 'if we build a fire,

maybe the people of the plain 'll take a notion to
come an' stir us up.'

'Pho! not they,' said Mbonavindongo, with unconscious contempt for the superstitions of his own race.
'They will think we are the *luve ni wai* (children of
the waters), and be glad enough to let us alone.
Besides, you have your clubs. Speak to them with
those, and if they come, they will go down again fast
enough.'

'That's likely,' returned Eli ; 'but we don't want
it to come to that.   Have it your own way, though.'

The fire was lit, and the simple supper prepared,
and though the whites were at first loth to partake of
the nauseous *yangona*, politeness compelled them to
accept the cup presented to them, and they were
agreeably surprised at the fillip the drug gave to their
tired nerves.

The night was divided into short watches of two
hours apiece, of which Eli took the first and the last,
and when shortly after dawn he heard afar on the
plain the faint cry of the king's herald, '*Yangona!*'
he roused Mbonavindongo, and requested him to in-
struct the messengers while he prepared the gift,
which consisted of two whales' teeth, a strong clasp
knife, and a *yangona* root.

They waited until the shout of the people, rolling
through the town from end to end, proclaimed that
the king had drunk his morning bowl, and then,
standing together upon the summit of the hill,
watched the messengers depart upon their errand.
They had no doubt as to the result, for, in addition
to the valuable presents entrusted to them, the
heralds had been instructed by Mbonavindongo to

make promise of even greater things when the favour
for which they craved had been granted.

Meantime, the watchers on the hill calmly ate their
breakfast, which bore a remarkable and not too
pleasing resemblance to their dinner of the day before
and their supper of the previous night.

But what was their surprise and dismay as they
slowly munched, keeping their eyes upon the *rara*,
where the king, surrounded by his courtiers, had
received the heralds, to see one of the latter suddenly
stricken to the ground by a heavy stroke with a club,
while the other, breaking through the angry crowd,
who struck furiously at his body, ran back at top
speed towards the mountain. He was not followed,
and at last he reached the summit, out of breath, and
bruised and bleeding from the rough treatment he
had received.

'How now! Would the king not hear you ? Are
the men of Mbau before us ? ' asked Mbonavindongo,
who, though very angry, did not seem at all surprised.

'Not so,' panted the herald. 'They are ignorant
fools who have never even heard of Naitasiri, much
less of Mbau. We had but begun our message when
the king cried out: "Where is Naitasiri ? Where is
Mbau ? Who are the men of one or the other that I
should be troubled with their quarrels ? These are
they of whom the priests prophesied last night when
the *luve ni wai* were gathered together on the
mountain. We knew there was mischief in the air,
but the people of Koro Dabea (Eel-town) are wise,
and know that whoso sheds the first blood shall be
the victors. Wherefore slay me one of those fellows,

dash his head against the great stone of the *Mbure
ni Kalou*, and bake him straightway. Let the other
return to them that sent him, and tell them to go
back the way they came, or to come down and be
eaten." So Na Visako they slew, but me they allowed
to return.'

Mbonavindongo's eyes flashed. 'Said he so?' he
cried. 'Then by the bones of those I have eaten
I swear I will eat him too. How is he called, this
king of Koro Dabea?'

'Na Kende Kende' (the Mountain), was the reply.

Mbonavindongo advanced a step, and shook his club
in the direction of the town.

'Na Kende Kende, Tui ni na Koro Dabea,' he
screamed, 'I will come down and beat you, mountain
that you are, until you are as flat as the plain upon
which you stand.' The conceit pleased him, and he
turned to Eli with a grin. 'At the same time,' he
said through Faatu, 'I don't see how I am going to
do it.'

'Same here,' assented Eli. 'I 'magine the only
thing to be done is to move a bit east or west, an'
look fer a more accommodatin' Tui. This one's
breakfast has disagreed with him, I guess.'

'What a pity,' said Guy disconsolately. 'Such fine
canoes to choose from, and such a beautiful beach.
Never mind. Better luck next time. I've no fancy
for going down there to be eaten.'

'Look! Oh, look!' cried Jerry. 'I do believe it
is—Oh! if it should be!'

Every one turned and followed his pointing finger.
Down the long hill behind them, the last they had
descended on that weary march yesterday, wound a

long black column, which even now was half way to the valley.

Eli took a long look. 'My land, it's him got on our track, after all,' he exclaimed at last. 'Boys, git your guns ready, fer down into that town we must go. We're 'twixt convict and cannibal now, and no mistake.'

CHAPTER XXII.

'TWIXT convict and cannibal!' The harsh syllables grated upon the ears of the listeners. What was to be done? Instinctively all eyes were turned upon Eli, and even Mbonavindongo, though nominally the leader of the expedition, held up his hand to stop the excited jabber of his men, and looked expectantly at the Virginian, ready to receive his opinion as to what was to be done.

Eli took the plug of tobacco from his haversack, slowly bit off a piece, chewed it thoughtfully for three or four minutes, turned it in his cheek, and finally repeated his first opinion, 'We must go down.'

'Yes,' he went on; 'thar's no help fer it. To stay hyar is to be chawed up sure and certain. Thar's five hundred comin' on behind us, an' thar's five hundred, or more, I should say, waitin' fer us in front. But the five hundred behind know what to expect, an' they'll come on, spite o' all we can do, wharas the five hundred in front don't know what we have in store for 'em, an' they'll give back—that is, at first. An' when they give back we must rush the

canoes and grab one or two, accordin' to size.   I
should judge by our own performance yesterday that
it will be two hours before Larkin sets foot upon the
plain, maybe less.   Anyhow, we've got to start at
once an' try our luck.'

'I hope we shall be able to avoid a collision with
the men of Koro Dabea,' said Guy.   'They have
never done us any harm.'

'Waal, they're quite ready to begin to do it now,'
said Eli drily, while Faatu rapidly translated his
remarks to Mbonavindongo, who nodded approval.
'See hyar, boys, thar must be no half measures now,
no firin' overhead or sech like.   If we have to draw
trigger, an' I jedge it'll come to that, every bullet
must be sent home.   The niggers on the plain will
likely be frightened at the row, I grant ye; but ef no
one's hurt it's not in reason to suppose they won't
git over their fright mighty quick, an' then it's all
Verginny to a cob o' corn we never git a chance o'
gittin' through.   I don't feel we're called upon to
throw our lives away.   We didn't bring this situation
on ourselves, and sence thar's only one way out o' it,
why, I reckon that's the way we're bound to take.'

'Right!' exclaimed Anthony.   'Let us stop talking
and move forward.'

'Hold on,' said Eli quietly.   'Thar's no sense in
hurryin'.   Either we'll git to them canoes at the first
rush, or we'll not git to them at all, fer thar's jest
a chance they may not give back.   Wharfore, it's fer
us to look ahead an' study the next move ef they
don't.—Faatu, pay partic'ler attention to what I say,
an' let Boney have it ez I go along.   We will go down
the hill in column, steadily an' quietly, no rushin' an'

no howlin'. We four whites will march abreast in
advance, with Faatu alongside, in case a word will do
instead o' a blow. At an interval of ten paces will
march Boney and his men, two deep, which 'll make
'em look more than they are. Mind, thar 's to be no
shoutin' or cussin', or *boley-boleyin*',* no insultin' o'
the Eel-towners, fer that 's sure to bring on the fuss.
Faatu will take the word from me, an' ef they won't
hear reason, the attack will be begun by us. Ef they
scatter an' give back, which please the Lord they will,
Boney an' his men will rush the canoes an git .'em
launched, while we whites face about an' cover the
movement. Ef they don't give back, we must hold
'em off the best way we kin, march up to that wooded
hill or mound, an' make a stand thar. It will be the
best thing we kin do. Now, is all cl'ar ? '

'Perfectly,' exclaimed his auditors, while Mbonavindongo, who with Faatu's help had closely followed
every word, nodded his head and gave utterance to
an emphatic ' *Vinaka !* '

'Wait a minute,' cried Jerry. 'I don't see where
I come in.'

'Jerry, my dear,' said Eli, looking wistfully at
him, ' seein' we 're tryin to do the best we kin fer
you, you 'll be a good boy, an' give no more trouble
than you kin help. Give up your musket to Faatu
along with your haversack an' ammunition, an' you
an' the Baker set yourselves in the very middle o' the
Fiji men. You 'll be safe thar to start with, an' ef it
comes to a real fuss, trust us to look after you while
the breath is in our bodies. Come now, Jerry.'

'But,' began the boy with a very mutinous expres-

---

* *Bole-bole.* Fijian, ' to challenge.'

sion of face, and then choked back the words upon
his lips, and handed his musket to Faatu.

'Thar, I know'd you would,' said Eli, beaming
upon him. 'You're high-sperrited an' all, but——
By time! I'll give you suthin' to do ez'll keep you
from feelin' so much out o' the game.'

He seized an axe, and, felling a couple of light
saplings with a few blows, rapidly lopped off the
branches and twigs, and taking the British and
American ensigns from the bag in which they were,
fixed them on to the poles.

'Thar,' he said, handing the proud red-white-and-
blue to Jerry, 'old England'll be safe in your hands,
I guess, while——hyar Baker, you kin hev the honour
an' glory o' upholdin' Uncle Sam.——Form up, boys!'
He threw a glance at the long winding column upon
the hill behind them. 'Larkin an' his gang hev
almost reached the valley. Ready? Forward! Not
a sound now! March!'

Down the long hill they stepped in the order
arranged, the vanguard looking to the priming of
their muskets, the column of Fijians trembling with
excitement, and longing, though not daring, to break
out into their accustomed shouts and yells; while, set
in the midst of them, Jerry and Mbeka, stepping
proudly forward, waved their brilliant ensigns in
the morning breeze.

No sooner had they started than a considerable
stir began among the men of Koro Dabea, who had
been watching intently from below. Numbers of
them darted into their houses, to reappear presently
with their faces and breasts hastily daubed with
war paint, and bearing their most tried and trusty

weapons in their hands. The chief Kende Kende took somewhat longer, and it was not until the column had reached the foot of the hill, and begun to advance over the plain that he issued from his house, a very embodiment of the pomp and circumstance of glorious war. His face was barred, black, white, and red stripes alternating; his elbows and knees were encircled with bunches of coloured grasses and twisted vines; his gauzy *sala*, newly adjusted for the occasion, shone in snowy whiteness above his terrific countenance, and his robe of gray figured *masi*, instead of trailing behind him, was caught up gracefully over his right shoulder, and passed from back to front under his left armpit. In his left hand he waved his great war fan, made from the leaf of the *niu viu*, the palm sacred to the chiefs, and in his right he bore without effort his enormous battle club, the head of which was painted an ominous red. He cast a glance at the advancing column, the T-shaped form of which evidently puzzled him, as did the gaudy banners in its midst, and then in a few words made his dispositions to resist the attack, arranging his forces in three rude squares, one upon each wing and the third in the centre, where he stationed himself with his *Mata* and personal bodyguard.

'Who are these that come here in this silent fashion?' he inquired of his *Mata*, Na Mbandira. 'Are they all dumb men, or have they lost their tongues by reason of the fear which fills their hearts? Shout and see if they are deaf as well as dumb. At this the Dabeans set up a terrible howling, but the men of Naitasiri, faithful to their chief's command,

came on in silence till but fifty yards separated them
from their foes.

'Halt!' cried Eli suddenly; and the column came
to a stand-still.

'Now Faatu, speak,' said Eli, 'and be quick about
it.'

Stepping a pace to the front, Faatu began: 'O
Kende Kende,' he said, 'behold we come in peace, if
you will have peace. But if you choose war, you
shall have it in plenty, and more than you desire:
for there be men here who come from a far country,
and they carry in their hands strange and terrible
clubs that will speak when they bid them, and whenever they open their mouths a man will fall dead.
But they do not wish to speak or to harm you.
Therefore let them pass and give them canoes, and
they will pay you well with whales' teeth, and
knives, and axes of a kind you know not, and
perhaps they will give you one of the talking clubs, and so shall you have power over your
enemies. But if you will not hearken, or if you
try to stop them, then they will grow very angry,
and they will let their clubs talk to you, and they
will sweep you into the arms of death, and the
road to Mbulu * shall be filled with your spirits,
and the land which is yours shall know you no
more.'

To this not over-pacific speech the *Mata* made
haste to reply on behalf of Kende Kende. 'Who are
you?' he cried. 'Who are you that boast so loud
with a tongue that sounds strange in our ears, and is
hard to understand? Are you gods that you stand

* The Fijian abode of the dead.

there, you few, and dare the warriors of Na Koro
Dabea? Behold we will not let you go. As for
your tale of clubs that talk, it is a lie. We will send
your spirits on the road to Mbulu; but your bodies,
ha! those we will bake and eat, and to-night there
shall be feasting in Koro Dabea. Forward! Dabeans,
and sweep these boasters from in front of you. See
how few they are. Ha! They will not give so
much trouble as would a drove of pigs. Upon
them!'

Faatu stepped hastily backwards, knowing what
was coming, and while the centre remained stationary,
the two wings with resounding yells sprang to the
charge.

'Fire with me, Anthony and Whitson,' shouted
Eli. 'Faatu and Guy, reserve your shots till we
have reloaded, if thar's time. Ready! Present!'

Right and left the Dabeans came on, each wing
led by a party of so-called 'invulnerables,' who,
waving large fans and brandishing their clubs, dashed
confidently on.

'Fire!'

A stream of flame, three sharp reports, and down
went three 'invulnerables' never to rise again.

A yell of terror broke from the opposing host.
Like a snow-flake in the sunshine the centre melted
away, and tumbling over one another in their eager-
ness to escape, the warriors of the wings checked
their headlong rush, and, turning, fled after their
bewildered and disheartened chief.

'Hurrah!' roared Eli. Then, as he saw what was
going forward: 'By heaven! We are lost! They
have taken to the canoes!'

It was too true. Frightened almost out of his senses, but yet retaining sufficient presence of mind to realise that his safest course would be to place as great a distance as he possibly could between himself and these mysterious strangers, who slew men afar off without themselves moving from their places, Kende Kende, followed by his screaming, terror-stricken subjects, raced madly to the beach. Scores of willing hands, strengthened by fear, seized the canoes and ran them into the water, and before the men of Naitasiri had fairly realised what was happening, the canoes one and all were afloat, crowded with yelling, jabbering Dabeans, who, with swift, unsteady strokes sent them spinning out upon the sparkling waves. With something like despair at his heart, Eli swung round and glanced at the mountain behind them. As yet no sign of Larkin and his company. Was it possible that they had halted in the valley to rest, ignorant of how near they were to their prey? It was just possible. But then the shots. In that clear air the sound would travel an immense distance, and they would surely be heard. At all events, what was to be done? Right or left they did not dare to go, for they knew not with what opposition they might be met, and the pursuit would be too hot. But one refuge remained—the wooded mound. There they would make their last stand, and there they would, if it must be, die. Eli raised his musket, and with it pointed to the hill. 'Make for that, O Mbonavindongo,' he cried, 'and bid your men be silent still; for it may be that we have not been heard. Tell him, Faatu, quick!'

He set off at a run, followed by the entire com-

pany, some few of whom stayed to raise the bodies of
the slain Dabeans and bring them along.   Guessing
the dreadful purpose that underlay this, Guy swerved
and made towards them; but Eli darted after him
and dragged him forcibly back.

'Let 'em alone,' he said.   'It's horrible, I admit;
but we can't help it.   Ef they choose to eat 'em they
must eat 'em, an' we daren't say 'em nay.   To offend
'em, to fall out with 'em now means death.   Come
on, an' put your feelings in your pocket.'

A great noise of lamentation arose as they swept
through the town, for the women and children and
the old men, cowering in the houses, expected nothing else than instant death.   But no one paid any
heed to them, and when presently, surprised at finding themselves unmolested, they stole to the doors and
peeped out, a ringing measured sound held their
attention fixed, and the silence of a great fear fell
upon them, so that they could neither speak nor cry
out, for, awful desecration, the strangers were cutting
down the sacred grove of Ndengei.   Certainly
Mbonavindongo did not know that the grove was
sacred to Ndengei, or he would have shrunk in
horror from the sacrilege; but if he thought about
the matter at all he probably imagined that the place
was the abode of the tutelary deity, who, considering
the poor care he had taken of his worshippers, was
entitled to nothing but contempt.   At all events he
offered no objection when at Eli's orders the half
dozen axemen among the company began to chop
vigorously right and left, felling the slender trees,
while the others dragged the severed trunks into
position to form a barricade or breastwork from

behind which the white men might deliver their fire. Although when all was done it was a poor affair, yet bad as it was, it was the best they could hope for under the circumstances, and with such scant time at their disposal.

The *Mbure ni kalou*, which stood in the centre of the grove, was a curious building with low walls and a most disproportionately tall sugar-loaf-shaped roof, at right angles to the apex of whose cone projected on both sides a long ridge-pole of carved wood. The house itself was reared upon a mound of stones about twelve feet high, at the top of which was a circular ledge 'or platform three or four feet wide. Four narrow, notched planks, dividing the mound into as many triangles, formed the means of ascent to the *Mbure*, the strategic value of which Eli had recognised at a glance.

The barricade of logs was so arranged as to form a complete, though small, circle round the mound, and the Fijians were still busily employed in strengthening it with earth and lopped branches when Eli, who, puzzled by the non-appearance of Larkin's force, had turned his attention to the Dabeans, uttered an exclamation of surprise.

'They've got over their fright and are coming back,' he cried.

It was true. Furious at this wholesale desecration of the temple of their god, the Dabeans, though by no means liking the task, had determined to return and make a vigorous effort to dislodge the bold intruders. They felt a sense of shame, too, at having allowed themselves to be so easily routed by so very few, and burned to wipe out the stain upon their

honour. Certainly the strangers were possessed of
some wonderful weapons, but they were but men
after all, and not gods, else why did they show fear
and make those elaborate preparations for defence?
At any rate Na Kende Kende resolved to have
another bout with them, and this time it should not
be his fault if he came off second best. So he gave
the order to turn the prows of the canoes towards
the shore, and presently formed his men in battle
array upon the beach, leaving a certain number
in the canoes in case a second retreat became necessary. Scarcely had he done so when the crest of
the mountain became suddenly black with men.

'Hyar they come!' shouted Eli; 'an' ez ef that
warn't enough, them pesky critters on the beach is
goin' to rush us. No matter. Let 'em come. We'll
give 'em beans.—Faatu, run up the flags.—Up to
the house, Guy, with Jerry an' the Baker. Keep
Faatu with you, an' you an' him loophole the place
in case we have to come up. Fire from the platform
when you git the chance.'

The boys obeyed, while Faatu, scaling the roof of
the *Mbure*, planted a flagstaff upon each side of
the apex of the thatch.

Eli ran hither and thither, posting his men advan-
tageously behind the barricades; while the Naitasirians,
loosed from the obnoxious prohibition, yelled defiance
indiscriminately at the men of Dabea and Mbau;
though, so far as the latter were concerned, they
might have saved their breath, for they were too far
off to hear.

The Dabeans heard though, and stayed their advance. Who were these men, pouring down the

mountain side? Were they friends or foes? They would go and see. Was all the world to be allowed to come tramping through Dabea with never a check? Certainly not. So, turning their backs upon the desecrated grove for the moment, they hurried over the plain to meet the new-comers.

'Hurrah!' shouted Anthony when he saw this. 'Set a thief to catch a thief. Eh, Eli?'

'I reckon,' said Eli with a quiet grin. 'Now thar'll be doin's.'

There were. As they touched the plain, the Mbauans closed up, and with the white men concealed in their midst, advanced rapidly.

On their part the Dabeans moved slowly, the *Mata* rehearsing great swelling words in which to address the strangers and demand the purpose of their coming. But ere the opportunity arose the compact column in his front opened out, disclosing the grim line of white men, with muskets levelled.

At this unexpected sight the Dabeans came to a sudden halt, rooted to the spot with horror; and before they could recover their wits, the rolling volley crashed, the men of Mbau broke into a run, and in a moment all was mad strife and conflict.

The rally was short and sharp. The watchers at the fort beheld a wild commotion of tumultuously waving arms, spears flying, and clubs rising and falling, and then, as by mutual consent, the contending bodies separated, recoiled in opposite directions, and stood still, glaring at one another.

Only for a moment, and then as the deadly rattle of musketry sounded again and the venomous bullets

found their billets or clove the air overhead with angry
'wheep!' the miserable Dabeans turned tail, and
fled headlong towards the beach, hotly pursued by
the Mbauans, whose blood was up and who gave
short shrift to any unfortunate whom they over-
took.

In rear of the pursuit, the white men moved along
at the double, and to his immense satisfaction Eli
saw as they came nearer that the opening act of
the combat had reduced their number to sixteen.

'D' you see how it is, boys?' he cried. 'That
Larkin has overreached himself this time an' jumped
to the conclusion that we had j'ined that mob. Wait
till he ketches sight o' the flags an' he 'll give us a
turn. No matter. They 're only four to one now,
an' who cares for niggers?'

'Here they come,' said Anthony. 'Let us give
them a volley as they go by. We may get rid of
two or three more that way.'

'You 're right,' answered Eli. 'Nothin' like strikin'
the first blow. Ready above there, Guy?'

'Yes,' replied Guy, as with pale face and compressed
lips he jerked his musket to his shoulder.

On they came, pursuers and pursued, sweeping
through the town in a wild skurry, the white men
trotting in the rear, their muskets at the trail, and
all laughing and talking, and unconscious of the
danger on their left, till just as they came abreast of
the mound, an appalling yell burst from the Naitasirians, five muskets cracked almost simultaneously,
and two of the convicts fell upon their faces, dead.

With a shout of wrath, the rest swung round, and,
seeing whence the attack had come, poured in their

fire, and hastened after their black allies to get out of range and consult upon this new development.

'Bad shootin' all round,' growled Eli.   'We ought to hev got two more anyway.'

'Just as well for us they were flurried,' said Anthony, holding up his musket to show where a bullet had glanced off the stock.   'Look at that.'

'And look at that!' shrieked Guy.   'Stop him! Stop him!'

But before any one could attempt to do so, or even had time to realise his intention, Jerry, with Mbeka hard behind him, had slid down from the *Mbure*, leaped the slight barricade, and rushing to where the dead convicts lay, caught up their arms and ammunition, and was back in the fort in a twinkling.

'I didn't see why I should stay up there to be shot,' he said coolly, as he rapidly loaded both muskets.   'That's as good as two more men to you. I'll load while you fire.'

'You imp!' exclaimed Eli admiringly.   He had no time to say more, for a loud yell announced that the next act of the tragedy had begun.

It was entirely unexpected.   Seeing the terrific charge of the Mbauans, and mindful only of their own safety, the men in the canoes had poled rapidly away from the shore, deaf to the cries of their panic-stricken friends, who, finding their retreat thus summarily cut off, had no resource but to turn and make a desperate stand upon the beach.   In another moment the battle would have begun again, when Larkin, who at the fire from the fort had leaped to a conclusion, and this time the right one, roared to Palavali, the Tongan, to order a halt.

'Stop them!' he shouted. 'We are fighting our
friends. Stop them!'

But it was no easy matter to balk the Mbauans of
their prey, and it was only when Larkin, at the
imminent risk of his own life, sprang between them
and the cowering Dabeans that they fell back, growl-
ing angrily.

'Tell them we are sorry,' shouted Larkin, well-
nigh beside himself with excitement. 'There are
the men who have caused all the trouble. There in
that fort. Let us make common cause and sweep
them away. Afterwards the men of Mbau will make
atonement for their mistake.'

It did not take the astute Kende Kende long to
grasp the facts as thus presented. He was very angry,
but he was still more badly frightened. To escape
upon such easy terms was a delightful surprise. With
a face that beamed with satisfaction, he intimated his
entire concurrence with the views of the white chief,
and with shouts and cries, his followers merged themselves in the still sullen and wrathful men of Mbau,
whose opinion was that they could quite well have
finished off the Dabeans first and stormed the fort
afterwards.

Sweeping forward in two long curving lines, with
the white men ten paces in the rear, the united forces
came on at the double, but when within a hundred
yards of the fort they slowed down to a walk.

'Look out!' called Eli. 'The centre will open
presently to let the whites fire. Be ready, and the
moment it does, let drive all together and lie down
flat.'

Bang! A solitary shot rang out from the *Mbure*

and the man next to Larkin flung up his arms and pitched heavily to the ground.

'I've done it,' muttered Guy through his set teeth, and, sliding down from the platform just in time to escape half-a-dozen bullets fired at him, tossed his empty musket to Jerry and caught up a loaded one.

'Bullee!' cried Eli. 'That drawed some o' their teeth. Look out! Fire!'

Bang! Rattle! Crash! Volley from above and volley from below rang out together. Three of the Mbauans fell, and one of the convicts sprawled on the ground with a broken leg.

With a groan Whitson fell upon his back and lay still; while Guy, staggering to a log, sat down and began feebly to wipe away the blood that poured down his face from a graze along the scalp.

'Good land!' began Eli; but Guy sprang to his feet. 'I'm not hurt,' he cried. 'Look out! Here they come!' Then he spun round and fell full length upon the ground as the Mbauans dashed up to the barricade.

Four shots met and for an instant checked them, but with vindictive yells they leaped forward, swarmed over the feeble barrier and a furious hand-to-hand conflict began.

But the men of Naitasiri were of sterner stuff than they of Dabea, and with their bodies pressed close up against the barricade they met the wild rush like men, club rattling against club, spear clashing against spear, while Mbonavindongo, swinging the bright axe that Eli had given him, cleft a skull with every downward stroke.

Shouting to some of the Naitasirians to join him,
Faatu seized Jerry and dragged him into the centre
of a hurriedly-formed ring, within which the boy,
panting with excitement, his empty musket fast
gripped by the barrel, was borne backwards and
forwards, this way and that, as rank after rank of
the Mbauans dashed and was shattered against the
sturdy phalanx which protected him.

Everywhere the fighting was terrific ; with a howl
of wrath the Mbauan *Mata* rushed at Eli and struck
fiercely at him with his club. The Virginian parried
the blow with his musket, but, though turned, it fell
with such force upon his shoulder that he staggered
and sank upon one knee. Once again the ponderous
club was swung upwards, but ere it could descend,
Anthony, bursting through the savages who stood
between, leaped upon the *Mata*, and seizing him by
the throat with one hand, with the other tore the
club from his grasp and flung it far away. Then
they closed.

Now began a battle of giants. Backwards and
forwards they rocked, from side to side they swayed
in that deadly grapple, each striving by every trick
of the wrestler to throw the other. Once a Fijian
sprang at Anthony and raised his club to brain him,
but the rushing tide of the battle swept the fellow
away, and still the two strong men fought on, their
sides heaving as the labouring breath came in thick
sobs from between their parted lips, their fierce eyes
glaring, their great muscles rolling and swelling,
shortening and lengthening, as one after another
came into play.

And now, of a sudden, the shouts were hushed,

and the fight for the time being ceased as 'friends
and foes in dumb surprise, with parted lips and
straining eyes' watched that mighty struggle.
Mbauans and Naitasirians gave back from one
another, and, standing in two crescents, the horns of
which almost touched, waited for the end.

Fiercer and fiercer raged the Homeric combat.
Now one supple body swayed from side to side like
a poplar in a storm; now the other writhed and
curled and twisted like a giant snake, seeking its
chance to strike; now a foot was raised, now a leg
bent, and yet so closely were the antagonists matched
that it seemed to the amazed beholders of the strife
that there was not a point to choose between
them.

Suddenly and simultaneously they loosed their
hold of one another, sprang apart a pace or two,
stood for one instant glaring like angry lions, and
then rushed once more together with a mighty
shock.

Back and forth, up and down they rocked and
reeled, and all the time Anthony's hands were slowly
sliding lower and lower until at last they locked
about the *Mata's* waist. A moment's pause, and then
the broad back bent in a great curve, straightened
swiftly like an unstrung bow and with a hoarse
shriek Mbitakau was torn from his foothold and flung
clear over Anthony's head to the ground behind,
where he lay without sense or motion.

A roar of delight went up from the men of
Naitasiri, and without waiting for the word they
charged home upon the Mbauans, who, astounded at
the fall of their redoubtable chief, faltered before the

last supreme rush of the heroic defenders, broke, swarmed the barricade, and fled down the slope to join the disgusted convicts.

'Keep off!' shouted Eli, beating back several of the Naitasirians, who came rushing up to batter the life out of the unconscious Mbitakau. 'He fought well, and if he's got a chance, he's going to be allowed to make the most of it. Are you all right, Anthony?' For the young man was lying upon the ground, sighing and sobbing for breath.

'Here's your musket,' said Jerry, running up to him. 'I've loaded it. I'm all right.'

'Thank God!' panted Anthony, looking round at Eli, who was now bending over Whitson. Guy was sitting up, binding the *sala* of a dead Fijian round his wounded head. Amid the jumble of dead and wounded it was impossible to distinguish friend from foe, but at one side of the enclosure Mbeka was busily engaged in sucking at a jagged spear-wound in Mbonavindongo's shoulder, and at another, Faatu, with a most disconsolate expression of countenance, was nursing a broken arm.

'Poor Whitson's gone,' said Eli sorrowfully. 'Waal, waal, he was a good man, an' so fur ez I know he was ready. Anthony, we're done fer ef they come agen. My collar-bone's broke; an' look at the rest of us—a quarter killed an' more'n half wounded.'

'Load up, Jerry,' said Guy faintly. 'They will only pause to re-form.'

'No need! No need!' shouted Anthony. 'Look at that.'

When the convicts came up with the Mbauans,

T

who had passed them at a gallop, Larkin flung himself into their midst at a white heat of rage.

'Back, you cowards, back!' he cried, gesticulating
wildly. 'One more rush like the last, and the place
is ours.'

But the Mbauans had had enough for the present,
and the tone of this speech as translated by Palavali
grated upon their ears.

'Send in the Dabeans,' replied the chief upon
whom the command had devolved after the fall of
the *Mata.* 'Why should we be torn to pieces while
they run away?' Which indeed the Eel-towners
had made haste to do at the first shock. But then
they had already had their share. 'Moreover,' went
on the chief, 'why do you not try it yourselves?
You stay far away and your clubs speak. But they
have forgotten how to kill. They are grown old, and
you are cowards yourselves, and liars, for you promised that none of us should die. Now see what
has happened because we trusted you.'

A murmur of approbation went round the
Mbauans; but Larkin, his face livid with passion,
rushed at the chief.

'Dog!' he cried. 'Who are you to argue with
me?' And raising his musket, shot him dead.

It was then that Anthony cried out, for with
screams of wrath the men of Mbau lifted their clubs
and sprang like tigers, each upon the white man
nearest to him, and smote to slay. Then the crowd
closed in and shut the convicts from sight.

For a moment there was a tossing to and fro of
lithe black bodies, a succession of ear-piercing shrieks,
and then out from the mass burst one solitary man,

staggered, reeled, fell to his knees, struggled to his feet, and rushed with what poor speed he might in the direction of the fort.

It was Larkin.

With scornful laughter a dozen Mbauans started upon his track, going slowly, for they knew that he could not escape, and they meant to inflict the torture of hope.

The blood was flowing down Larkin's face from a deep wound in his head, and his eyes were blinded by the red stream, but still he stumbled on, his hands held out imploringly in front of him.

What was this? Coming at him from the front a wild black figure that brandished an axe and shouted as it ran. He stopped, looking this way and that, and groping uncertainly. A Mbauan ran forward and cast his throwing club after him. The huge knob caught him where the head is set upon the spine, and without a sound he fell upon his face, twisted for a moment as one convulsed, and then turned over upon his back, and lay feebly twitching. As one in a dream he saw that savage figure bounding by; heard the crash of splintering bone as the axe cleft the skull of the nearest pursuer; saw the Mbauans give back, jeering as they went; felt himself lifted in strong arms; heard the voice of Anthony in his ears, hoarse, but kind and encouraging, and without one note of vengeance, 'All right, Larkin. I'll bring you safe in.' Heard it, saw it all as a dying man sees and hears, murmured once: 'For—give!—God!' shuddered strongly, and lay a dead weight in his would-be rescuer's arms.

When Anthony passed him over the barrier he was

quite dead. They laid him down beside Whitson, and turned again with their faces to the foe. A miserable remnant they were, and the Mbauans, joined once more with the men of Dabea, laughed as they came on in their long curved lines.

'It is the end,' said Eli solemnly. 'Fire!'

The muskets spat their sharp and sudden death for the last time, but the savages were sworn to have them now, and came on unfalteringly.

Eli swung Jerry up in his arms and kissed him. Then he set him down without a word, and with their arms encircling one another's necks, the four comrades knelt by Whitson's body.

'Ready!' cried Eli springing up.

'Ready!' echoed the others, and with shining faces rose to their feet and clubbed their muskets.

Then Jerry did a strange thing.

Springing up the steps of the *Mbure*, he scaled the thatch and tore the standards down and, standing on the ledge with one in each hand, began to sing. And as he sang the others joined in, Anthony's deep bass ringing defiantly as he shook his empty musket at the advancing foe.

And this is what they sang:

> 'God save our gracious King!
> Long live our noble King!
> God save the King!'

At this the savages stayed their rush, and halted, bewildered and uncertain whether to advance or to go back, while a confused murmuring arose from their ranks.

'See,' they cried, 'they are calling on their God. Ha! It is *kalou!* Their God is powerful. Let us

not kill them lest a worse thing befall us. Go on !
Slay them and spare not. Have they not slain the
men of Mbau. Let us kill them and prepare them
for the cooking pot. Not so, they are too strong.
Go back. Go on.'

But with a roar of rage a tall chief swept to the
front, and silencing the murmurers with a wave of his
hand, shouted, ' What mean you, O you of little heart.
Will you stay now when the death-dealers are face
to face with death ? Behold they have slain your
brothers, men of Mbau. Ha ! There shall be weeping this night in your houses, men of Dabea, because
of your young men that are slain. But the slayers
can slay no more. Ha ! Lo ! they have no more food
for the clubs that spit death. The clubs are hungry
and will not speak till they are fed, and, ha ! they
have nought with which to feed them. So they call
upon their God; but Ndengei is greater and fights
for us. Forward my brothers. Forward and slay
them all, and to-night shall be feasting and laughter.
Forward !'

But as the dark host pressed on once more, shouting vengefully, Palavali, the Tongan, broke from
among them and fled towards the mountain, screaming, ' Behold their God has heard. It is true. He
is greater than Ndengei. Fly ! O my brothers !'

For he had seen a sight that lent wings unto his
feet.

Boom ! boom ! boom !

Three round-shots, one after the other, in quick
succession, tearing a hideous path through the long
black lines.

' Ié ! Ié !' shrieked Faatu, speeding round

the *Mbure.* 'Big gun all same like um Tonga! *Aioo!'*

Jerry raced round the platform and was back again in an instant.

'A man-of-war!' he shouted. 'His Majesty's ship *Endymion,* or I'm a Dutchman! Hurrah!'

'Hurrah! Hurrah! Thank God! Thank God! *Aioo! Ié! Ai-oo! Whoo-oo!'*

Helter-skelter they poured over the barricade, and rushed to the back of the *Mbure* to get a view of the stately frigate, and while Mbauans and Dabeans, blended now in one inextricable mass, fled madly towards the mountain, above the yells of the half delighted, wholly terrified men of Naitasiri, swelled again and again, strong and triumphant, the deep-toned British 'Hurrah!'

CHAPTER XXIII

HOMEWARD BOUND.

'BELAY, men; back water. We must not go any closer.—Major, there is something very queer about this. There is not a white man among them, yet we certainly heard the cheering. See, the beggars have got the flags.'

The speaker was the first lieutenant of the *Endymion*, who was directing operations in the long boat, which, at the captain's orders, had been manned and despatched with a landing party to the shore.

Major Hawkins did not reply at once. He glanced first at his brothers-in-law, who were with him in the boat, and then his anxious eyes wandered towards the beach, where the Naitasirians, their fears at rest, thanks to Faatu's explanations, were apparently trying to discover which of them could yell the loudest.

'They are making a dreadful noise,' said the Major at last, 'but, in my opinion, they are peaceably inclined. Look at that little chap with the British ensign, and the tall chap with the yellow hair. They are certainly making signals to us to come ashore. Take us in a little closer, Mr Rowley, if you please, and let us try to fathom the mystery.'

'Give way, men,' said the lieutenant, laconically, and the sturdy tars bent to the oars once more.

The yells were redoubled in intensity, the small standard-bearer was apparently engaged in a duel to the death with another about his own size, who carried the American ensign, for the two charged backwards and forwards, belabouring each other with the staves they held, and leaped and danced like maniacs, while the yellow-haired chief, who was armed with a musket, brandished his weapon furiously, and howled inarticulate syllables, which might have meant peace, but certainly did not sound like it.

'That will do,' said Major Hawkins, when the boat was within fifty yards of the beach; 'you must not run any risks on our account. I will endeavour to show them that we mean them no harm.'

He laid his musket in the bottom of the boat and stood up, extending his arms towards the crowd on the shore.

There was a simultaneous shriek, 'Father! Uncle Tony!' The small standard-bearer tossed away his flag, the yellow-haired chief sent his musket spinning into the air, and into the shallows they dashed together, and splashed their way to the boat.

Over the side sprang Major Hawkins and Dr Blake, and swam to meet them, while poor Captain Trimball anxiously scanned the line of dusky faces in search of his son.

The four met in deep water, rushed into each other's arms, and sank out of sight. In a moment they rose, sputtering and gasping. 'Father! father!' 'My dear boy! My dear, dear boy!' Then down they went again.

'Come ashore,' panted Anthony. 'Plenty, much, big shark here, as Faatu would say.'

He turned and led the way, the boat following, and in a few moments they had reached the beach, where they fell to laughing, crying, and hugging once more.

Suddenly Jerry tore himself from his father's embrace, and flung himself into the arms of Captain Trimball, who was standing disconsolately apart.

'It's all right, Uncle Bob,' he cried; 'Guy is safe. He was wounded in the head, and just as we were starting from the fort he fainted. See, here he comes with Eli.'

With a cry of joy Captain Trimball hastened to meet his son, who, with his arm thrown round Eli's shoulder, was advancing slowly and painfully from the fort.

'My dear, dear boy! Thank God, you are safe!' exclaimed the Captain in heartfelt tones. 'I began to think—— Here, Blake, quick! He has fainted again.'

'No, I haven't,' said Guy in a weak voice; 'there's not much the matter with me. Father, dearest father, how good it is to see you again! Where did you come from? How did you get here? What—oh! I don't know how to be thankful enough. Mother and Aunt Mary'——

'Are well,' interrupted the Captain. 'At least, they were when we left home, though, to be sure, they were in a pretty state of mind about you youngsters. They are staying with the Governor's lady.'

Guy's eyes were moist. 'Darling mother!' he murmured; then, gently pushing Eli forward, he

exclaimed: 'I say, has no one a word for Eli?
But for him you would never have seen us again.'

A word for him! No, there was not one. But
Major Hawkins and Captain Trimball grasped each a
hand of him, while Dr Blake held on to his arm, and
all three looked at him with brimming eyes. But
never a word did they say.

'Oh, come now,' said Eli, laughing rather huskily;
'that Guy is always thinkin' o' somebody else.
Waal, waal, I guess this is a joy. How are you,
Major? Captain, Doctor, my respects. Waal, waal,
I did what I could; but thar, the Lord is above us,
an' I jedge it's Him, an' not me, ez ought to be
thanked.'

'That's true,' agreed the Major; 'but while we
give deep and heartfelt thanks to God, we need not
forget his instruments. Banks, dear, faithful friend,
I—I—we don't know what to say to you.'

'Waal, then, Major, I wouldn't try,' returned Eli;
'thar'll be heaps to say presently without botherin'
about me. Ez to what I did, ef it wasn't less, it
cert'nly wasn't more, than what any one else did. Ef
you want to thank the right critters, why, turn your
tongues loose on Boney and Fatty.'

'Boney and Fatty!' echoed the Major, with a
laugh. 'What do you mean by that?'

'An' what's more, you mustn't fergit the Baker,'
went on Eli; and in a few words he outlined what
had taken place since their escape from Mbau. 'We
can tell you the rest once we're comfortably afloat,' he
concluded. 'Meantime, Fatty, say to his majesty
ez I hope he'll permit me to present the fathers o'
these hyar boys to him. He has seen what the sons

can do, so he ought to respect their pa's. By time,
yes! King, the Major, the Captain, and the Doctor.
Major, Captain, Doctor, the King.'

Mbonavindongo advanced to where the gentlemen
were standing, and, after gently pressing their hands
between his own, greeted each of them with the
Fijian kiss of peace.

'Sa *loloma*, my lords,' he said, with the aid of
Faatu. 'I am glad to see you. Indeed, you came
only just in time. I had said that I would flatten
the impudent Kende Kende, yet, but for you, I and all
those with me would have been in his cooking pot
ere now. Indeed, my lords, I have done nothing.
What have I done? I was greedy of what Eli promised me. I wanted the clubs that can speak, so I
came to show them the way. Besides, there was
Jelly-my-boy-Jelly-not-Jelly-stupid, and I loved him.
Ha! what have I done?'

'Don't laugh, Major,' put in Eli, in an undertone,
as a smile flitted over the faces of the listeners.

'I loved him,' went on the chief, drawing Jerry to
his side. 'I would have done more for him than I
have done. Ha! I wish there had been more to do.
I said I would do all for him that he desired of me.
Ha! and so I will.'

'I'll bind you down to that presently, my boy,'
muttered Jerry, and the king concluded:

'Behold, I am king in Naitasiri, and perhaps I
shall become king in Mbau ere many days are on.
For the Mbauans have fled before me, and I will demand a *soro* of Na Ulivou. But if he will not give
me a *soro*, ha! then I will give him one. Yes, I
will carry him a little bit of earth from Naitasiri.

So shall there be peace between us, for we are
both mighty men of valour, and together we will fall
upon the Rewans, and both of us shall smite the men
of Viwa, and we two shall be kings in Viti. I have
finished. But I would ask to see the great canoe
that floats upon the bosom of the ocean as a duck
upon the surface of a lagoon. I do not say that I
must see it, for, ha! I am not a fool, and I know
that you are greater than I. Also, I would know
by what magic you came here at the right time,
for that knowledge would be useful. Teach me the
way it is done.'

'Oh, great king,' answered Major Hawkins, 'my
brothers and I have no words in which to thank you
for giving us back our sons, who are dearer to us
than our own lives. But for you we should have
lost them.' His voice shook. 'Through you those
we mourned as dead have been given back to us,
and we thank you, and we thank God, who softened
your heart, and made you good to those who were
in trouble.'

'Ah, that is right,' said the king, as Major
Hawkins paused. 'If Ndengei had not fought for us,
we could not have won. I offered him a *soro* last
night upon the mountains.'

'Mbonavindongo, there is a greater God than
Ndengei, and it was He who fought for us,' said Guy.

'No, that is not possible,' answered the king
simply. 'There is no greater god than Ndengei.'

'Some day you will know,' said Guy, with a smile.

'And you, too, my good fellow,' exclaimed the
Major, grasping Faatu's hand. 'I don't know the
particulars of what you have done, but it is enough

for us that you have been the means, under God, of giving us back our sons. We are very, very grateful.'

'And we mustn't forget the Baker, as you call him,' added Dr Blake. 'He seems to be your particular chum, Jerry.' For Mbeka was standing with his arm thrown affectionately round Jerry's shoulders.

'Oh, he is,' answered Jerry. 'Just wait till you hear all he did for me.'

Dr Blake detached the gold chain from his watch.

'Here, my boy,' he said to Mbeka, 'here is something that will please you.'

With a shrill cry of delight, Mbeka seized the glittering chain and passed it through the hole of his left ear. Mbonavindongo eyed him with sparkling eyes. 'Give that to me,' he said briefly.

'No, no, king,' interposed Major Hawkins, as the Baker, with a burst of tears, prepared to obey; 'let the boy keep it. Here is mine for you, and when you come on board, we will give you plenty of things, as much as your heart can desire.'

'Well now, father,' said Anthony, 'you have not answered the king's question as to how you came here. I wish you would, for we are extremely anxious to know. Our own story is too long to tell in a breath.'

'Ours is easily told,' answered the Major. 'Alarmed at the thought that your party might encounter the convicts, your Uncle Blake hastened to the rendezvous, only to find that you were not there. The number of footsteps above the tide level, however, gave him a faint idea of what might have occurred, and he came hurrying back to the settlement with the news. Our first suspicion was that you had been carried 'inland, and would be held as hostages, but next day two dead bodies were washed ashore on the south side of the harbour. They both bore marks of violence, and when brought to the settlement were at once recognised as those of the captain and one of the crew of the brig. It then became evident that Larkin's plan had been a deep one, and that he had made off with the vessel. The best that we could hope was that he had taken you all with him, though we feared that you must have met with a more cruel fate at his hands. By the way, where is he now?' he broke off to ask.

'He is dead,' said Anthony briefly; 'he died in my arms. Go on.'

'Well, well, it is better so,' said the Major gravely. 'We were at our wits' end what to do,' he resumed, 'for there was no ship in port; but, to our unbounded delight, the *Endymion* returned just then from Norfolk Island. She was not an hour longer in Sydney Cove than was necessary to take in supplies, and then we bowled away upon your track.'

'But how did you know which way to steer?' inquired Mbonavindongo, who, assisted by Faatu, was following the narrative with the greatest interest.

'The God who is greater than Ndengei helped us,' replied the Major. 'Of course, boys, we had no certain knowledge, but the captain of the *Endymion* suggested that the most likely place towards which the rascals would make would be the China Sea; so we shaped our course accordingly.'

'The same violent storm that you encountered blew us out of our course,' put in the lieutenant, 'and we came to the north of this island. After most anxious deliberation we concluded to beat round it in case, by any possibility, you might have got stranded somewhere upon it. Providentially we dropped down the west coast instead of the east. We should even thus have missed you, I believe, had it not been that the lookout spied the flags from the masthead. The rest you know.'

'It was providential, ez you say,' observed Eli. 'But thar, I jedge sech boys ez these hyar were much too good to be wasted on a lot o' cannibals. Not but what thar ain't some good ones among 'em,' he added, with an apologetic nod in the direction of Mbonavindongo.

'Well, let us return on board,' said Major Hawkins. 'Captain Pearson must be getting impatient. Lieutenant Ellmer, I suppose a party will be sent ashore to bury the dead? King, are you ready? Will you go in a canoe or in the boat with us?'

'Wait a moment,' answered Mbonavindongo, and turned to issue an order to some of his men.

Jerry sprang to Faatu's side and whispered something. The Tongan nodded.

'Then translate for me,' cried Jerry. 'Listen to me, king. You promised to grant me whatever I asked of you?'

'That is true,' admitted Mbonavindongo frankly. 'What would you have?'

'You have given orders that the bodies of our enemies should be cooked,' replied Jerry. 'Do this for my sake. Let them be buried instead.'

Mbonavindongo looked considerably taken aback.

A decided negative sprang to his lips, but, after a sharp struggle, he choked it back.

'I am not a liar,' he said laconically; 'let them be buried.'

.　　.　　.　　.　　.　　.

It was a week later. The surviving Naitasirians, who had seized the canoes of the Dabeans as spoils of war, had returned by water to the mouth of the Rewa river, escorted by the frigate. The fleet lay all around the great ship, at the gangway of which stood Mbonavindongo, reluctant to say farewell to his white friends. Around him clustered his companions on the march, with Faatu and Mbeka, who had been persuaded to visit Sydney, on the understanding that they were to be brought back to Tonga later on. Big tears were rolling down the king's face, and again and again he drew Jerry to him and sniffed affectionately at the boy's cheeks.

'Farewell,' he said brokenly, 'Jelly-my-boy-Jelly-not-Jelly-stupid, farewell. I shall never see you again.'

'But you will hear of us,' said Jerry cheerfully, when Faatu had explained. 'We will teach Mbeka of the God who is greater than Ndengei, and he shall come back and tell you about Him.'

'Yes,' echoed Guy, 'and if God spare me, I will come with him. Jerry, sing to him once more.'

The sun was sinking, and as the last notes of the evening hymn died softly and sweetly away, a mournful cry went up from the rapt Fijians in the canoes:

'*Sa lakki mothe!* Good-night! Farewell!'

Edinburgh: Printed by W. & R. Chambers, Limited.

CPSIA information can be obtained at www.ICGtesting.com
Printed in the USA
BVOW04s1318221113

337073BV00015B/629/P